Odyssey of a Soul

...A Poetic Memoir

By
Olachi Joy Mezu-Ndubuisi

BLACK ACADEMY PRESS, INC.
BALTIMORE MARYLAND **21208**

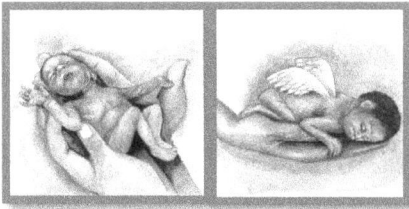

All book sales will benefit Obiolarose Twin Angels Foundation, a subsidiary of MI Foundation, to support parents of premature infants and provide humanitarian aid to improve medical care in under-served areas.
www.obiolarosefoundation.org

1

All Rights Reserved
Including the right of reproduction
in whole or in part in any form

No part of this publication may be reproduced, stored in a retrieval
system, or transmitted in any form or by any means –for example,
electronic, photocopy, recording – without the prior written
permission of the publishers.

Copyright © 2016 by Black Academy Press, Inc.
Printed in the United States of America

ISBN   0-87831-136-X   9780878311361 paper

First Published in USA in 2016
by
BLACK ACADEMY PRESS, INC.
4015 Old Court Road
BALTIMORE, MARYLAND 21208

www.blackacademypress.com

Dedication

To GOD for showing me His Divine Mercy :
I believe, I trust and I submit to
Your Holy will in my Life

To my twin Angels, OlaRose and Obiola, whose courage
and will to live gave me the strength to fight for
their lives: You are an eternal testament of God's love
for me

To my family who have been a great source of
strength and support throughout my journey:
Your unconditional love is my rock

To all I encounter daily:
You are the face of Christ in my life

...These are lyrics to the songs emanating from the depths of my soul during life's odyssey...

~Olachi

Contents

Preface

Odyssey of a Soul … A Poetic memoir is a four book collection of poetry, prose and personal life experiences written over a seventeen year period (1999-2016). It is a story of life, love, loss, and faith in divine providence. It makes for a heart-warming reading and a real solace to anyone who believes in God, love, family, and miracles. This poetic memoir is an indeed refreshing and soul-searching sequel to the author's first book of poetry as a teenager, *Image of a Soul*. We are immersed in it as the child becomes a woman, and gives back to life as good as she gets.

Book One: *The Evolution of Millie Ola* shows the maturity of the author's youthful, romantic dreams as she explores the thrills of life's twists and turns to discover her chosen path and imbibe the gripping realities of the joys, pains and phantoms of love, faith, and life.

Book Two: *The Journey of OlaRose & Obiola, my NICU babies …, With love to Obiola, our twin angel and hero*, is a mother's brave, nostalgic and spiritually uplifting account of a high risk twin pregnancy and the struggles, trials, sorrows and triumphs that followed.

    Part One: *Before I formed you in the womb* - is a testimony of the struggle of two innocent souls from the moment of conception.

    Part Two: *Poems to my Twin Angels: Echoes from the womb* - The author takes one through a remarkable and intense bittersweet journey, as she awaits the birth of her miracle babies: OlaRose and Obiola, who are eventually born premature. It is a collection of poems written during her hospitalization for pregnancy complications, giving her courage, solace and hope in the midst of a lot of uncertainty and fear of the unknown, as she bravely chooses to continue her pregnancy. She pours out her thoughts, fears, hopes, prayers, and conversations with her babies through their ordeal: true echoes of the womb. It takes one into the real personalities of these babies and their surreal connection with their mother.

Part Three: *In memory of Obiola, our angel and hero* – The author takes us through the passionate journey of premature birth of her babies, losing her son, and the deep emotions stirred in a close-knit family and community. It is a soulful collection of poems and tribute to Obiola, the little angel and hero, from the extended family on his memorial, showing how the loss of an innocent soul affects an entire community.

Part Four: *The NICU Diary of OlaRose* – The author keeps a diary as she cares for her precious, one pound daughter, OlaRose, in the neonatal intensive care unit (NICU). Through her eyes, one has a deeper understanding of the emotional experience of being a mother of a micro preemie in the NICU, and the impact of losing a child from the unique perspective of not just a mother, but a NICU physician. It is a personal journey of hope, pain, loss, and the will to survive. This diary gives healthcare professionals an understanding of the over-whelming emotions NICU parents' experience, and parents in similar situations, a glimpse of what lies ahead and hope to endure.

Book Three: A Divine Mercy Experience, is an amazing story of how the author's life is divinely saved from the life-threatening consequences of an unsuspecting ruptured brain aneurysm and her miraculous recovery to full health. It shows how this intimate encounter with God's Fatherly love and mercy permeates the author's life and work, as she struggles to stay true to herself in life's troubling waters.

Book Four, The Way of Trust and Love: The author seeks the peace and joy that comes with a total abandon to God's will in her life and complete trust in His unwavering love. It is poetry, it is art, it is life... as she bares her soul... and in so doing finds strength and peace within... It can be whatever you want it to be. Hopefully, you'll find in it a little bit of your own.

Black Academy Press Inc.

Book One
The Evolution of Millie Ola

Yuletide's Grace In White (a sonnet)

Handballs of fun hurled around at dawn
rolling in a blanket of white in the chill of morn
Love's own creation, still and white as cotton
with a carrot-mouthed grin and gleaming eyes of button
A dry blast of chill on my cheeks a mere caress
as I savor the picturesque awe of nature's prowess
Little icy flakes warm our hearts from skies so empty
and like a chastising torrent, form an envelope of purity
As if to hide the world's flaws and mendacities
A consequent veil of our blatant iniquities
Indeed a show of divine goodwill, this is
for the season's new birth comes in peace
And as You fill the world with Your grace, I pray
Do so to my penitent soul , my Lord, and stay

December, 1998
First White Christmas
Randallstown, Maryland

The Journey Begins

Here at last,
In quest of my dreams
In pursuit of my heart's choice,
Here at last

A land so faraway
Across oceans and plains alike
away from friends and loves
a land so far away

Nay, shall I fret
For alone I am not
with my Lord and friends above
Nay, shall I fret

With His grace alone
I will be the best I can,
and excel in all I plough
With his grace alone

My destiny's stars shine so
With scenery so bright and alive
and faces hope-laden and warm
My destiny's stars shine so

I do commend my life
O Lord, my path do walk
Guide, guard, and safely keep
My life I do commend

Aug, 1999;
Ross University School of Medicine, Dominica

Chills From Within

Silent nights, so lonely
Goose pimples spring out
like tiny anthills
The autumn chill,
tomb freezing

A heartbeat resounds
in the crippling stillness
Propagating transverse waves
all across the Atlantic

Did you hear it?...a sob
torn from a lonely heart
longing for its deprived warmth

Feeling encased in somber clouds
though right on the sun's pinnacle
surrounded by neon lights
that have lost their sparkle

Cold lips touch the cherished sapphire
-the heart's sole console
calling forth memories so dear
bringing promises of
unending warmth....
....a heartbeat away.

October, 1999

The Heart in my hands

What a wonder, lying in my palms
the essence of your being
the soul of your existence
barely one-fist large

Blessed you are, though no more
You're a sacrifice for knowledge, so divine
Lifeless on a cold, steel table
while your body, once lived in
 is dissected regionally
your muscles numbered
your nerves counted and severed

A wonder indeed
human existence is
Our complexity, still perplexing
and more so the awareness that
a single beat of this organ sustains,
and none thereof puts an end to
life so precious, so real

I feel my own heart
with each systole and diastole
My soul do guard Lord, now and for aye
Its last beat I commend to thee
to keep in your fist for aye

Oct, 1999 *after first anatomy lab dissection experience*
Ross University School of Medicine, Dominica Campus

Sunset on the Caribbean Sea

At peace with the world
At one with the sea
mesmerized by the golden tones
at the world's brink

Little canoes and boats
paddling across the ocean's silvery ripples
The shimmering golden blue waters
with the salutary lap of the waves at my feet
A picturesque blend at dusk

I see past the colorful skies
I see beyond its fathomable depths
To the other side of the world
To the other side of my dreams

I wonder deep into the clouds
A blend of blue and gold alike
On the banks of the Caribbean sands
With one or two lovers in awe at nature
As she displays her sovereign glamour

Alone, I wonder and marvel
It will be okay
It will be alright
My goals and dreams
will be one in time.

October 1999
Island of Dominica

Reawakened

Love left me sore with hurt
but you caressed my wounded heart

I was torn with cries of betrayal
but you kissed my pain away

It took your warm, safe arms to ignite
the emotions I had caged in fright

I tried to erase and pulverize memories of dreams destroyed
and now I can make new hopes and dreams of love

Gone was my faith in promises, empty and bare
but your gaze held truth crystal-clear

Words were unnecessary, your eyes said it all
Together we'll rediscover the love path after all

Re-awakened my dreams now are
With you, I'll love again for sure

February 2000

Ten Chants to You

You've groomed us like delicate roses
And watched all 10 as we blossomed
You've chanted words of wisdom
And carved indelible graces in our hearts
You've taught us to give exuberantly
And not count how much is left
You've showered our lives with joy
And added surreal colors to the sun
You've made us stretch our potentials
And shoot for the distant stars
You've created a palatial home within us
And we're united though spread across the seas.
You've led us through life's thickest woods
And shielded us from the piercing thorns
You've laid awake nights unending
And tried to ease our falls and pains
You've unraveled the essence of true love
And exuded it like a fountain to us
You've helped us count our God-given blessings
And Mum & Dad, you are the best of them.

September 6th, 2001

Anniversary Poem to Mom and Dad. Read during their 33rd wedding anniversary party, Olive Branch, Pikesville, MD

The Story of The Rose

With a scent one lifetime old
a dozen rose buds unfold
a ne'er ending tale
laden with memories
joys, tears, alike

Each petal
a soul full of grace, dreams, hopes
and yet more

Bundled together
in a chord of love
and Godly might

A song
in the trees,
its mellifluous labyrinth
unfolding like a rose
at the crack of dawn.

November 12th 2001
In honor of Mom's (Dr. Rose Ure Mezu) birthday

You and Me

Life is full of themes
some important, some senseless
an array of words truthful or bare
but when all is said and done,
it's all about you and me

Life is full of strings
binding us to traditions
laboring us to expectations
but whether knotted or not
it's all about you and me

Life is full of uncertainties
Yesterdays' problems are no clearer today
and tomorrow's tunnel is seemingly bleak
but whether the sun sets or rises,
it's all about you and me

Life is full of people
some friends, some foes
entwined in our day to day
but whether they are or not,
it's only about YOU and ME

February 2002
West Hills, California

Petals of Love

A dozen petals of love
A dozen stems of strength
arrayed in a vase, crystal clear
indeed my very own rose garden
A symbol of our affection
A seal of our commitment
 my heart fluttering at the first glimpse
as I whispered, "I love you, too..."

February 2002
Elizabeth, NJ

The Lovers' Prayer

Dear Lord,
We humbly come to your presence
with our hearts as one to seek your favor
We thank you for the many blessings
of our lives, families, friends, good health and careers
We particularly invoke your continued protection
on our families far and wide

Sweet Jesus, we've lived separate lives so far
trying to utilize our God-given graces in our various endeavors,
and yet our paths crossed again and again.
God of love, we are praying for your blessing and protection
as we seek to share our lives together.

Take our love, we beseech you,
nurture it, and help it to grow daily.
Teach us to love each other like you did your disciples:
selflessly, patiently, and completely without reserve.

Writer of our destiny, do complete this love story of ours
and like the wedding at Cana
officiate at our union
that we may multiply in your name

Jesus our age, be our friend, intercede for us to the father
Give us strength to overcome temptations:
physically, spiritually, emotionally,
and from unseen forces of evil beyond our control

Wipe away our past misgivings,
and create a fresh path leading to our future together
We seek shelter in your arms as we begin this journey of love
Divert the straying arrow, distract the preying wolves
Even though the path might be rocky, with you by our side
and through the intercession of your servant, St. Anthony
we shall get to the foot of your altar

March 2002

A Sonnet to my love

I'm so drunk in love
with your dewdrops of Irish cream
and my tender shot of chocolate rum
so tantalizing, my soul flutters like a butterfly
drawn to you like pure, raw nectar
Overwhelmed by your strong, virile essence, I am
consumed with your passion, so fiery
intoxicated with your presence so real
hypnotized by your kiss, so sweet
inebriated by your promises, so true
dazzled by your smile, so sensual
swaying to your touch, so gentle
buzzing to your laughter, so pleasant
Indeed I'm drunk in love.

March 2002

My Heart

My heart, my love
My lips will never tire to say your name
in different sounds of life
whispering, speaking
blushing, laughing

My soul will never tire to sing our love
in different cords of life
blues, jazz
flute, harp

My mind will never tire to draw your face
in different shades of life
waking, sleeping
dreaming, living

My life from hence
is seemingly all about
my love,
my heart, *my "OBI"*

March 2002
Elizabeth, NJ

My One and Only

Let's not turn anthills into mountains
or pebbles into bricks
If I were a magician
the world would belong to us
If I were a deity
we would live forever
But since we're only human
with our strengths and failings,
Let's live our day to day
doing the bit we can
and hopeful for those we can't
I'd do anything for you
I'd give anything to make you happy
But the best gift of all
Is the love we share, you and I

April 2002
Elizabeth, New Jersey

The reason I'm all smiles

I smile when I think about you,
knowing that you are thinking about me too
I smile when I think about you,
knowing that you are like a rainbow in my life
I smile when I think about you,
knowing that you're in my heart, so close, so near,
so sure that no distance, seas, or skies can drift us apart
I smile when I think about you, knowing that you love me too

April, 2002
Elizabeth, NJ

Tell Me The Meaning of Love

When you tell me that you love me, what does it mean to you...?
Is it the conventional, appropriate statement
to someone you feel deeply for...
Or is it because it sounds passionate and sexy to verbalize?
Is it a commitment to me to be faithful and true...
Or is it merely a diversion from pressures of reality...?
Is it saying that I'm the dearest person to your heart for now...
Or are there limits and boundaries beyond which I can't reach?
Is it a promise to seek my happiness or pleasure in all you do...
Or are there thrills reserved for your private sojourns?
Is it unconditional and oblivious to physical and material stock...
Or is it a surrogate contract for what we have to offer?
When I say I love you; it means BODY, MIND, AND SOUL...

May 2002
Brooklyn, New York

The Story of Us

A story of two lives
A tale of two hearts
In a parallel world they lived
Till one summer day in July
When a buzz of the phone
Triggered a lifetime connection

You were my hotline stranger
through whom I lived my fantasies
I was your mystery girl
Often heard of, but never seen.

Six hours and some of talk time
spiraled a deep soul searching
Erupting a force so strong
we were engulfed in a sea of fire

The buzz of the doorbell
chimed a harmony, well anticipated
For in flesh stood the object of desire
A first sight captured in the memory of time

We wined, dined and rode through fantasy land
Our youthful hearts soaring to heights unimaginable
And at the end of a long, hot summer
it was sealed with a kiss...

Aaah! The kiss...
Brief, sweet, innocent and so full of promise
A promise so silent, it was missed
We were oblivious to the unspoken talisman
that was to follow us through the years apart.

We went on our parallel paths a yonder
Soaking in life's lessons and treasures
Of knowledge, love, and war
Separated by seas and miles of silence for five or so odd years

Till one fateful summer night
the weary souls returned
To yet again relive the dial-up connection
Testing the waters.....braving the wind
so unsure....yet so right
Was this a trick of fate?

Twice strangers, but never again
For the second meeting was déjà vu
At the buzz of the doorbell on February 19th
We gazed a second too long
into each other's eyes.... that smile....that gleam
Time had been kind and good
All blossomed, all grown, but the very same soul

A trip to the city of lights sealed our fates
As we swayed to the rhythm of life
A perfect blend of body and soul
Our names entwined in the book of love

The heart and the Jewel together at last
In destiny's love boat, we'll ride
and make sweet music so enchanting
that we'll tango for the rest of our lives.

June 2002,
Brooklyn, New York

The Lovers' Plea to the Blessed Mother

Dearest Mother, betrothed of St. Joseph
We, your children, choose you to be our sponsor and patroness
as we pledge our commitment to each other for the rest of our lives.
Let the splendor of your grace shine on us
that we may learn to love and cherish each other.
Bestow on us the humility and graciousness
to support each other always, tolerate each other's failings,
learn from our mistakes and grow together through life.
Empower us with the light of your love
that we may love each other completely without reserve.
Enkindle in us a fiery passion that will burn in our hearts for all time,
and never be quenched by the torrents of envy, ill will, or evil

Seat of Wisdom, we dedicate our different careers to you
May our work bring us closer, as we seek to conquer the world
and maximize the talents your son has bestowed on us.
Oversee all our endeavors and make them fruitful
so that we may always lend a helping hand
to your people in need, all for the glory of your name
Bring our families together in a union of peace,
that we may all share a bond of love, harmony, and kindness.
Bless and protect our families, and may they
forever be a source of support and counsel to us.

We dedicate this year to you sweet mother, as we prepare
to be joined together as man and wife, in the presence of your son
Bless us as we make our promises
to honor, cherish, and be faithful to each other through thick and thin.
And when the time is right,
bless us with the fruit of the womb, healthy and whole
that we may teach the life's pearls and the love of God to a new being.
Queen of Heaven, intercede for us to your son for his blessings
as we confidently fly to your patronage.

January 2003

Prayer To The Sacred Heart

Most Sacred Heart of Jesus
we come to seek your favor
Illuminate our hollow hearts
with your divine love and grace
that we may be enriched and nourished
from your ominous fountain

Our love is young and still feeble,
so do strengthen it
that no wave of doubt, insecurities,
or uncertainties can shake it

Bestow on us the patience that love needs
to harvest everlasting roots in our hearts.
May we be not just lovers,
but best friends and soul mates to each other

As we walk to the altar,
guide us and our families as we plan
and prepare to celebrate our union
We ask for good and strong health for all.

Bless our budding careers
that we may work passionately and be productive
and as the need arises
may we have the means to plan our special day

Sweet Jesus, model of love
we pray for kindness to each other
Teach us to be gentle as you are
that we may always cherish each other,
as we become man and wife
We ask of these through your most divine heart.

September 2003

A Dream of You

I woke up with a smile on my face,
This has not happened for a while now
I imagined I slept all wrapped up in your arms, and
that I could feel your breath next to mine.

My dream last night was filled with visions of us
drowning in each other's love,
igniting sparks so raw,
savoring every bit of rum and cream.
Aah the sweet, lingering scent
of the after love,
with your whispers of undying love
reverberating in my ears...
 saying "I will always love you , ..."
No wonder, even though
beside me was void of you,
I still woke up with a smile on my face.

November 3, 2003

Two Hearts As One

Ours is a tale of Two Hearts, Two Souls
Sojourning and seeking our own true grail
Threading parallel paths on life's seamless trail
Oblivious to destiny's conjoined goals

First unseen, our voices met at bay
Potent, striking, soothing, exciting vocals
Reminiscing from dreams of old, familiar echoes
Resonating across a chance phone call one summer day

Soon we were face to face in muse
and the enigma, no more to be
As we searched mesmerized to see
Through sheer depths of caramel hues

An illusion it had to be, we thought
For real life is not a fairy tale state
Where one's deepest desires are incarnate
So let go we must of the formless moth

But then came fate's unyielding tune
as our paths crossed again by chance, it seemed
And second sight was the charm indeed
'cos five years felt like yesterday's noon

Like clouds after a storm it was clear
That you and I were meant to be fashioned
In Andromeda's mystical garlands of scented passion
Consuming our souls in sweet surrender

We pray thee Lord for our sage and seal
To bless the union of our two hearts and souls
As we vow through thick and thin to carouse
As one and the same for aye and for real.

November 2003, *printed in church wedding brochure held on December 30, 2003 Assumpta Cathedral, Owerri, Imo State*

Pride

A vice worse than any
Making a man a shadow of himself
Pulling a man apart from his soul
Stopping a man from reaching for gold
Turning a man to a dark, sinister soul
Tearing a man away from love
Causing a man to lose his charm
Forming a man that thinks not twice of
Breaking his lover's teary heart
A vice I pray to be saved from
More than any

March 2005

Thief of Hearts

I heard it loud and clear
A big "thud!"
A loud crash in the still of the night
The sound of my heart
breaking into a thousand pieces

Like a thief
you crawled into my life
not once, but twice
you stole my heart away
With promises of love and life

Promises you never meant to keep
It was all a game
My heart, the unsuspecting goal
A price too dear to pay

All these years
were an illusion
All the love and laughter
were all part of your sinister plot
To take away the essence of my youth
To tear down my ideals of romance
To steal my heart and cause it to break
Not into two, but a thousand pieces.

March 25th, 2005

Lost Love

And then it was no more
Gone into oblivion
Faded into nothingness
A puff in the air
A cloud in the storm

And then it was gone
Never to return
As if a mere figment
of a vivid imagination
A memory only in my mind

And then it was lost
In the still of night
a whisper of the dusk
A phantom of the dawn

And then it was no more
Forever it was gone
Completely I had lost
the love of my life

March 2005

Betrayal

It hurts so much
like a second degree burn
It bleeds so much
like an arterial puncture
It aches so much
like a vaso-occlusive crises

It cares so little
if a skin graft is needed
It cares so little
if the heart is in failure
It cares so little
if analgesia is available

It's blind to its vision
It's deaf to its noise
It's numb to its feeling
It hurts so much more
that you betrayed our love
by caring so little

March 2005

Not Good Enough

I'm too good for you? Now I know
I'm too good for you, you knew it all along
I'm too good for you, which you could not stand
That's why you dared to woo me and win me
That's why you dared to hide your faults and insecurities
That's why you dared to hurt me and leave me
That's why you dared to lie about love
Because you knew before I did
That you were not good enough for me

March 25th, 2005

Voice Within

Say No to the urge to hurt
Say No to the urge to leave
Say No to the urge to harm
Say No to the urge to make
a footstool of your love.

Say No 'cos you can't turn back
the hand of time..
Say No 'cos you can't bring back
a life gone in vain
Say No 'cos you can't wipe out
words of hurt impaled on a soul
Say No 'cos you can't forgive
yourself if you lose your love.

March 2005

Broken Promises

You promised me the moon
in its fullness and grace
You promised me the stars
in its splendor and charm
You promised me the earth
in its bounty and truth
You promised me the sun
in its glory and power
You promised me the love
 of your heart forever
You promised me the life
of a queen in your soul
You promised me the beauty
of life's precious gems

Alas, you forgot to promise
always to keep your word
'Cos now I'm alone and forlorn
in a galaxy of darkness and gloom
embowered by so many promises broken
just like my broken heart.

March 2005
Shreveport, LA

Waiting for a Dream

I waited all my life for a dream
I waited while others frolicked
I waited while others laughed
I waited all my life for you

You came and claimed my heart
You came and romanced my soul
You came and caressed my life
You came but not for long

'Cos the dream became a nightmare
The dance, became a battle
The laughter, turned to tears
For soon you were gone

Alas I waited in vain....
Maybe if I sleep again
I'll awake to see it all a dream
and you are truly still the one.

March 2005
Shreveport, LA

After You

I want my life back,
so I can live again
I want my heart back,
so I can love again
I want my dreams back,
so I can sleep again
I want my will back,
so I can work again
I want my strength back,
so I can fight again
Fight to regain my sanity
Fight to start a new life
after you are gone.

March 2005

Time

Tick! Tock!
It's the sound of time
one second after another
going with or without me
Tick! Tock!
It's the sound of time
changing into another day
and move on I must
'cos time waits for no man.

March 2005
Pikesville, MD

A Sonnet to My Family

You are my rock
holding me steady in the wind
You are my shelter
keeping me safe from the storm
You are my light
showing me the way in the dark
You are my hope
keeping me looking for tomorrow
You are my treasure
enriching me when I've lost all
You are my eternal fountain
quenching my thirst for love
You are my truth
teaching me to trust again.

March 2005
Mezuville America, Pikesville, MD

Time to Think about the End of the "Year of my Life"

It was supposed to be the best year of my life
The first year we live our love together as one
The year to learn to cherish and to hold
Each other dear, but alas, it was not so
There were some tender moments, some laughs
But you turned out not to be the prince charming I had thought
You turned not to be the man of my dreams
For soon, I was living a nightmare

You were so angry; You could not bear to hear the truth
You did not live up to your basic responsibilities
You were uncaring and ungiving of your time, self, and emotions
And would lose control at a whim...

At first I thought you did not mean it?
I had faith in you, in us, in love
I was faithful to my vows and promises to God
I was going to make it work, so I bore all in silence
But it meant nothing to you, for my silence gave you courage
You got angrier, more hurtful - I was trapped in a nightmare
After ten long months, I cried out desperately for help
To those that love and care; and you ran off, leaving truth behind
But, I would no longer succumb to your lies and tyranny
And that ended the year of our life.

Did it make you feel strong to see me hurt and helpless?
Did you smile secretly to see me in tears and in pain?
Did you get empowered seeing me in quiet agony?
It must have been so, for you are deny it all now.
You lied about being sorry for all the pain you caused me
You really meant to hurt me for you are weak in character and spirit
I'm supposed to forgive you in private and accept your lies in public?
No, only the truth can save our love and heal the pain
Else, it is truly the end of the year of our life.

March 2005 *Shreveport, LA*

Time to Decide the Rest of My Life

There's been too much hurt and pain
I need time to decide about the rest of my life
Things didn't have to be this way, if there was love at all
Was trying to control and neglecting to care so important?
It doesn't seem that way now
I did not feel loved or appreciated - I felt used
Doesn't the loved one care and seek the beloved's happiness?
You did know what could make me happy
Not gold nor silver; just love... And it was too much to ask?

I don't want to spend the rest of my life wishing I had left him
I don't want a love without trust or truth
I don't want a love that seeks to control and subdue
I don't want a love that puts me second place, chasing shadows
I don't want to waste my life and love on him anymore
The cost is dear – it's taking too much from me
I just realized the past three years were all a lie
All the romance and promises a phantom
I don't want to waste another minute, if he will not change
He appears sorry now and professes love with such emotions, so pure
He says he can't live without me and cannot bear to lose me
He says he will cherish, love and care with all his heart now
Poetry pours from his soul, my heart aches with joy,
It sounds true, so sincere; but how long will the remorse last?
He says he's sorry he hurt me and lost my trust
He says he's sorry he betrayed our love
How long before he needs to assert his dominion and hurts me again?

I could forgive him; but I don't think I could forget
All the hurt, lies, and promises failed
I could forgive him; but I don't think I could forget
that he's tarnished our love so pure
our cherished memories with pain, scorn, shame...
I don't think I could live with that

Now he is professing his love, saying he cannot live without me

He says he's sorry for the pain he caused
He says he did not know what came over him
He says he lost control and did not know what he was doing?
He says he didn't mean to cause me pain...
I had believed him then...each time I forgave him
But he knew it was causing me pain, but still did all that anyways
Now I feel like a fool ..A fool for forgiving him
A fool for keeping silent and not telling for months
A fool for seeking to save our love
Till I could not bear it anymore, else I died

He left me for months without looking back
Now I am supposed to forgive and start anew
And believe promises of love and truth?
How do I know he won't do it again?
How do I know the dark secrets harbored in all the months of silence?
How do I know this is not a ploy to save his skin, freedom and ego?
How do I know his heart will not become vengeful?
How do I trust him with my life, my love, my future, my heart... How?
So, I need time to be assured that last year,
my supposed honeymoon turned nightmare will never happen again
How can he convince me of that?
If I ever think he'll hurt me again,
I'm going to move on now and never look back
Nothing is worth the pain I've endured this past year

I need answers, Lord...
I have kept silent not trusting myself to speak to him
Else I show how much he has hurt me or I still care
He has communicated by emails, letters and family for months
I don't know if people change overnight
But I know that I'd rather be alone than be this unhappy
I pray for guidance, Lord; Do I give love another chance?
My heart cannot withstand another heartbreak or agony
Show me the way, else I make a decision that'll haunt me forever
I will trust in the saying, "He gives the best to those who let him make
the choice. So, Lord, please choose my destiny."

June 2005

Promise No More

Don't promise to be there, when you know you won't
Don't promise to make me happy, when you know sorrow's lurking.
Don't promise me sunshine, when a storm is brewing.
Don't make promises to me, when you know they'll be broken.

Promise me bliss, only when you sing for joy
Promise me stars, only when the moonlit sky is clear
Promise me a cruise around the world, only when you'll sail with me
Promise me a home, only when we'll build as one
Promise me no more, for I'll rather live in my dreams,
Than awake to a trail of broken promises.

November, 2005
Shreveport, LA

Memories of Yesterday

I hold my breath a moment longer
Not wanting to make a sound
Listening to the howls
Of the roaring winds of time
As it caresses my cheeks
I want to hold on to this phantom
For as long as I can
Else the moment will be gone
Else the essence will be lost
Of all I had endured yesterday

They are mine…. Yes they are
Scars deep in my soul
Bearing witness to tears shed
Over life's twisting bends
Holding on to fading threads of hope
Praying with every breath exhaled
That the next corner turns into sunlit plains
From which fruits of lessons learned sprout
And indeed make worthwhile
Those painful memories of yesterday

December 2005
Shreveport, LA

Parts of Love

Eyes that looked at me with love
Ears that listened to my hopes and dreams
Lips that kissed so tenderly
Arms that kept me warm and safe
Legs that walked through life with me
Body that molded my frame so gently
Soul that merged as one with mine
Where are you my love, my heart?
Forever, these parts of you remain in my mind

December 2005

Sounds of Souls

Cries for Justice
Echoes of anguish
Shouts of outrage
Sounds of turmoil
Voices of despair
Searing across the globe
Into the depths of our souls

Do you not hear their sorrow?
Do you not see their turmoil?
Do you not feel their pain?
Do you not know their plight?
Will you not O brothers and sisters
Come to the rescue
In the wake of nature's devastating blow?

Be strong you victims
Hold on you survivors
Keep the courage you that rescue
Forge on you that live
Lend a hand you that are spared
Love a little you that watch
Rest in peace you souls so innocent

Victims of Katrina, your pain and tales will live forever
In the sea of life
In the sands of time
In the souls of man
In the logs of history
In the bosom of the Omega
Victory indeed is yours for aye

December 9, 2005

Cruise To the Bahamas

Day 1, Departure:
It was an experience of a lifetime,
and I can only try to recapture the sheer rhapsody
of the moments spent aboard the *Norwegian Sun.*
We set out early on Tuesday, January 17th, 2006
on a well-deserved vacation.
We drove two hours from Shreveport, Louisiana
to the Dallas International Airport where we parked our car,
and boarded the American airlines flight to Miami.

It was a smooth , uneventful flight,
and I was full of both excitement and apprehension about the trip.
Neither of us could swim,
and it did nothing to calm my fears whenever I remembered
that our stateroom was one of the ship's finest:
an ocean view with balcony.
"I'll have to remember to wear my lifejacket to bed,"
I thought to myself.
Looking over at him, we shared a smile, and I felt reassured that
we would enjoy our 3-night, 4-day ship cruise to the Bahamas.

We arrived at Miami International Airport
at 4.30pm on Tuesday, January 17th,
and took a cab to the port of Miami, twenty minutes away.
The drive through the palm-tree lined streets
and highways of the sunshine state was like deja-vu,
reminding me fondly of my seven month stay in Miami five years ago
during my medical school rotations.

As we pulled up to the port of Miami,
we stared in awe at the first glimpse
of the massive vessel in pristine white. It was beautiful!
As we would later learn, the Norwegian Sun,
part of the Norwegian cruise line of ships,
was completed in 2001 in Germany after two years of designing
at a cost of over 400 million dollars.
It was an amazing work of art.

We joined a queue for immigration checks of our passport
and luggage scanning before boarding the ship.

All Aboard:
I held my breath as we stepped into sheer luxury.
The interior of the ship was decorated in pure gold and brass,
with exquisitely regal, rich draperies lining the walls and windows.
Spiraling, golden stairways stood in the center.
We were escorted through the reception area
into one of the large dining rooms
which was used as a workstation with over twenty computers
to check in the 2,400 guests on board.
We had our pictures taken,
and our passports and I.D's reviewed again,
before we were handed our electronic room key-cards
which would serve also as a credit card
for any miscellaneous purchases on the ship
in order to discourage guests
from carrying cash around for security reasons.

There were about 12 elevators onboard the ship
and we took one of them to deck 8 were our room was located.
The ship is composed of 15 decks with 990 staterooms;
has a capacity for 2500 guests
and the ship crew is composed of 960 crew members
at our beck and call.
Our room was just like a luxury room in a five-star hotel,
and we had a marvelous view of the ocean right from our balcony.

The ship had not yet set sail,
but it was breathtaking to feel the cool breeze
of the Atlantic ocean on our faces
and stare straight into the deep still waters below.
We made several calls to wish our family and friends goodbye
and let them know we were onboard the ship.
By then, it was about 8pm, and we got ready for dinner
before proceeding to explore the ship and find the restaurants.
There are 10 restaurants onboard the ship:
2 main restaurants (seven seas and four seasons' restaurant)

offer freestyle waiter-service dinning 24hrs a day with open seating;
the Garden café and Great Outdoor Restaurant
offer Buffet Style service 24hrs a day;
and 6 specialty restaurants offer dishes
from around the world (e.g. French, Italian, Japanese..etc.)
Meals are all-inclusive in the trip cost,
But you pay for alcoholic beverages and sodas.
Unlimited ice tea and water are offered complimentary on the ship.
Only the 6 specialty restaurants require a cover charge of $10-$15
and you can order anything on the menu - and I mean anything.

For the sail away special,
 the specialty restaurants were offering half price
on their cover charges,
so we decided to try the Italian restaurant, *Il Adagio,* the first night.
We had a six course dinner that was absolutely scrumptious
Mediterranean seafood cocktail appetizer;
steak and Milanese chicken pasta entrées,
and authentic Italian tiramisu for dessert,
and a hot cup of cappuccino, to name a few.

The dress code is resort style casual for the rest of the ship,
but strictly evening formal
for all the formal restaurants from 5.30pm
(no jeans, shorts or tanks allowed).
It was fun dressing up for dinner every night.
The ship set sail eventually at 11.30pm
and we took the elevators to the outer deck area on deck 6 mid
to watch the ship sail away,
and strangers waved to us
as they drove along the busy Miami highways.
It was fun standing on the deck
as we enjoyed the cool fresh ocean night breeze
while the outdoor band played Caribbean music.
We retired early that night a little bit exhausted from the traveling.

Day 2, January 18th:
We woke up at 5.30am
to watch the sunrise seemingly over the Atlantic ocean.

It was surreal indeed with the aqua sheen of the crisp waters
bouncing in small waves alongside the ship.
The clean, fresh, intoxicating scent of the ocean rifted through the air,
and I felt the soft caress of the wind of my cheeks. Aaah! heavenly.

I had watched beautiful sunrises before;
but nothing compares to being right on the ocean
and watching the rays stretch and blend
in the horizon at the edge of the world like an illusion.
Our day starts with the captain greeting everyone over the
loudspeakers about 7.30am in a sea captain drool
telling us where we were docking:
"Good morning ladies and gentlemen, boys and girls;
 this is your captain speaking…".

The staterooms were equipped with cable TV and a channel
that had a view of the ship in motion along with the weather report.
The ship printed a daily brochure called *Freestyle Daily*,
that told us where we were docking and activities to do on the island;
as well as hour by hour schedule of activities offered on the ship:
from movie theatre viewing, comedy shows, Broadway-like ballet
musical operas, casino, karaoke sing-alongs, video arcade, fully
equipped 24hr fitness gym, aerobics and yoga classes, golf range;
volleyball court, a library with lots of board games;
over a dozen bars and lounges;
country music, disco and hip-hop night clubs;
24hr internet café ; Art Gallery; and *Mandara* Spa services.

The sheer magnitude of the vessel
was like five huge five-star hotels together,
and some guests were getting lost
despite the picture maps on every elevator floor.
The crew was extremely polite and catered to our every whim,
and treated us like royalty.
There was 24hr room service with the staterooms cleaned twice daily,
and more often if you requested.

In the morning, we worked out in the gym before showering
and getting a mouth-watering buffet style breakfast

in the garden café.
At 9.30am, the emergency alarm sounded
heralding time for the safety drill.
We returned to our staterooms to put on our lifejackets
before proceeding to our allotted lifeboat stations.
The drill lasted for twenty minutes
during which our drill captain showed us
how to properly wear a lifejacket
and what to do in the rare case
of emergency dis-embankment of the ship with lifeboats.
All the lifeboats were fully equipped
with bottled water, snack foods, and emergency medical supply,
and strong enough to contain 50 people each.
I felt more confident about being on the ship after the drill.

We docked at the port of Nassau, Bahamas
at 10am on January 18th.
It was a picturesque site as a pilot boat from the island
drove to our ship to lead us safely to the docking area.
A flock of birds flew around our balconies,
adding to the beauty of the moment
as some guest tried to feed the birds.
Other ships were docked already and they all looked small
as our Norwegian Sun towered over them.

As we exited the ship, our room key cards were swiped, as usual,
with each exit or entry for identification.
Also equipped at every door and room in the ship
were automatic sanitary hand wash liquid dispensers
to maintain a high state of sanitation onboard.
Nassau is the capital of Bahamas
founded in 1656 with a population of 185,000 people,
predominantly black
They were British colonized until July 10, 1973
when they got their independence.
They use an equivalent dollar currency,
 but with the queen's image on it.
Their source of income in mainly tourism,

hence the city is always clean and well-kept with brightly, colored
colonial buildings that added to the tourist appeal.

We boarded an air-conditioned new tour bus
and the driver, Frank, an well-informed indigene,
took us along with a few other tourists
on a guided tour of the city cultural landmarks.
The city had no mountains, few hills and mainly low-lying areas,
with a high cost of living; and well-known
for their locally brewed Bacardi rum.
As in most tropical countries, homes were built
with concrete and steel for storm protection.
We also visited the Prince George dock,
Forte Charlotte, and Forte Fincastle.

The grand finale of the tour
was the visit to the world renowned Atlantis Hotel on paradise island.
The hotel was an epitome of luxury
with chandeliers, golden pillars, exquisite sculptures and artwork.
We took lots of pictures, my favorite were the flying Pegasus horses,
The blue marlans (national fish of the island); and the famous
underwater marine life.
Atlantis, it appears, stands on water
and has the best view of the marine life in the world
from the hotel aquarium.
We visited the local stores where they were lots of
colorful straw hats, bags, tee-shirts,
seashell jewelry and beach wraps or sarongs.

We returned to the ship
for a hearty buffet lunch in the Great Outdoors café.
As we sailed away from Nassau at 6pm,
amidst the loud horn of the steam engine,
After indulging in a session at the Mandara Spa.
I decided to try the ionithermie treatment
that was reputed to remove inches off your waist.
The hour long spa treatment was wonderful.

We had dinner that night
 at the Le Bistro, French restaurant
and indulged ourselves to a five course dinner
comprising French escargots for appetizer,
 perfectly grilled filet mignon and
 honey-glazed salmon a L'Oseille entrées,
 with crème brulee` and chocolate fondue for dessert,
 and a cup of authentic espresso to end it.
 I took a picture with the captain of the ship at the end of dinner.
 We then spent the rest of the night
 swaying to the beat of reggae music from the live-band on deck 11
 as we leisurely sipped a tropical fruit-flavored alcoholic drink from a
real pineapple, and ended the night with a visit to the casino
and hip-hop night club on deck 6.

Day 3:
By the time we awoke the next day, January 19th,
we were already docked at the next Bahamian island, Freeport,
this was just as colorful as Nassau.
We visited the straw market, and danced merrily
to the Caribbean live-band
stationed at the dock along with other guests.
After lunch onboard, we toured the ship
and stopped by the library to play a game of checkers.
Then we played ping-pong with fellow guests on outer deck 11.

I watched the sunset as it formed a mirage
over the deep, blue waters as we sailed away again at 5.45pm
with my little adorable friend Sarah from Kentucky,
who would not leave my side all evening, keeping me entertained.
As the ship sailed away, the band started playing calypso and mambo
beats to kick off the sail-away party as guests lounged on the poolside
deck. We joined the group of guests swaying to the beat, and formed
a dancing line around the pool area, and later the band lead singer
taught the ecstatic crowd a famous Caribbean dance: "move to the
right, move to the left… back and front" with everyone gyrating their
waists in fun.

Before dinner that night, we had fun at the Karaoke bar

and I joined a few brave guests and crooned my solo rendition
of Madonna's *La Isla Bonita and* Toni Braxton's *Unbreak my heart*.
Dinner that night was splendid at the seven seas restaurant
with our exquisite waiters in their crisp penguin colors.
It was a tasteful four-course dinner with citrus compote appetizer,
mushroom soup, beef fettuccini entrée; and for dessert there was
orange sherbet, sundae and vanilla-caramel pudding.

After dinner, it was off to the grand finale show for the night:
a musical ballet opera rendition of Peter Pan in the theatre.
It was just magical and splendid with skillful set decoration
and ballet dancing by fairies, captain hook,
 and the Neverland characters.
After the show, 50 or so crew members
came in a musical procession to thank us
for coming on board the Norwegian Sun.
It was quite a heartwarming, and we gave them a standing ovation
with tear filled eyes of gratitude.
They spent 10 months a year on the ship.
We ended the night at the disco lounge where we had a cocktail and
enjoyed the swing dance competition for the 50's couples;
and later an Elvis impersonation contest
that had us roaring in laughter.

I woke up on January 20th, with a regretful sigh: the cruise was over!
I could see the port of Miami in the horizon
as the sun rose in the east of the Atlantic ocean.
We were back to reality, back to land.
We would be disembarking after breakfast in Miami.
I felt like staying back on the ship, on the live-size fantasy island,
indeed a moving holiday resort.
It was indeed the best vacation ever.
A three-day luxury cruise across the Atlantic ocean
on the Norwegian Sun with my hubby.

January, 2006

Book Two

The Journey of OlaRose and Obiola, The Twin Angels

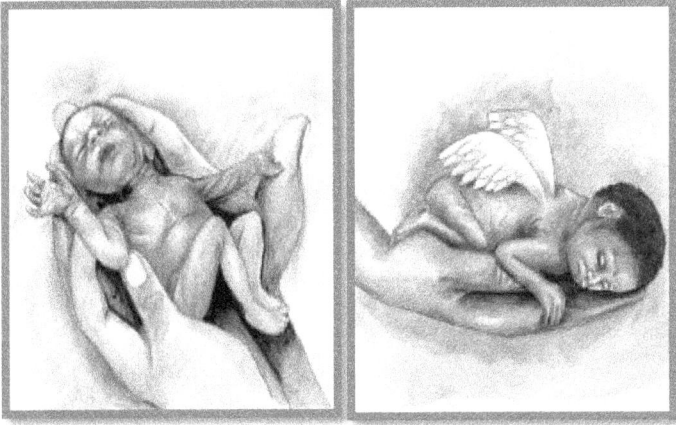

...With love to Obiola, our twin angel and hero

Part One:
Before I formed you in the womb... "

The Miracle of Life

God is great !!
I have witnessed his hand in a true miracle.
Every day of our lives should be a miracle,
but this was evidence that God is all powerful,
and man's finite knowledge is no match for His infinite wisdom.
We are just a fragment of his Heavenly genius mind.

I want to testify with all my heart
and shout it from the rooftops.
Though my tongue and weak spirit hold me back,
I still owe it to God to spread HIS MIGHT
and tell of his miracle in my life.

A man without God has no faith
and gives up easily with no respect for life or creation...!
"You are dead..." he says to the unborn innocents,
 "there's no life in thee."
Despair sets in as ominous visions of death and decay abound
Alas, no safe haven was found within.
Without man's power, none can be or so it seemed.

All reason gone, my soul soars!
It can't be! There must be a God!
I cried! I wept! I fought for life!!
Beloved of mine, pray with me !
Let's beckon to the heavenly powers above
to save and banish evil from around us
for hades will not prevail!!!
Life there is, with every breath I take, I believe

So I beckon to thee, "O ye innocents" of the Father
"Live, I bid to you. Be strong and hold on tight...
Fight for your souls

Any mortal there exists with but a thread of faith,
So from there, will fate prevail
So that even though laid to rest as is,
Arise you will from hades cove
To become seeds of hope
And spring forth the fountain of life!
And indeed they did.

He who doubted shall be full of shame
He will not renounce despair
Nor see the hand of God
But will say "..so it is in the world of man...
A game of chance, probability, or gambler's luck."
Alas, he will not give honor to Him above.
"Good, fortunate," is all he says.
But nay, it is but for the grace of God
Who plants and reaps where he sows.

Sing from the mountain top all you that believe
Whatever ye seek from God above
Bread, Water, Life, Hope
Let this tale inspire you
To hold on to the good within
And keep the flag of faith flying
Suffering and loss may come your way
But God knows best and bids his time
If you believe and call upon the heavenly hosts
With all knees bent together in prayer
You will be vindicated
And life bestowed on you.

Beckon to the heavenly mother and the Spirit Divine
But beware of temptation that will come from the angel of death
Who will be mad at you and God
and try to shut the ray of light from entering your heart.

He'll tempt you with despair, doubt, anger, and fear;
And put you at logger heads with those you love
When you need them the most.

This is a powerful battle for souls between heaven and hell.
God creating life, and the devil trying to take it;
And so you will find yourself in the midst
of such potent unearthly forces.
Call on all you hold dear to see you through
as your soul may be weakened from seeking the light.
Be on your guard that you may prevail
For at last, the storm will calm!
Heaven will be victorious and you will laugh again!
My sojourns brought me and my love as one
No matter our faults and imperfections
That is the miracle of life!!!
The joyous souls within me bountiful and whole...
To God be the Glory....!!!

October 2006
Westminster, Maryland

Our Family Prayer

Dear Father,
We come to you with humility and trust
asking for your infinite blessing and grace on our new family.
We, your children, thank you
for the precious gift of the womb you have bestowed on us.
We thank you for our two beautiful souls, our twin angels,
our daughter and son: the two new additions to our family.
We feel unworthy for your divine gift to us
and pray that you give us the grace
to take good care of our heavenly gifts.
Watch over our careers and business
that they may flourish and be successful,
and give us our daily bread
so we can provide a home, adequate care
and nourishment for our new family.

Holy Father, our maker and our God,
nurture our little ones with your grace
that they may grow healthy and strong with each passing day.
Give them the food of life to sustain them,
the drink from the fountain of your spirit to invigorate them
and let their guardian angels keep watch over them
as they reside in their mother's womb,
all three hearts beating as one.
Keep mother and children healthy and whole,
and when the time comes,
let the heavenly choir sing for joy and herald to this world,
our two wonderful angels.

Dear Holy Family,
we ask that you teach us to love each other
completely without reserve;
to give and not wait to receive,
to help each other when in need;
to be patient and tolerant of each other;
to forgive one another for errors and mistakes,
 to vow not to hurt each other's feelings with words or omissions;

to aim to please and not to be pleased;
to be faithful to our holy vows before God
and cherish one another more and more each passing day;
and above all, to bring up our God-given children
in a warm, loving, and stable Christian home.
Bless Heavenly Father, our families with peace and good health,
and may they be a source of moral strength
and love for our new family.

Jesus, son of Mary,
become the age of our little ones,
watch over them and be their friend forever.
Mary ,Virgin Queen and Mother
intercede for us with your beloved son.
St. Joseph, our model for husband and father
intercede for us to the heavenly Father to grant our petition, Amen.

December, 2006
Westminster, MD

Part Two:
Poems to my Twins - Echoes from the Womb

Foreword:

As I lay in the labor and delivery ward for four weeks after spending two weeks earlier admitted in two other hospitals, I was spent, sad, terrified, in deep anguish and nothing could allay my fears. I believed I was either going to die trying to prolong this pregnancy against medical advice or my babies may die from weakness or lack of blood flow in my womb as a result of my severe pre-eclampsia. Suddenly my whole world came crumbling down. I had come in to see my obstetrician for a routine check, and here I lay with no clue as to how this saga would end. Developing severe pre-eclampsia at 20 weeks was uncommon, and with severe fetal growth restriction due to blood flow compromise to the babies, the doctors expressed no hope that my babies wouldl survive. I was being strongly asked to terminate the pregnancy to save my life – my clinical condition was deteriorating. I was devastated, to say the least.

At the first request from the doctors for me to terminate my pregnancy, I said vehemently "No!" How could anyone even think such? I would not let anyone harm my babies! They tried to reason with me saying my life was in danger; but I continued to say NO!!. I was not sure I would make it through the morning, but I was not going to let any harm come to my babies.

My family kept watch day and night at my bedside. The flow of people traffic in and out of my room was like grand central station. Coming from a large family with ten siblings, there was no wonder. My parents were a huge rock of support for me. They took turns keeping watch day and night.

My mother, a woman of deep faith in God, kept a prayerful vigil at my bedside going through rosaries and prayers. Early in my ordeal faced with a grim and bleak prognosis, I sometimes got too weak in spirit to pray with her. She would continue without me; and in despair, I would ask her not to pray out loud. I ,at that time, could not understand why God would allow such a calamity to befall me after all my prayers to Him. She would continue in silence, not giving up. She had great faith in God's power of miracles, and a great faith in my babies. She believed they would be okay, especially OlaRose who had the worst prognosis. "She is dying, any minute now.." we were first told after the definitive ultrasound upon ambulance transfer to the teaching hospital. She had no end-diastolic blood flow. The only blood flow seems to be going to her brain. The consequence of that was not known: preservation or massive intraventricular bleeding at the expense of other organs which were getting no perfusion. In the womb, we were all more worried for OlaRose. Obiola still had some placental blood flow. He was a lot more active, while OlaRose lay really still with no movement at all; but through it all, their heartbeat were strong on the doppler checks. "Whatever blood flow she is getting will be enough for her... it will be enough for her God to sustain her," my mother would say repeatedly.

As the days went by, I lay on strict bed rest in the labor and delivery ward, pondering solemnly, my life and my fate. Just three months earlier, I had thought "Life, could get no better!" – I was doing my neonatology fellowship; my husband and I had bought our first home in Maryland; and we were expecting our twins – soon found to be a boy and a girl. Life indeed couldn't be better! And now, I was about to lose everything that mattered to me. How could God allow this calamity to befall me? I had dedicated my life, my love, and my babies to Him. Why did He let this happen to me? Why has He abandoned me in the darkest hour of my life? I was alone in my suffering, or so I thought.
One day, light infused my soul. I soon began to realize that God had not abandoned me. God had saved me and my babies' lives. He had known what was going to happen to me at this point in time, and He had been preparing me mentally and emotional my whole life for this period of reckoning in my life: the strong yearning to go on to medical school after a long professional training in optometry,... directing me to pediatrics, when every muscle in my being wanted to be an ophthalmologist; the sudden intense urge to continue a training in

neonatology, rejecting great job offers at the time in pediatrics; the decision to choose a training program close to my family, even though I had great offers in other top institutions farther from home.

It soon all made sense. He knew all along what was going to happen... He was preparing me for this day and time. It was left for me to rise in faith knowing that He would not abandon me in my hour of need. I would trust in Him who knew tomorrow to lead the way to the light. Thus, I could say "no" to the medical advice to terminate my pregnancy at 21 weeks even though I was warned of possible impending doom to me from severe pre-eclampsia. Thus, my little knowledge of medicine empowered me to say 'no' throughout my stay in the labor and delivery ward to requests to induce the pregnancy and terminate it. The team were kind and respectful of my bid to continue the pregnancy, even though they couldn't understand why I was holding on to a pregnancy that could yield developmentally disabled babies because of the level of placental compromise. "You could have more babies if you end this pregnancy now," I was told. "We will not deliver for the babies because they are not viable.. They have to first reach the limit of viability of 24weeks and show steady weight gain... If we have to go to the OR emergently due to your condition declining... we don't know what may happen. You could bleed profusely and we may need to remove your uterus; and you may never have any more kids. It is not worth destroying your body and health, if you do survive this. Your kidney function is declining, you could end up on the ventilator, if you survive this... you may have destroyed your health or body for future pregnancies. If you end this pregnancy now, it will all reverse to normal while there is still little damage to your internal organs."

I was 30 yrs old at the time. I could have more babies, but it was not that simple. I wanted these babies.. I already had names for them: OlaRose and Obiola... they were my God-given twins. I was attached to them. I held steadfast in my decision to keep going, and knew they would humor me only up to a certain point. I was getting checked several times a day for mental status changes, seizures, etc. or signs of worsening to eclampsia, which they told me would take the decision out of their hands; and the pregnancy would be ended regardless of my wishes.

One morning after my first few days in the teaching hospital, my father brought to me, my book of poem, " Image of a soul," and my first novel, "A Dream Come True," first published at the age of nineteen in 1996, according to him to keep myself occupied. "You know, you could write down your thoughts like you used to as a young girl," he said. "This experience is the only one of this kind you will ever have… You may never feel like this again. Write down your thoughts every day and what you are going through." I shook my head in despair. "No Daddy," I said. "I can't do that right now." How could he talk about me writing poetry at a time like this? I wondered in disbelief and slight chagrin. I just wanted to be left alone with my pain! I wanted to be consumed in the anguish of now and the unknown. No-one knew how I felt, and I did not want anyone to tell me how to feel. My parents were writers, poets, and indeed literary giants of their time, and have always inspired us to express ourselves through poetry from a young age. It had brought me solace and direction through my teen years – but how could I think of poetry at a time like this?? He went home that night, but returned the next day with a red ruled notebook and a pen. "Here you go," he said. "Take your time. This is for whenever you feel you are ready to write." I stared blankly at the book in disbelief. That is my Dad… ever gently urging us to our greatest potential. Even when you lose faith in yourself, he never loses faith in you. He is my biggest champion and supporter. I didn't touch the book while he was there. I didn't have the will or energy to write a thing, I thought. Then he sat silently for a couple hours across from me like he does every day, a silent companion to my pain. I didn't say a word.

After he got up and left, I continued to stare long and hard at the red notebook, before picking it up and flipping through the empty pages. How does one put in words this pain, this feeling that was tearing me apart? In the quiet and still of the morning, left alone, I started to write, slowly at first, in hesitation, then purposefully as if my life depended on it. I wanted to pray and I could not, so I thought I would write down my plea to God the Father to save my babies; I would write down the echoes resonating from my womb, the unheard cry for help from my unborn babies. I began to write down my hopes, my fears, my emotions, day to day, in the way I always did as an introverted, shy child and teenager. I began to write the way I knew best… in poetry of words .. lyrics flowing like a song from my soul. As I wrote, I felt safe; I felt comforted; I felt at peace. As I wrote, I felt an open gateway to communicate with God. I felt He was listening. I felt He was with me – though unseen. It was a powerful feeling. I hid my writings for a few days, and would read it over and over as a prayer throughout the day. It was my prayer to God. I wrote till the notebook was almost filled.

My dear mother found the book one day, on one of her daily visits; and I was reluctant to share it at first. She opened to "Make them Whole", and asked permission to read it. After she did, she said softly "This is a powerful prayer, my daughter. I will join you to pray it." She was referring to "Make them Whole." She took to reading out it out aloud, and my other poems as well, as I lay exhausted on the bed for weeks. Soon, my sister, Ngozi, my faithful companion throughout my pregnancy saga would read it out loud to me; and then my husband and I would pray it together on the nights he stayed over. We would read daily: Make them Whole, The Visitation, The Struggle in my Womb, My twin angels, Litany of Hope and Healing, Well with my soul, Prayer of Thanks, I've made my peace with God. Ngozi suggested I send it by email to the rest of our siblings; and that's how the whole family started praying it as a novena for me and my babies…. Make them Whole, Litany of Hope and Healing (said on the rosary beads) throughout my stay in the L & D. The prayers were empowering… They were invigorating…they were my hope in the face of hopelessness, in my darkest hour.

****

Make Them Whole

God the Father, give them life
Creator of souls, save them
Maker of Us, make them whole
God the Son, be with them
Word made flesh, save them
Blood of Christ, inebriate them
Body of Christ, make them whole
God the Holy Spirit, possess their souls
Giver of Life, breathe for them
Spirit of life, fill their souls
Healer of souls, make them whole

Jesus, the child, be their age
Stay with them, comfort them
Hold their hands, play with them
So they never feel alone
Guardian angel, keep them safe
Keep watch day and night
Ward off all evil and demons
Guide their blood flow and keep them whole

Mary our Queen and Mother dear
Embrace them and wrap them in your bosom
Pour your graces unto them
Care for them and love them as your own
Heavenly hosts, keep watch over them
Nourish them, body and soul
Heal their body, give them courage
Let the blood of life flow within them
Make them whole

Father, Son and Spirit divine
I commend my darling angels to you
OlaRose and Obiola, my precious twins;
Keep them healthy and whole for aye.
March 3, 2007 *Baltimore, MD written while hospitalized for high risk pregnancy complications.*

The Struggle in My Womb

Before you formed them in my womb
You knew them through and through
You gave them to be mine
Please don't take them away.

Once you formed them in my womb
I knew them through and through
I knew them to be mine
heavenly gifts from you divine
Please now, don't take them away.

Each day they spend in my womb
I feel them to be mine
Beating in unison with my heart
Blood of my blood, flesh of my flesh
Please don't now take them away

Each week they spend in my womb
Their souls are blended with mine
My spirit and theirs are one
Their suffering and pain, I feel
I feel them fighting for their lives
Clinging to hopes, last strands
So how can I give up on them
Please don't take my babies away.

Each month they've spent in my womb
Their lives have become mine
I love them with all my heart
I love them more than life itself
Now I'm asked to choose
Between my life and theirs
Don't make me choose
between my daughter or son
Please don't take them away
I'll give up my life for them
So please don't take my babies away from me ...

Each minute they've spent in my womb
I hear them cry out these days
"Mummy help us!, Mummy don't let go!"
Never my darlings! I say
As long as you fight for your lives
I fight for you with all my life
So I implore you Father, Creator give them back life
I implore you Jesus, give them strength,
I implore you Holy Spirit, renew their weak bodies and blood
Keep my organs vital and well
That I do not have to choose
between my life and theirs
Please keep my blood pressure stable
Preserve my brain, kidneys, liver, lungs and heart
from the ill demons of preeclampsia
from the toxins of their ill placenta
Channel the blood away from any obstacles,
so it can get to be anew
To fill them, heal them and save them
Please don't take them away

Each second they spend in my womb
I hear their cries all day long in my head
Mummy don't give up on us!
Never, my darlings! How can I when I feel you move?
How can I when every day I hear
your Doppler heart beats, strong and purposeful
How can I when I see you squirm
Kick and roll over in the ultrasound.
Glimpses that bring such joy to my soul.
I'll never give up on you, my babies
Each second you're in my womb fighting for your lives.
So please Father, preserve us three
And don't take my babies away from me.

March 3, 2007, Baltimore, MD

written while hospitalized for high risk pregnancy complications.

My Twin Angels: OlaRose And Obiola

OlaRose, my darling
My first daughter from God
My precious twin girl
Lodged all curled up in your sac.

Anchored to a failing placenta
Sending toxins that weaken you
Depriving you from growing big
Cutting back the nourishing blood you seek
No flow during diastole, the Doppler shows
But a strong spirit you are indeed
For you adapted all so well
Rerouting blood to your brain
And shunting through a narrow channel
to nourish and sustain your body.
So my darling, hang on tight
OlaRose my darling don't give up
Mummy is here for you always.

Obiola, my heart, My first son from God
My precious twin boy
All sprawled in your own sac too
More spacious than your sister's,
So you crawl and swim about
Though anchored to a weak placenta
from a thrombosis all spontaneous
But still functioning unlike your sister
Filled with brotherly love
you summon up courage despite your own struggle
You swim across to her side daily
Seemingly to comfort and show your love
Saying "Hold on sister dear"
Letting her know she is not alone.

Each day, we search for you on the doppler;
But I know exactly where to find you.
Visiting on the left above your sister

Your head cradled above hers as she clings to life
Letting her hear your heart beat as one.
And the next doppler check eight hours later
you're back in your own corner,
Fighting to strengthen yourself .. Fighting for survival too.

OlaRose and Obiola, my precious angels
Mummy is fighting for you too
They say you cannot survive
on a compromised placenta and reduced blood flow
But I believe the God I worship
is nourishing you and will keep you alive.
They say you are dying, not worth risking my life for
But how can that be?
Don't they see how brave and resilient you are.
Never have I seen such courage
Each day you breathe and live, they marvel
A true medical mystery
They said you will not survive past a day
That was a twenty-three weeks and two days
But each day you prove them wrong,
Strengthening my resolve to keep on hoping and fighting
As we count day by day, four days now gone by.

OlaRose and Obiola
They say you are at the limit of viability
And worse off for being growth restricted.
I know too well what they mean.
Being a neonatology fellow, it drives too close to home.
Poor prognosis, poor survival rate
Increased morbidity and mortality
The heart-wrenching neonatal diseases:
respiratory distress syndrome (RDS), Necrotizing Enterocolitis (NEC),
Patent Ductus Arteriosus (PDA) , ventilator dependency,
Chronic Lung Disease (CLD), Retinopathy of Prematurity (ROP) -
leading to blindness, Hypoxic-ischemic encephalopathy (HIE),
Cerebral Palsy (CP)

tube-feeding, multiple surgeries and infections
A life of suffering and pains if you are born too early and do survive
How can any mother wish that for her children?

I am torn between my knowledge as a physician
and my emotions as a mother.
How do I end their lives before it begins?
They say my life comes first
I know that's reasonable
but I pray God preserve my organs.
I've made my peace with God
So my darling angels, Obiola and OlaRose
Be friends to each other and sustain each other
in that dark and lonely place.
It's just for a short time
While mummy pleads with God
for each day that passes by.
To buy you more time to grow big and strong
So even though you come out extremely premature
your survival rate and prognosis improves.
I need to give you a fighting chance
I owe that much to you as your mother
So hold on tight, OlaRose and Obiola
Mummy and Daddy will be here for you, now and for aye.

March 3, 2007,
*Baltimore, MD written while hospitalized for high risk pregnancy
complications.*

The Visitation

Come to me O blessed Mother
Virgin Immaculate
Visit me in my hour of need
Like you did your cousin Elizabeth
Let the light of your presence
Shine forth on the fruits of my womb
And my soul will be glad
That my two angels may jump for joy
at your holy countenance
And in the presence of your divine Son
Just as St. John felt while resting in the womb

Come to be with me O blessed Mother
Comfort me in my hour of distress
Still the raging fires in my body
Calm the torment in my soul
Pour forth your grace on me
that my body may heal and be strong
So that I may carry my precious gifts within
to a safe delivery, healthy and strong.
Come to me O blessed Mother
Visit me in my hour of need.

March 4, 2007
Baltimore, MD written while hospitalized for high risk twin pregnancy.

Litany of Hope and Healing

OlaRose, my darling, Mummy and Daddy love you (2x)
Obiola, my darling, Mummy and Daddy love you (2x)
Hold on tight, OlaRose, Mummy's here for you (2x)
Hold on tight, Obiola, Mummy's here for you (2x)
Fight for your life, baby girl, Mummy's here for you (2x)
Fight for your life, baby boy, Mummy's here for you (2x)
Don't be scared my daughter, Mummy will never leave you
Don't be scared my son, Mummy will never leave you.
God the Father, give them life
God the son, give them strength
God the Holy Spirit, give them hope
Spirit of Christ, guide them
Waters from the side of Christ, cleanse them
Blood of Christ, heal them
Body of Christ, feed them
Holy Spirit, breathe for them
Holy Mary Mother of God, pray for us
Holy Virgin, conceived of the Holy Spirit, pray for us
Mother of Christ, vessel of grace, pray for us

Refrain: O Jesus deliver them
From the powers of the enemy, O Jesus deliver them
From the spirit of darkness, O Jesus deliver them
From despair and anguish, O Jesus deliver them
From pain and suffering, O Jesus deliver them
From hunger and thirst, O Jesus deliver them
From the dangers of prematurity, O Jesus deliver them
From the clutches of death, O Jesus deliver them
From the sin of abortion, O Jesus deliver them

Refrain: O Jesus heal them
With your divine grace, O Jesus heal them
With the waters of salvation, O Jesus heal them
With the food of life, O Jesus heal them
With the power of your touch, O Jesus heal them
With your saving blood, O Jesus heal them

For all sick infants that suffer today, O Jesus heal them
For all expectant mothers suffering an illness, O Jesus heal them

Nourish them with your body and blood O Jesus,
that they might grow big and strong
Empower them with your spirit O, Jesus,
that they might cling steadfastly to your light
Don't give up OlaRose,
Don't give up Obiola,
Mummy and Daddy are here for you.

March 4, 2007
*Baltimore, MD written while hospitalized for high risk pregnancy
complications and prayed daily for 3 weeks till the delivery of the
babies*

I've made my Peace with God

I've made my peace with God
My soul is now at rest
My spirit no longer will fear
Unseen shadows or faceless demons
My soul has confessed to my maker
My countenance now lifted up high
Anointed with his divine oil
I've made my peace with God

I've made my peace with God
His body I've daily received
To heal my ails and strengthen me
For the spiritual battle that rages within
the giver of life cannot want me
to take innocent lives just to save mine
That cannot be just or true
So my resolve is steadfast and firm
as long as their hearts beat and they move within
To the end will I keep the fight
despite worsening blood work and labs,
rising creatinine and uric acids
Warning of failing kidney function
Chart tipping values of proteinuria
confirming renal damage, dialysis need and concern;
Dropping platelets daily,
heralding a life-threatening hemorrhage

 Persistent anemia depletes my energy and strength
Alarming high blood pressures
heralds the impending doom of seizures and mental state change
that could take my life or leave me a vegetable for ever
Now I'm kept ready to be rushed to surgery any minute
All are shadows, my soul believes
the Lord is my light and my salvation
He gives and takes at will, not man
So whom shall I fear?
He cannot give me more than I can bear

So willingly my cross I carry with faith
Believe he is washing my ills away
Taking each sunrise as a sign of his love
Indeed, I've made my peace with God

I've made my peace with God
Seven days gone now, it's a marvel I'm still pregnant.
They expected my babies to die in my womb
Or me to go into shock or multi-organ failure
Due to the stress of severe pre-eclampsia
Empowered by His body that I daily receive
And strengthened by his anointing oil
I firmly said "I'll make it through the week-end.
I'll see you all on Monday," to my caretakers.
As they looked sadly and said their goodbyes
Smiling with unwavering faith I said:
"My babies and I will be here on Monday."
Because, I know I've made my peace with God.

March 5, 2007
*Baltimore, MD written while hospitalized for high risk pregnancy
complicationes.*

Well with my Soul

It is well, I believe
It is well, I know
It is well, It is well
With my soul

Peace flows, I believe
Peace flows, I know
It is well, It is well
With my soul.

Healing waters come to me
From my Lord's stricken side
Cleanse my body
Heal my soul

It is well, I believe it
It is well, I know
It is well, It is well
With my soul.

March 5, 2007
*Baltimore, MD written while hospitalized for high risk pregnancy
complications.*

Prayer of Thanks

Thank You God for another day
Thank You Lord for another dawn
Thank You Lord for another breath
Thank You for Your saving grace.

My faith is renewed
My hope is restored
My spirit is revived
By Your infinite mercy

Thank You God for another smile
Thank You Lord for daily bread
Thank You Lord for healing touch
Thank You for your saving grace

March 6, 2007
Baltimore, MD written while hospitalized.

Miracles do Happen

Miracles do happen
Yes they do
I bear witness indeed
Staring at the ultrasound and doppler
The heads together in the pelvic area
"They turned ... they turned ..."
I echoed in disbelief.
"She turned. She turned..." my strong angel
Lying face up transversely head down
Positioned vertex and head down, he lay
Daily she regained her strength
And finally did make that turn
Miracles indeed do happen!

Miracles do happen
No end diastolic flow, was her initial assessment
But today her doppler shows blood flow
 in systole and diastole too.
Perfectly formed they both are
All organs intact, their activity great
A perfect biophysical profile score of eight over eight (8/8)
Despite notching of the uterine arteries
Indicating the on-going pre-eclampsia
Their prognosis initially was poor
Now they remain healthy, strong and nourished.
A testimony that miracles do happen

Tuesday March 6, 2007
Baltimore, MD

God's Plan for Me

How often in our life
Have we wanted something with all our heart
Have we worked hard to achieve something
Have we prayed earnestly for something.
How often in our lives
Have we moved mountains to get some where
Have we made sacrifices to get something
Yet no matter how much we did
It didn't happen
Yet no matter how hard we worked
It did not come to be
Because it was not God's plan for us.

Now I see that what I want and need
May sometimes be different from
God's wishes and plan for me.
Even if my intentions are true
Even if my wishes hurt no one
Even if my desires are well deserved
Even if I work and pray the hardest
What I want for myself
May not be what God wants for me
At that point in time - now I see.

Now I have learned
After times of misery over misfortune
After moments of longing for what I can't have
After hours of toiling for elusive dreams,
Of self-pity, of pride for unfulfilled wishes
to let go and let God, as Mummy always says,
To work and pray as hard as I can
And leave the rest to Him above.
Because He gives the best to those
Who let Him make the choice in their lives.
Now indeed, I've learned, to accept God's plan in my life.

Saturday, March 10, 2007

Thy Will Be Done

Thy will be done, O Lord
My life indeed is yours
My destiny in You will be fulfilled
My life story You already wrote
The ending You already know
Even though the clouds are dark
I will not be glum
Even though the nights are eerie
I will not be afraid
Cause You and only You know for sure
What my future holds
My Father and savior
My life I commend to You
Saying with full confidence
Thy will be done, O Lord

Wednesday, March 14, 2007
Baltimore, MD written while hospitalized.

What Do I Do?

Two and a half weeks now gone by
Since you've been fighting for your lives
Since I've been fighting for you two.
Then you were pre-viable
Now your chances are improved to fifty per cent
at 25 weeks and 4 days today.
Then my life was in danger
and the choice was easier for me
For I could not end your lives
Just to save myself from organ damage.

So to God I placed our lives
and he has preserved us so far.
Now your lives are in great danger
due to continued placental insufficiency
from persistent severe pre-eclampsia
From no end-diastolic flow to reverse flow
The doppler studies are concerning indeed
So the choice is harder now.
Do I keep going trying to buy each day I can?
but risk hypoxemia, fetal distress and death to you?
Or do I let you be delivered now
while your heart still beats strongly
and give you a fighting chance outside the womb
and expose you to the rigors and risks
and uncertainties of premature birth.

What do I do?
For at the crossroads, I am now.
I'll go to my Lord as always
My creator, the giver and taker of life
You make the choice for me God
The definitive doppler studies are approaching
Studies say it's impossible for reverse flow to improve.
They say their condition can only get worse.
I need a miracle today, dear Father.

Let the doppler studies show the same
Or show improvement and I will keep going
following your guiding light.
But if the doppler is worse,
I'll take it as a sign that it is time
To let my precious angels out to the world
Before their brain and organs suffer damage
Before they lose strength and will to live
before hypoxemia claims them.
Despite my pleural effusion abdominal ascites and
worsening labs and renal function, I would go on,
 but I'm so filled with concern for my babies worsening
due to reduced blood flow and nutrition.
I'll trust in the Lord
And let Him lead the way
I'll let Him make the choice.

March 14, 2007
Baltimore, MD written while hospitalized for high risk pregnancy
complications.

Running Out of Time

I fear not of worsening pleural effusions
compromising my lung function
With threatening respiratory distress/failure
I fear not of increasing ascites
from prolonged severe proteinuria
due to leaky capillaries and declining renal function

What I fear really is running out of time
to give my babies each extra day they need
to grow and receive nourishment
despite severe placental Insufficiency

What I fear is the onset of hypoxemia
from compromised vascular flow to my babies
that may soon put them in distress and rob them
of the strength to fight for their lives

What I fear is that I may not be there
to see them cry, smile, and grow
to watch them crawl, walk and speak
if my organs indeed do fail

What I fear is not death or pain itself
It's the possibility that I may not be here
to hug, cuddle and kiss their faces
If I keep going on

We're running out of time, O Lord
You've brought us so far
It seems a miracle to all that see
Even my doctor marvel and exclaim
"You've exceeded our expectations.
We didn't think you'd last a day,
Now look almost three weeks gone and counting.
Keep doing what you are, cause it's working."
"It's the prayers to God," I testified
For indeed an international chain of prayers

had been formed joining family, friends the world over
And all that heard our plight for life.
God cannot be blind or deaf to our cries.
or indeed he works a miracle each day
when all hope seems to be gone.

Now I feel greedy for asking for more time
Three weeks earlier, I had asked for a few days
and at most two weeks now,
I pray for more days and another 2 weeks
Still trusting in your mercy and compassion
For I believe you gave these angels to me
To be a testimony of your love and power
And not to take them away in vain.
So in you I will continue to trust
even though I'm running out of time it seems
The good Lord who has seen us so far
Will see us through to the end.

March, 15, 2007.
Baltimore, MD written while hospitalized.

My Faith

Faith is believing without seeing
Hoping when all hope is gone
Trusting in the unknown
Saying "Yes" when all say "No!"
Marching boldly ahead while blindfolded
Putting all your eggs in one basket
Letting God lead you where He pleases
Faith is all I have left now.

Concerned that OlaRose had not gained any weight in 2 weeks
While Obiola gained about 110 g,
The neonatologists advised delivery for both
The obstetrics doctors thought there is no guarantee
that her heart will still beat tomorrow.
Delivery may or may not save her, they thought,
Since she's still not viable,
I am 25 weeks and 6 days,
but she still measures barely 22 weeks at 440g
"Why subject him to extreme prematurity by delivery now?
Let him be, at 660g, and keep going," they said
"And let nature take its course with her; she is sure to die
Her demise will not affect him with separate placentas."

I will not choose between either of them, I cried
I want them both, my daughter and son
I'll deliver now if I thought she'll be gone tomorrow
And give them both a fighting chance.
I'm not worried about my health or labs
I'm worried about my darling angels
They are suffering so, yet so brave.
Dear God, show me the way to go, I prayed
My daughter is starving it seems
But still her heart beats so strongly
Her maker indeed must be nourishing her with his body and blood.
I don't believe God wants me to choose
I don't believe God will take them away.

He is testing my faith now or so it seems
Since no-one knows tomorrow or the next
I'll trust in HE who knows tomorrow.
For after all, he's brought us three so far.
3 weeks gone by, and no-one thought we'd make it each day
I trust he'll nourish their body and soul
Despite their compromised placenta
So blindly, I'll follow where He leads
That's what faith is
Truly believing in the unknown.

I'll keep going each day at a time
Till Monday when daily biophysicals start
As long as they both have perfect scores
We'll keep trudging on in faith
And see how far the Lord will take us.
Once their biophysical score drops, I'll take it
As a sign that it is time
To let them both out to the world
So God can complete the miracle he started
For how can he manifest His power
if there is no adversity
How can I testify of His goodness
if there is no suffering
So with Faith I'll keep going
and I'll make my covenant with the Lord
To glorify Him in all I do
as he preserves my precious angels
and gives them life.
So even though as small as a mustard seed,
My faith will move mountains indeed.

March 16, 2007
*Baltimore, MD written while hospitalized for high risk pregnancy
complications.*

I Choose Life For Them

I chose life for them
theirs over mine,
Insisting on continuing the pregnancy
even though my life was in jeopardy
from progressive, severe pre-eclampsia and
God sustained me so far
Keeping my organs vital and stable
despite worsening labs
as I bought my babies maturity
And with each passing day within my womb,
their chances of survival increased by 2-3 %

I choose life now
theirs over mine
I want to be delivered for fetal indications
for any signs of distress from either baby
and not for maternal concerns of 22 grams per day of proteinuria,
hypertension or poor renal function
Or any other signs of declining clinical status
Because I believe my maker will preserve my organs and life
so He can continue His work of sustaining
and nurturing my divine fruits within
who so bravely fight for life
A marvel they are still growing
despite 3 weeks of compromised placental blood flow.

I choose life again, faced with the heart-breaking decision
of watching her life end
just to preserve his a little while longer even if for a day
I'm asked to delay delivery even if she is in distress
and so long as I am clinically stable.
That's a choice I cannot make
My poor daughter has fought so hard
Three weeks of no placental flow and reverse flow
She barely has enough to sustain her
And I feel her lying really still all day
trying to conserve her energy.

She grows weaker each day, it seems
Her heartbeat taking longer to find
She's fought so hard to be alive
How can anyone ask me to give up on her?
He seems to be getting weaker too.

Today the Doppler shows no end-diastolic flow
At mid-cord for him.
His biophysical are still a perfect 8 out of 8 score
While hers now a 6 due to declining amniotic fluid
Today my heart almost skipped a beat
As she would not breath or move for minutes.
The ultrasound probe poked to no avail.
Her brother who was lying on top of her
prodded gently on her chest with his tiny feet
and she moved in response to him
As we watched in vain for practice breathing,
I prayed and called slowly onto my patron saints in heaven
Saints Anthony, Rita, Jude, Gerard, Pope John Paul the II
and St. Joseph whose feast is today to pray for her
As I chanted, her chest began to rise
And I knew my prayers were being heard
"Go on girl, listen to mummy," said the ultrasound technician
As we all stared at the miracle unfold.
Her brother prodded with his feet on her chest
And she began to breath and would not stop.
That's all the sign I needed to know
That she will live despite the odds
I will fight for her life despite the risk
Cause God promised me two not one baby
And He has never been known to fail.

I choose life over and over again
Delivery will put both babies at risk, I am warned
She most likely will not survive now or later, they say
You risk losing him too
When a little while longer might have bought him more maturity
But may cause her death
"Let her go and do nothing," they say

"Her death will not affect him due to separate placentas
So he can keep going daily as long as he can.
You've suffered so much and put your life at risk for so long
You deserve to come out of this
with at least one healthy baby.. which might be him," I'm told
That sounds reasonable, but my faith is strong
That I will be victorious in the end, God will manifest his power for all
I will have my two babies in the end
So, her life I'll choose right now

Because she is weaker and is dying according to science;
At any sign of a biophysical score less than 6
or decelerations of heart rate from either of them on the monitor
I will deliver and take my chances.
God will see them through resuscitation
 and throughout the NICU stay.
He will use the doctors as an instrument of his healing touch and life
guiding their care and treatment of my precious babies
whenever they arrive
Be it today, tomorrow or whenever.
Q6 hour biophysicals we'll keep going
till I see that her health and strength are failing
or he shows any signs of decline too.
My health will be preserved by God,
as long as they can survive in my womb
So whenever given a choice between life and death of another soul
I'll always choose life
Any other choice is for our maker above, not man.

Monday, March 19th, 2007 @ 10.30am.

*At 300pm on March 13th, OlaRose was believed dead due to no
detectable heart beat on ultrasound. Despite medical advice to let
OlaRose die due to the life-threatening risks of going to surgery at that
time for the mother, she insisted vehemently on having a C-section to
deliver both babies to save OlaRose. Both twins were delivered alive.*

Part Three:
In Memory of Obiola, Our Angel and Hero

On Wednesday, March 28th 2007, family members, close friends, colleagues and well-wishers came together to pay their respects to little Obiola Julian Anthony Ndubuisi, whose story of courage, sacrifice, and love had spread across state and country lines to live in people's hearts.

My Angel From God by Olachi Mezu Ndubuisi

Obiola Julian Anthony
My brave little boy
My handsome son
Why did God take you from me?
Why Father, why? I asked as I held you in my arms,
as the spirit left from you
They were my miracle babies: OlaRose and Obiola
The story is not complete if he doesn't live, I wept.
How will the story be complete without Obiola?

How do I begin to say how wonderful you were?
How do I tell your brave little life's story ?
I'll start from the beginning
When God put you in my womb
Along with your sister, OlaRose Adaobi Rita
At 6 weeks, only one gestational sac was seen on ultrasound
Now I believe that was just OlaRose
A week later, a second sac was found,
And that was you Obiola, I now believe
You were an angel that God placed in my womb
to protect OlaRose and I, and keep us safe.
At 9 weeks I had prolonged bleeding
I believe you protected your sister from threatened fetal demise.

First hospitalized at barely 21 weeks gestation
for poor fetal growth and early pre-eclampsia, the saga began
By 23 weeks and 2 days, confirmed with pre-eclampsia, severe
proteinuria, declining renal function and severe hypertension
I was advised to terminate the pregnancy in order to save my life
The babies are not viable , I was warned,
and have severely compromised placentas.
My little girl was worse off due to no end-diastolic flow, reverse flow,
and declining amniotic fluid causing growth restriction.
They would not survive if I had been delivered then
I chose their life over mine ...
I will not end their lives, God cannot ask that of me, I cried
As long as their heart beats strongly on the Doppler,
I swore to keep going
Only God can take a life
So don't ask me to take innocent lives, I cried
Then, I made my peace with God and was not afraid
Daily, his body I received and was anointed
The Lord is my light and salvation
Whom shall I fear?
He would preserve me as long as I needed to give them life.

So day and night we prayed to God, family and friends
to give my babies and I each day they needed to grow big and strong.
Every minute I prayed saying" God the Father give them life,
God the son give them strength, Holy Spirit breathe for them."
I called every day on our Virgin Mother, Mary
to visit me and comfort me like she did her cousin Elizabeth.
I called everyday on St. Joseph,
the foster father of Jesus to pray for us.
I called every minute on the heavenly hosts and angels
to protect my babies
I called every minute upon the holy saints:
St. Gerard, Patron of expectant mothers,
St. Anthony worker of miracles,
St. Rita Patron of Impossible cases, St. Jude hope of the Hopeless,
Pope John Paul the second,
my deceased elder brother Obinna Julian Mezu, my parents' first born

Whom God called at just one year old.
I called daily upon the God who says yes, when everyone says no!

It was like an international prayer chain
As family and friends all over the world prayed for our lives,
all three of us.
Each day, God performed a miracle and kept all three hearts beating
"You have exceeded our expectations," the doctors said.
"We can't believe you're still pregnant.
Keep doing whatever you are doing because its working,"
"It's the power of prayers," I said.
I had asked God for a few days to get to 24 weeks, the limit of viability
so that I might receive the steroid shots
that would facilitate their lung maturity.
On getting there, I asked again for two weeks from God,
that they may add some weight to sustain them
through the rigors and stress of premature birth, if it comes.
All those three weeks in the labor and delivery unit
as I battled the complications of pre-eclampsia
including ascites and pleural effusion,
I spoke to my babies telling them
"Mummy loves you, hang on tight my babies,
Mummy will never leave you.
Don't be scared my babies, mummy is praying for you.
Don't give up, OlaRose and ObiOla,
Mummy is fighting for you."

At 25 and 5 days, after three weeks of hanging on,
I was told OlaRose was still dying.
even though all their organs had formed well,
she had not gained any weight in 3 weeks.
She had no nutrition or blood flow.
Her umbilical blood flow was totally reverse
and her amniotic fluid severely depleted.
I was told to let her die and keep going as long
as my clinical situation did not deteriorate.
That her death will not affect him
since they were di-di twins with different placentas.
My heart was breaking.

I will not choose between my son and daughter, I cried
How could I give up on my baby girl?
She was fighting so hard.
Each day I heard her strong doppler heart beats
Each day I saw her all curled up on the ultrasound,
conserving her energy.
My brave little boy took care of his sister.
their heart beating in synchrony
He was positioned on the upper right quadrant,
but during each doppler check, his heart beat could not be located,
and on using the ultrasound to scan,
he would be visualized lying on the far left, on top his sister,
his head cradled on hers.
I imagined him telling her
"Hang on sister dear, I'm here for you… don't give up."
Ten hours later, he would be found back in his original position
resting, gathering strength and fighting for his life too.
My brave little hero

All through that weekend, as we prayed for her life;
we particularly prayed through St. Joseph
because his feast day was on the Monday, the19th.
All through the weekend,
you lay right on top of her and would not move,
giving her warmth, giving her life….
Now I know cause she was born hypothermic.
Obiola, my son, my beautiful son…
you gave your life to save your sister and me.
On that Monday morning, on March 19th, around 9am,
The ultrasound showed that Obiola
now had no end-diastolic flow in mid cord ,
and OlaRose still had reverse flow.
She was not moving, and her heart was beating a little slower.
"She does not respond to the ultrasound probe," the tech said,
"but moves only when her brother touches her."
OlaRose's chest was not rising
Then Obiola who was lying on top of her
started to thump on her chest with his tiny little feet
and suddenly her chest started to rise for a few minutes,

he was resuscitating her
Then her chest stopped and for about a minute we stared horrified
and as I prayed…. God the father give her life…. St. Joseph pray for her.
Suddenly, her chest started moving up and down and would not stop.
The ultrasound tech was excited and said,
 " Go on girl, listen to mummy..,listen to mummy."
A miracle had unfolded in front of our eyes.

I was concerned when it took OlaRose so long to breathe
and I spoke to the maternal-fetal specialists
who reiterated that her chances of survival was close to nil
and since I've been through so much,
they would want me to come out of it with at least one baby.
I was advised to let her go and keep going
for as long as I could for Obiola who was bigger.
I might lose both of them, if delivered now
I was devastated.
How could I watch her die and do nothing?
How could I live with myself?
She's fought so hard, what sort of mother would I be?
Due to my concern for her, a repeat biophysical profile
was scheduled for 12 hrs later about 9pm.
I was monitored for an hour
and Obiola was noted to have repeated decelerations of his heart rate
I feared both lives were now in danger.
About 2pm, I was in deep prayer with family and friends
And we had just shared the story of Jarius' daughter
whom Jesus raised from the dead.
When I panicked saying," I have not felt them move in a while.
I called for the doctor hurriedly for an ultrasound.
As we stared at the screen, she had no chest movement at all,
and her heart had slowly stopped beating.
I whispered in tears, "God the Father, give her life, God the son, give
her strength. Holy spirit breathe for her…" I kept chanting.
That caused one or two chest rises, and no movement was seen again.
It was too late. She was gone, it seemed.
"I want a C-section right now, " I cried. "I can't watch her die.
 I can't live with myself if I do nothing." It was 3pm.
I had made my decision and there was no going back.

I was taken to the operating room,
not knowing if any of them were alive.
Praying the Lord is my shepherd and saying "Jesus, I love you."
20 minutes into the C-section, she was delivered.
For a second, there was silence, and then I heard,
"She's crying..." my soul wept tears of joy. M
A minute later at 4.54pm, Obiola was delivered crying too.
Her Apgars were 7 and 8 and his were 9 and 9.
They were active, perfect and pink.
That was a miracle to me. They were perfect, beautiful babies.
Both were soon electively intubated because of their low birthweight.

Obiola, my son...
You were born on March 19th, 2007
On the Feast of St. Joseph
I pound 7.5 ounces (675g), 12 inches.
While your sister was 1 pound 0.6oz.(470g), 11and half inches.
I loved you and your sister in the womb,
I felt closer to you as we fought for our lives
I loved you even more when I saw you face to face.
Your full black hair, your smooth oval face,
your exquisite angelic features
My handsome son.....
We had joked all through the months of ultrasound
that OlaRose would look like her daddy and you would look like me.
And indeed you did, but you had your daddy's nose ,
 long limbs and beautiful smile.
I was recovering from the C-section
but I had to see your beautiful faces every minute I could.
Each day, I would visit morning, afternoon and night
I would watch you in your incubator fighting for your life.
My brave boy, I realized you had used all your strength
to take care of your sister
And now, you were exhausted and in severe respiratory distress
due to your prematurity.
I would sing to you and your sister everyday:
"Mummy loves you, Daddy loves you, but Jesus loves you more..."

Mummy and Daddy love you, Obiola we do,

Mummy and Daddy love you, O yes we do.
Mummy and Daddy love you, Obiola we do
And we'll pray for you everyday

Jesus loves you, Obiola he does
Jesus loves you, Obiola he does
Jesus loves you, Obiola he does
And his angels will watch over you.

Little did I know then that you were an angel
Given to me by God
He placed you in my womb
that you may save OlaRose and myself
You saw your sister to a safe delivery,
giving her warmth and sustaining her
when her placenta was compromised
You saved my life too
No matter that my renal function declined
or my blood pressure escalated
Despite the pleural effusion and ascites, you preserved my organs
So that even after delivery, my fast recovery was a miracle indeed
It was all you, my valiant hero
My god-sent angel

I had told God I did not want to choose between my son and daughter
And he didn't make me choose.
He brought you two out safely for all to see and marvel.
But shortly after birth, your clinical condition deteriorated
Day after day of maximum FiO2 on the oscillatory ventilator
With fluctuating oxygen saturation,
 as your lungs were overcome by their immaturity
I prayed by your side calling on my litany of Saints and guardian angels
to pray for you and the baby Jesus to comfort you
and be with you and OlaRose
As you suffered, OlaRose stayed stable on minimal respiratory support
my 1 pound miracle, and all were amazed.
But I didn't realize then you were giving up your life for her

On Wednesday, March 21st

when you had prolonged desaturations
that was a sign from God that you would not be here for long.
So with your grandparents, Sebastian and Rose, present,
your daddy and I got your baptized
Your innocent souls were recruited and saved as children of God.
Every day it seemed, I had a priest come and bless you and your sister
To give you the strength to keep going on
As family and friends prayed daily for your healing
Obiola, my son, on Friday at bedtime
you gave me another sign that the end was near
They said you were deteriorating,
 and I spoke to you through the phone.
I called on the Father to give you your life back
and the Son, to give you your strength,
and the spirit to breathe for you
And they answered my prayers as you improved
as I spoke and sang to you.
You knew Mummy was not ready to let you God at that time,
so you waited and hung on to life to give mummy more time with you.

On Sunday, the reading was about Lazarus being raised from the dead
As Obi and I read it together,
we marveled at the power and mercy of God
Little did we know that it was a sign
that you were going to be raised from the dead that very Sunday
We came with a priest that Sunday afternoon
to bless you and pray for you
You looked so peaceful as I talked to you,
stroked your hair and sang to you
It tore me apart to leave you that day, now I know why….
At 7pm while at home, I started to have chills and feel sick inside..
that was the point when you deteriorated.
When I got the call that you were dying,
I cried "No! Please give him the phone so I can talk to him"
They put the phone in your incubator
"I said Obiola my son, Obiola my son….
Be strong baby, Hang on tight to your life
Please wait for mummy… You are not going anywhere
Mummy is coming.

It will take Daddy 50 mins
but mummy will talk to you all the way.
Don't be scared my baby, mummy's here….
Don't be scared, mummy's praying for you..
Baby Jesus is in the incubator with you…he is holding your hand,
Don't be scared… you're not alone..
Mary our mother is hugging you to her bosom.
Your guardian angels are with you…
at the head and the foot of your bed..
Your patron saints are praying for you.
God the Father, give you life…
God the son, give you strength…
The Holy Spirit will breathe for you,….
The Holy Spirit, will breathe for you!
I know you are tired, baby, hold on tight, my son…
Mummy will be there soon."

I got there and you were still waiting for me.
I kept talking to you and praying;
Calling on the heavenly hosts and your patron saints:
As your oxygen saturations, heart rate and blood pressure declined
I stroked your hair, and tiny hands and feet,
and you moved each time in response to my touch.
I said, "Mary, my mother hold him close to your heart
like you did your son, Jesus.
Press his head to your bosom, so he is not afraid.
God the Father give him back his life,
God the Son give him strength,
Holy Spirit, breathe for him, breathe for him…"
I soon cradled you in my arms and kissed your beautiful face,
and your tiny hands and feet.

For over two hours I had barely held him through the incubator
as I prayed and wept, while the doctors took turns
hand bagging him off the ventilator
Suddenly, he was laid in my arms, "Olachi, hold your son. He has been
without oxygen for over 2 hours. It's time to say goodbye,"
I was told by the one of the medical team.
The oxygen tubing was disconnected from his endotracheal tube.

My heart wept as I held him for only a couple minutes
I cried, "Breathe my son...breathe...
please God, don't take my son from me."
I cried till your heart stopped and your chest stopped moving.
I pressed my fingers gently to your chest
and felt your tiny heart skip a beat and stop.
My heart stopped too.
 "God the Father, you are the maker of us, creator and taker of life...
Please give my son, back his life.
 Mary, my mother, you also held your dying son in your arms,
please ask your son to give my son back his life," I cried softly
My tears could not run any faster as I poured out my anguish.
"Your will be done Father, but do this one miracle for me
and bring him back to life like Lazarus
and I will dedicate my work as a neonatologist to you,
 I will love all those sick babies as my own
...and glorify your name in all I do.
Give him back his life and I will give my life to you.
I am a sinner... but I am his mother and I am praying for him.
Jesus, I still believe.... I have faith.... I still believe," I cried.

All the vital signs on the screen had zeroed out finally.
I cried and I cried, "Holy Spirit breathe life into him..."
Suddenly, I felt your chest move and your heart started beating slowly.
The numbers on the screen started rising
your heart rate with from zero to 80,
your oxygen saturation rose from zero to 60%.
I felt the spirit in you stir,
Suddenly, you opened your eyes ever so slowly...
You opened your eyes ... and looked at me... you looked at me...
 and squeezed my finger that held your tiny fingers..
You squeezed my finger so gently and firmly.
 "He is alive..." I cried through my tears. Alive forever....
You saw me your mother
and I stared into the depths of your beautiful dark eyes....
Obiola , my son, ... Obiola, my son.... Mummy loves you.
Your eyes slowly closed and all was silent.

Through my tears and anguish,

I smiled peacefully as I gazed at your beautiful face…
I felt a warm sensation course my being
I felt so LOVED by God! I felt His presence within me
God had answered my prayers…
He brought you back for the few seconds
to show me His mighty power…
but still say No to an earthly life!
Obiola is not of this world, God seemed to say
"His mission is finished.
I have called him back to the heavenly choir of angels
where he came from."
"Thank you Father,… thank you Jesus…. Jesus, his age hold his hand.
Guardian angles and patron saints lead him into the Kingdom of God.
Mary my mother, I give you my son, You know how I feel for you've
held your dead son in your arms too carry my son in your arms into
the arms of God the Father. Lord, I still believe…. I still believe.
Be it done to me according to your will," I cried.
My heart was broken, my tears overflowing, but I felt such joy

Obiola, my son…. Obiola, my son
My beautiful boy, my first son
My angel from heaven; You are my hero
I wanted to see you grow up; To take care of you and love you
Watch you play basketball with your father
And get to scold you a little when you are naughty
And have you watch me grow old too
All Glory be to God above who loaned you to me,
For six and half months I carried you in my womb,
I was your mummy… the mother of an angel
How could I have deserved such an honor?

I asked God not to make me choose between you and your sister
And He didn't make me choose, but blessed me with your lives
You were born healthy and whole
I got to kiss you, hold you, sing to you and pray for you
I got to love you with my whole heart
I thank God for every precious minute we spent together
I thank God for seven days of pure joy and bliss…
the joy of loving and caring for you as your mother.

Seven days that will last me a whole life long
Your Daddy and I will never cease to love you
Our first born son

Obiola, my darling,
Ola's heart, My heart, my very own OBI
It's not farewell at all
You are our guardian angel now; Our intercessor with God, the Father
OlaRose misses you, but I tell her that you will always be with her
You are in the incubator with her, holding her hand
And she is as strong and well as can be now
A true miracle of life
Your innocent pure soul has soared to heaven to the Father
We are not sad; We only cry because we miss you,
We thank God for the brief but precious time spent with you
We celebrate your life
Did you Know Mummy is a Twin B too
to your Aunty Oge, who is expecting Little Ikechi?
At 34 weeks, he kicked up a storm in the womb the night you passed,
seemingly sad you would not meet face to face.
Your spirit shall always live in our souls
For you truly have not just been my Obiola "Ola's heart"
but indeed an Obiora, "Heart of the people...Everyone's heart",
Save a place for us in heaven, my son
Mummy Loves You; Daddy Loves You; OlaRose loves you , but Jesus
Loves you more.

Olachi Mezu Ndubuisi (Millie Ola)
March 26th, 2007
*Eulogy read during the funeral service of Obiola Julian Anthony on
March 28th, 2007 by his mother, Olachi.*

To My First Son by Obiora Anthony Ndubuisi

You came into this world for a short stay
You came into this world for a purpose
You came to protect your twin sister
You came to protect and save your lovely mother
You came to bless us

You are my little brave heart
Your bravery has inspired me
It gave me another reason to live and be fearless

I was looking forward to taking you to school
I was looking forward to kissing your forehead
I was looking forward to teaching you basketball
I was looking forward to your bright future
I was looking forward to dressing you as little O, and showing you off

But we know nothing as humans
We can't predict the next hour
God's will always takes precedence

Hope is not lost, because you gave us just that
You are truly a blessing to us
For that, we thank God
Pray for us as you rest in eternal peace
You will forever live in our hearts

Insha Allah, Love Always,
Dad, March 27, 2007
Eulogy to Obiola Anthony Ndubuisi Read by his father at the burial site after the funeral mass

Poems For Olachi Joy, OlaRose, and Obiola

"A bouncing baby boy who sacrificed his life
to save the selfless Mother who risked death
to choose life for her unborn babies.
In the womb, Obiola fed and protected his sister OlaRose
who was given no chance by Medical Science
'Greater Love Than This No Man Hath'"
---------- Dr. S. Okechukwu Mezu

OBIOLA JULIAN NDUBUISI
Tombstone
St. Charles Borromeo Catholic Church Cemetery
Pikesville, Maryland USA

Petition for Safety in a Difficult Pregnancy by Dr. Rose Ure
Mezu

Your Gracious Majesty, Dearest Savior,
We honor You, we worship and adore You
To keep Your promises to us, we trust in You.
You promised the Father will grant any good request
We ask in Your name. In Your name, Lord Jesus Christ.
We ask, we plead that Olachi, the twins- Obiola & OlaRose
Remain nourished, active and healthy while yet in her womb.

You tell us "Do Not Be Afraid!" – we are trying to not be afraid
Because we know that only You, Lord can grant all good requests.

Save the twins and keep them from all dangers
By keeping Olachi, their mother healthy.
To Olachi - Your own Jewel – You Lord have
Given special skills to save and nourish other lives.
Keep her safe that she may minister to Your people
And help save those little lives entrusted into her care.

Men and women of science have plotted the scenario.
Yes! we do thank You for their creative knowledge;
We laud You for their near exactitude of Knowledge,
But You Lord are the Beyond Science –You Are *MetaScience*.

The Twins' blood supply is little, the learned medics say.
Even that little, Lord Jesus, Our Savior, Giver of life,
Is all too sufficient, for it is You, Precious Blood
Who in truth is nourishing OlaRose and Obiola.
The waters from Your wounded side continue to
Wash, cleanse Olachi's Heart, lungs, liver, kidney, etc.
Your healing waters cradle the twins and their mother,
Nourishing, sustaining them until the fullness of time
When they will emerge alive to honor and exalt Your
Glorious name, Oh, wondrous Love and awesome Mercy!

We know that Your Mother Mary, Purest of women and
St. Joseph her cherishing spouse, are interceding for them.
All the saints and guardian angels do keep watch over them
Every second, minute of every day as they ask God for their
Wholesome lives and safety entrusted to Saints Gerald and Rita.
In the end, Olachi and all around her will in triumph witness
Everywhere to everyone the awesome miracle of their deliverances.
 Amen! Amen! And Again, Amen!

March 10, 2007

Olachi Joy: God's Incomparable Warrior by Rose Ure Mezu

See how she glides! Such beauty, such grace!
Hear her speak: such authority, such knowledge!
Read her words, such lyricism, such wise insights!

She is *Olachi* – God's precious jewel!
The incomparable Astorea – kpankpandu.
When life throws her a challenge
This shining star stands tall to meet it
When buffeted by winds of trouble
She bends like a reed, but refuses to break.

Given a choice, our *Igolo* readily lays down her life
Refusing to choose between her two children
"**I want them both**," were her constant cries.
Is she greedy, or stubborn, or selfless, or all of these?
Soldier on, peerless Queen, boon to the Mezu Clan!
Soldier on *Agunwanyi*, Christ's Lenten Warrior-Mother!

Faith sponges out Fear
Life offered up buys two other lives – her twins,
Her flesh and her bone.
Her life, a willing sacrifice that all may live
To praise God's mercy and bounty on this earth –
  in the land of the Living.
Thus, may the joy of my Joy be complete.
Hooray for Life's Warrior Princess – Olachi Joy!

Friday, March 16, 2007 .

Who Are You, God? by Rose Ure Mezu

Who are You, Lord?
Who really are You?
We call you God, and know You
by other names
But who truly are you, Lord?
Do you have a name?
Do You have a face?
Do you have an abode?

How do I know You?
How do I apprehend You?
How do I feel You?

For answers to these imponderables,
I must dig deep into my being:

      In my heart, You are my heartbeat
      In my veins, you are my blood strength
      In my mind, You are Wisdom
      In my very core, You are Wisdom and Courage
      In my eyes, You are Beauty Incomparable
      In my head, You are Unfathomable Mercy
      In my being, You are Endless Love.

Where are You, God?:
In me, You are the breath of life
and everywhere, in everything
Outside of me, **You are:**
The air that I breathe

      The wind that rustles the leaves
      The sun that gives warmth to life,
      Ripening ears of corn and all fruits
      The Rain that waters all living things,
      You are obeyed by Hurricanes and Tsunamis
      You are the torrents that float us a secure boat
      With which to row through life's choppy waters

You are Eternal Sunshine of Warmest Love
You are cool waters of the Lake of Purest Love
You are my Desire of the Everlasting Hills
You are the my Light of the Never-ending Day
You are the Fullness of Your Own Time
Hastening to us OlaRose and ObiOla.

March 16, 2007

I Could Swear I know them: OlaRose and Obiola by Rose Ure Mezu

I could swear I know them well
Their antics in the womb so funny
They defy all pundits of science.

The twins have galvanized our world
Into a human global chain of prayer
That even Ikechi Fortune, Jr. 32 weeks old
Still in the womb also kicks up a prayer storm
For being blood cousin to OlaRose and Obiola,
This son of Ogechi, twin to the twins' mother —
The three infants I had dreamt tumbling out
Months before they were even conceived.
I could swear I know them already.

Love can actually redeem our world, I thought
Suddenly, hearts have become sweet and kind
People have become so caring, so warmhearted
From East to West to South and North
Prayers cascade down in saintly torrents.

Who are these befuddling twins?
These amazing grandchildren of mine
Whose presences feel so well-known
So aptly named with all the graces one can count
They trigger so much warmth even in hard hearts.

One searches for Obiola with the sonogram machine
Only to see his head nestled above that of OlaRose
As if to say, "**Sister dear, hang on tight
I will share my warmth with you.**"
And so their two hearts would beat in unison.

When OlaRose's heartbeat fails to register
Obiola prods her with a kick and her heart restarts,
And the Nurse smiles as she registers the heart beats

"Not viable," they said at 23 weeks
 "Why jeopardize your life, Olachi?
Terminate them for you can have others."
Well, they've now past 26 weeks
Their heartbeats are now not so weak
Their biophysical profile still at 8/8

I've learnt so many new terms:
"Growth restricted, Reverse flow"
"Well," I thought to myself, "I know ONE Who
Can make 'Growth restricted' **be** 'Growth permitted'
ONE who can make 'reverse flow' **be** 'Direct flow'"

Indeed, I know these babies so very well:
OlaRose, so patiently stubborn, feisty as ever
Creative, she grabs her own food Wherever,
Whenever, and However so little, it feeds her well!
I indeed could swear I've known this twosome, ever!

These brave twins have such character, I say,
Colorful personalities, they are, Olachi's twins
As daily battling, they cling stubbornly to life.
Their bravery brings such smile to my face.
Thinking of them, laughter bubbles up to my lips
I really believe I've seen them before face to face!

Yet, I can't wait to meet you, dear Ones
For when I do, I surely will know you
Bone and Flesh of mine, you two are the ones.
I can hardly wait to welcome you into my world!

Sunday, March 18, 2007

Of Birth, Life and Miracles By Rose Ure Mezu

. . .And then they were born! After so much suffering, now they are here, I exulted – the famous twins. . . . OlaRose Rita came first, the baby girl that was thought to be dead: "I am the Resurrection and the Life," the Lord had said to Martha. Behold, OlaRose was alive! Later came her brother, ObiOla Julian Anthony – and they were both alive! My daughter, Dr. Olachi Joy Mezu-Ndubuisi readily laid down her life, and as the Lord Jesus promised, she got it back with her twins as added bonus. It was an occasion to celebrate, and a Day to remember!

. . . One of the many miracles that were manifested during this period is the wondrous love link between people - even strangers, through prayer. There has been a veritable global prayer chain of friends and relatives from the many states of Nigeria to England to America and beyond, through e-mails, through phones, with church groups, prayer ministries like Alan Ames, Silent Unity (very consoling prayers), my students and fellow teachers, and so many families. I solicited prayers everywhere from everyone I met. It has been wonderful how God has touched so many hearts, opened peoples' mouths and have inspired words of encouragement pour out, such that I am now firmly convinced that if we can show sustained kindness and compassion towards one another, love can recreate our world. People literally have been speaking in tongues.

. . . With baited breath, I had got ready for the Caesarean operation. I had for a while now through practice transported myself spiritually to a sphere beyond fear and doubt. Fear is a specter I have had to keep confronting and keep trying to defeat on many, many occasions. Once again, I remembered our confrontation – **Fear and I**- openly yesterday, March 18, 2007:

> **FEAR**
> "Do Not Be afraid, "is the divine injunction.
> But how do you "Not Be Afraid?"
> I think of the specter of Fear
> I stand upright to confront Fear
> And it looms so large and queer
> But I know fear is mere shadow

So, I exhale, stretch out my hand to scatter its
shadow
But I encounter no substance, no resistance.
Now, Fear has no *body*, the story goes.
Fear is like a cloud, fog or mist
I blow my hot breath into it and it dissolves
I slice it with a knife, it creates a pathway
If I simply walk through it, it gives way.

Yet Fear's shadow seems so large.
"*SEEMS*," that is the key word
For things are not always what they seem
Fear melts like ice water before my fiery Faith

And the way is suddenly clear when like
The near-spent sprinter, I throw out my chest
And cross the Finishing line beyond fear.
And then I behold the healing Light so Clear
Who is the Reality of good things to come.   –
03/18/07

The operation done, Dr. Algers her Ob announced to Olachi, "You have your twins and our work is done. The NICU unit, your group will now take over." All of the staff and the doctors, technicians, nurses, cleaners - have been great. Olachi never needed the blood for transfusion that was held ready. Her blood pressure had held stable. Heaven and prayerful wishes of people of goodwill had prevailed. **The first stage, the most important, was over**, I thought. Before now, we had no way of knowing if the twins would be born alive! Now, I thought, the real work of praying and tending to the new babies would begin. I remembered what Dr. Harmon, the renowned perinatologist had said,

> *No, I will not be surprised. In my long years of practicing medicine, I have seen enough to believe that the inexplicable can happen. I have seen a baby like her in the same position survive with no permanent damage and be quite normal. Even as we tell you what could happen based on medical findings, any*

person who claims to know for certain all that will happen tomorrow would be lying.

OlaRose was **that "baby"** Dr. Harmon spoke about. With humility, I thought to myself, how magnificent medical science is in this age, and how lucky we are to be living here and now! but also, I exulted that it was proved wrong, at least in two points – Olachi's vital signs held stable through faith prayers, and OlaRose did survive and is alive through the grace of Providence! While the one attending handled Obiola on one side of the room, the director from the opposite end asked me to come and behold my new grandchildren. I held the infinitely tiny hand of OlaRose and she actually squeezed my hand. I shouted with amazement. She squeezed me! My husband would thereafter tease me about my poem and the line that said, "**I can't wait to meet you, dear Ones / flesh and bone of mine.**" "Well,' Sebastian said, "she is telling you that they are now here." I then went to see ObiOla Julian Anthony. He was tall and bigger. That Monday night and also Tuesday, my husband and I slept for the first in about a month – blissfully and without nightmares, and for two days, I relished the joy of this miracle of salvation, of new lives that have arrived amidst so many difficulties. I was unwilling to hear any negative news.

But in the week that followed, we would be thrown back again into the temporal, material dimension of human concerns, into a world of tribulations and mental anguish. Anxiously, we waited, watched and prayed that the twins would make it. It had been a dramatic, action-packed, fast-paced and stress-filled one month. But little OlaRose, barely 1 lb, grew from strength to strength and gradually went off most of her medications, now needing only partially the ventilator. But ObiOla, her heroic supporter and shelter in the womb now struggled to keep going – male babies, the doctors had said, are more fragile. They seem to be right, for otherwise a perfect little man, his lungs were weak. A crisis first occurred on the night of Wednesday, March 21st. My daughter Dr. Ngozi Mezu quickly baptized Obiola with holy water that her sister Kelechi had brought from St. Jude's shrine. Later, the hospital chaplain Rev. Larry Schumester came and formally baptized both OlaRose and ObiOla. I was relieved that the twins had formally been welcomed into Christ's holy Church. Before we rushed in panic to the University Hospital, I stopped to send a message to Alan Ames, the Catholic mystic and healer:

"Alan, please pray for Obiola - my grandson with low blood pressure and failing lungs." Rose.

And "In a message dated 3/23/2007 9:11:27 A.M. Eastern Daylight Time, toheaven@iinet.net.au writes:
   I am praying for your grandson, God bless, Alan."

Again, on 3/24/2007 5:19:52 P.M., I wrote to him again:
   Dear Alan, Thank you. Keeping praying for God's immeasurable mercy and love for the unborn and the fragile newly-born babies. His sister OlaRose Rita - much smaller is however holding stable.

   ObiOla needs to start breathing more on his own. Their birth / survival thus far is already a major miracle. He has had two crises already - one last night and the first the night when I sent to you the one-line message to pray. He was revived on both occasions. Both babies need to get off oxygen.

   I am writing, and will soon send an account as it concerns my grandchildren's contact with your healing and prayer ministry. Thanks for your encouragement and consolation. ---Rose Ure Mezu

I thank Alan Ames and Beverly Burke among so many others for their prayers.

But finally, on the night of March 25, 2007 – feast of the Annunciation of the incarnation of Our Lord Jesus Christ, ObiOla would be called back to his Maker. His mother held ObiOla and rocked him crooning her prayerful lullabies, and pleadings,

"Spirit of God, please breathe for him;
ObiOla, my darling, you are not going anywhere;
Please Lord, let him live,
do not take away my beautiful son.
ObiOla, mummy and daddy love you,
please don't go!
"Breathe, my son, Breathe!"

But who is to know the mind of God! It was heart-wrenching watching my daughter go through what I went through thirty-three years ago, on March 30, 1974 when our first born son, 17 month-old Obinna Julian Mezu born at the Sisters of Charity Hospital, Buffalo, New York, USA equally died in my arms at the Holy Rosary Hospital, Emekuku, Owerri, Imo State, Nigeria. Now my daughter's first born son has died in her arms at the University of Maryland Hospital, U.S.A. So many parents go through this sorrow all the time. Olachi and I are not alone.

Indeed, I would say that our collective Faith in God and belief in miracles carried Olachi and her twins through to a successful delivery. Does the Lord calling ObiOla to heaven signify that our collective prayers were not fully answered? or that our faith was not strong enough? Again, who can discern the inscrutable will of God? I had to remind my daughter Olachi that even the saints we use as intercessors were those who even while alive most often did not have their prayers answered. They are not in heaven because they received every good thing out of life, but because even when they suffered, they still trusted. For them, and for us, it would always be, "Lord, may Thy Will be done!"

Now is Lent and for my family the passion of Christ becomes more poignant because of the human pain and suffering we were experiencing. We know what Christ's Mother

Mary must have felt as she carried her dead son in her arms: her dead adult son, *God-made-man, God-with-us, Lamb of God, Suffering Servant, Man of Sorrows* who carried all our ailments, all our sins / imperfections that for all ages to come we may be made perfect, deserving to see God.

So many members of Olachi's NICU unit were gathered in sorrow. The NICU Director who had taken charge of OlaRose once she was born was there; she came from her home to kept vigil with us; the attending on call, Dr. Alex and Olachi's friends were also around as was my indomitable daughter Dr. Nnenna Mezu Nwaba who shepherds her siblings as if she is their mother. The nurse who looked after ObiOla wept. Nurses and technicians came and embraced and consoled. I knew and felt all over again what my daughter was going through. Rev. Fr. Bill Spacek, priest at the University Hospital Catholic chapel who daily was bringing communion and comfort to Olachi was there, looking on with sorrow. My husband Sebastian started the hymn "**Trust and Obey**," and all joined in. We sang songs of praise to God for His wondrous presence among us. It could really have been worse! At the perfect moment of departure, little OlaRose's heart rate started dropping. Mystically linked to her heroic brother, after he passed, her heart rate went up again and stayed stable. ObiOla had fulfilled his mission, safely ushering his sister into this splendid but sometimes tragic world. I kept thinking of Christ's words: "*Greater love hath no man than this that a man lay down his life for his friends*" (John 15:13). Obiola's work was done. God's awesome presence is felt all through this ordeal, but my daughter was heartbroken and could hardly bear it. It was our veritable hour of darkness – our darkest night of the soul! Jesus words to Peter kept flashing through my mind like a neon light: "Simon, Simon, behold, Satan demanded to have you that he might sift you like wheat, *but I have prayed for you that your faith may not fail*; and when you have turned again, strengthen your brethren" (Luke 31-32). Frankly, I believed we had enough faith to literally move mountains and it did; this faith drew family friends and relations together and closer to God. It was simultaneously scary, sad and magnificently sublime.

The University Hospital NICU Training director was invaluable. She took Olachi into a room and lay her down. But would my daughter be comforted? I thought of the biblical Rachel weeping and who would not be consoled for losing her children. What mothers and fathers go through! I thought of the mysteries of life and the experiences that can rend our hearts; what attitudes that could get us through these difficult periods. As the Rev. Chaplain explained to Olachi:

> *"What is your profession?" he had queried Olachi; "you are a physician and your job is to save lives. Everyone has a purpose in life. ObioOla's purpose was to be a messenger to take care of his sister OlaRose. Just as Christ gave His life to save humanity, ObiOla gave his life to save his sister and you. Now, the passion of Christ from henceforth will no longer be abstract, but concrete to you. Just as MichelAngelo's Pieta shows Christ in His mother's arms, now you know concretely what Mary felt. The passion is real to you. You will never forget it. ObiOla is now a pure*

spirit, a wonderful messenger of love, he has gone to his real home."

Fr. Bill Spacek's words were very consoling to all who listened as he strove to soothe my daughter's pain as had done throughout this period the other priests, Frs. Austin Ochu - chaplain of the VA hospital, Val Awoyemi, chaplain of St. Joseph's Hospital chapel who first anointed Olachi and tended her, and Fr. Maurice Akwa who came to visit. During life's turbulence and complexities, I thank God for the many gifts like family and friends, for in-laws like the Ndubuisi family. Obiora's parents especially his mum, Barrister Dora Mary Urenna Ndubuisi called sometimes twice a day from Nigeria all through this Ordeal. At the exact moment when her daughter-in-law was being wheeled into the operating room, her call came urgent and insistent. She prayed all the more, I know. I thank the saints whose lives provide a model of faith, love and hope – instruments to help navigate the sometimes choppy waters of life. I thank God above all for the insuperable gift of Faith that provides us with spiritual backbone so that we do not break and fall into the sin of despair when our world is rocked. I laud God for His inscrutable wisdom and omniscience. Through our sufferings, we drew closer to Jesus, journeying with Him through Gethsemane to the crucifixion of Calvary. And we shall rise with Christ from sorrow. I applied to my family, Christ's words to Peter, "Simon, Simon, behold, Satan demanded to have you that he might sift you like wheat, *but I have prayed for you that your faith may not fail.*" Indeed, we have been sifted like wheat, but we will also experience our resurrection with Christ.

On Wednesday, March 28, a mass and burial were done for little ObiOla Julian Anthony Ndubuisi. His aunties sang the mass, led by Dr. Ure Laura Rita Mezu, the young Cardiologist from whom OlaRose got her middle name "Rita." Ure sang in Igbo in her lovely voice *"Ama Ya Zuru Oke – God's wisdom / grace is complete."* It was very moving. Then Olachi read her "Song of OBiOla" – carrying the church congregation tremulously with her lament and joy through her twins' ordeal, birth, survival, and the subsequent passing into eternity of ObiOla. It was simultaneously heartrending, sublime and transcendental – a slice of heaven. One felt transported to a dimension of pure spiritual joy, and I did not want to descend again to this "vale of tears." But there was closure. It was a special day and

ObiOla's spirit presence was more powerful dead than alive. We bow completely to God who sent HIS OWN ONLY Son to die for humans, He who is the Resurrection and the Life. I remembered the words: *"I will turn their mourning into joy, I will comfort them, and give them gladness for sorrow "* (Jeremiah 13: 13); *"In the morning, fill us with your joy / we shall exult and rejoice all our days / . . . give us joy to balance our affliction / for the days when she knew misfortune"* (Psalm 90: 14-5).

Little OlaRose Rita, **Twin A**, is growing daily. Her skin is filling in. She has been introduced to her mother's milk and has tolerated it. Her parents visit her daily. Her mother made a recording of her voice and songs to which the baby listens in her absence. When the baby hears Olachi's voice, she wriggles with joy, opens her eyes, squeezes her hand. OlaRose Rita still has a while to go before coming home to her parents. We pray every day for complete health. Olachi promises to tell her infant daughter about her hero brother who gave his life that she may live. ObiOla Julian Anthony's presence is always with us as is his uncle, my first born son Obinna Julian's even as we pray through these pure Christian souls. We have been sorely tried: *As iron is fashioned by fire and on the anvil, so in the fire of suffering and under the weight of trials, our souls receive that form which our Lord desires them to have -- St Madeline Sophie Barat.* Daily, we also live by faith and remember the miracle of life, birth and survival.

Who really knows the mind of God! That the twin who remained was the one who was written off as a fetus, the one assumed to have died in the womb - this little feisty **OlaRose Rita** who clings stubbornly to life. As exact as science can be, in this one mystery, I celebrate God, the Author of life for being the **Only Right One**, for being the **Only One** who knew, who really knows the **Mystery of Life and Death**! ------ Dr. Rose Ure Mezu

April 2007

Obiola, the cousin I never met by Adaure Nwaba

Little Obiola, our angel from heaven.
Little Obiola, a savior that's given.
Little Obiola, yet fragile but tall
Little Obiola, you saved your sister from a great fall
Little Obiola, we'll never forget you.
Little Obiola, I'll never regret you
Little Obiola, we never could see you.
Little Obiola, I wish I could greet you
Little Obiola, so young but brave
Little Obiola, we'll praise you for all our days.
Little Obiola, we'll always miss you.
Little Obiola, only a week could you stay.
Little Obiola, so innocent were you.
What evil have you done, to be taken so new.
Little Obiola, don't forget your sister.
Little Obiola, her sweet guardian angel.
Keep her in your prayers, day and night.
Little Obiola, we'll always remember
The miracles you provided for your dear little sister.
Little Obiola, why did you go
We never got the chance to say welcome home.
Little Obiola, we never thought you wouldn't make it
We thought you were here to stay
Pray for your sister,
Thank you for what you've done, you sent us a message,
And fulfilled the destiny you were sent here to give.
From the Almighty King and Lord,
Who makes the decisions for you and me.

Always & Forever I'll never forget.
Sweet Obiola, the cousin I never met
...love you always & forever
                    ~~Adaure Nwaba, March 27, 2007 (13 years)

Our little Obiola by Obinna Edward Jr., Nwaba

Our little Obiola,
Why did you leave us,
You were loved by all
You are missed by all
We all thought that you would make it
We now have two little Obi's in heaven

Why did you leave us
We cry everyday
We know you are doing fine
You would have been my best friend
You saved your sister

Why did you leave us
You angel on Earth
You stayed for such a short time
You were such a handsome boy

Why did you leave us
You were so healthy in the womb
We loved you so much
You will never be forgotten
You were so innocent
You were our family

Why did you leave us
Because you destiny was fulfilled
My little Obiola you are loved by all,
missed by all, and you were cared for by all
We will never forget you and you will always be loved
Juju will never forget you.
– Edward Jr. Obinna Nwaba 2007 (11 years old)
Juju Nwaba will never forget you –

Dear Little Soldier by Amy Amanda Uzoamaka Nwaba

Dear little soldier,
You left too soon,
My cousin Obiola,
I never saw you

Even though we never met,
Eye to eye
I am crying my eyes out
When I found out you died

My heart crumpled up
Broken and red
When my mommy cried out
Obiola is dead

Here I am in the car
At this time tonight
To comfort the parents
Of Obiola, who made things right

Letter to Obiola by Amy Amanda Uzoamaka Nwaba

Obiola Julian Anthony Ndubuisi, I call you to the honor of the Family's Little Soldier only because you fought and persevered until you were positive that you had finished the mission that God sent you here for. You are OlaRose's personal angel who she can thank, look up to, pray to, love and emulate. I love you very much and hope that I and many others will be able to look up to you and try to be like you. You were the cousin whom I thought, I imagined, would grow up and everyone would tell you how you saved the lives of Aunty Ola and OlaRose. Did you know that you were named after your uncle, Obinna Julian Mezu? I hope you know that even though you never met me, I knew everything I needed to know about you.

OBIOLA, YOU ARE A HERO! I love you Obiola and so did everyone else who knew you (or at least about you...) I may cry, but do you think that I would want you to suffer on this earth and learn all the cruel things about it? NO! I want you to be here, actually I need you to be here, but now I can feel emptiness inside my heart. I feel like part of me is missing. Probably the part that wanted to be a branch of your life, a part of that huge, brave tree that put you together. But that fraction of me is gone... so I thought, now I know that the way I am talking about you is all accurate, except for the part of it that said that I will never witness being with you again.

I am always with you just because you are Olarose's guardian angel does not mean that you are not with all your other admirers ... no, I am always with you, vice versa. I want you to be here, baby boy but now I will just have to pray to you and both you and OlaRose will hear it. You guys have bonded. Besides, when you passed away, your sister's heart rate dropped. Some way your hearts are connected and you can feel each other's presence. Someway by the power of God. I will miss you, Little Soldier.
Your cousin, Amy Amanda Uzoamaka Nwaba **– 10 years old.**

Obiola my son, The Day You Were Laid to Rest by Olachi Mezu-Ndubuisi

Obiola Julian Anthony, my son
My beautiful son,
My handsome son,
My valiant hero
My brave little boy
My angel from God
Who gave his life for
me and his twin sister
OlaRose
You job here was
done
And God called you to
Himself
Cause He loves
beautiful things

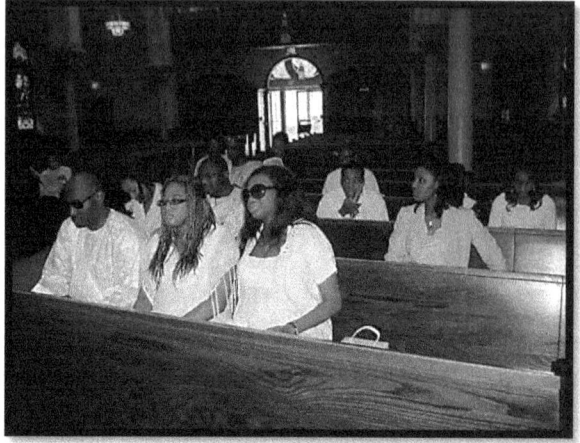

Obiola My son... Obiola My son.... Obiola My son....Obiola My son
My heart weeps for you
My soul aches like from a pierced arrow
Just because I miss you
Just because I can no longer touch you
And kiss your fine little face
Or stroke your soft little head
And your tiny little limbs
My beautiful boy
My handsome son

As you lay in that little golden casket
You looked like an angel
In your immaculate tiny white gown
Fair as the sun
Bright as a star
Peaceful as a dove
Cheeks pink as a rose
Lips soft as a feather
As I kissed them so gently; I wanted to stay there forever

Till I felt your breath again,
But I know your spirit lies within me now and forever

Obiola my son.. My first son from God
It was a beautiful day indeed
The day you were laid to rest
The winds were so gentle
The sun shone so brightly
The breeze was so cool
All of nature's elements paid homage it seems
To God's messenger on earth

Obiola.. my darling... my saving grace
All came from far and wide; emails poured from hearts
Phone calls and texts from all over the world
Streamed in to testify to your brave life and death
All hearts bled for the loss of a hero
It was midafternoon on Wednesday, March 28th
But the Church was full like on a regular Sunday
Most dressed in white to honor your purity
The songs were soul-warming, the singing angelic
As our voices were joined with the choir of angels
Heralding your soul's entrance into the Kingdom of God

"I am honored to embrace you, the female church warden said
You are the mother of a saint."
My heart fluttered with tears of joy and pain
I knew I was the mother of an angel
But the mother of a saint?
Of course a saint you are,
You were born of my womb, flesh of my flesh
You lived and you suffered during the passion of Christ
I had felt as one with my Virgin Mother Mary
who carried her dying son, Jesus
As I held my dying son in my arms on Sunday, March 25th
Giving him to her to carry on her bosom
And take my son to God the Father sitting on His heavenly throne
I had called on the herald of angels and saints
to lead the way to God's eternal abode

I begged Jesus to hold his hand and never let it go.
I kissed his dying lips, as the spirit left from him.
When his heart stopped and he was proclaimed dead, I cried out
 "I believe... O Lord.... I still believe ; God the Father, give him life.
God the son, give him strength, Holy Spirit breathe for him."
His spirit stirred within, his heart started beating again,
and his chest began to rise as he started to breathe,
and his tiny hands squeezed my finger.
God had answered my prayers for that moment
 to let me know He was God
But his messenger still had to go, since his work was complete
And so, his soul departed once again....
And my soul was at peace as I kissed his lips
Yes indeed he lived, suffered, and died during the passion of Christ
I am the mother of a saint
I must be loved by God; I feel blessed to be chosen
Who am I? But a poor sinner on earth.
Indeed I feel blessed that you chose to come into my life,
Obiola my son.

My beautiful angel,
No camera could capture your beauty
No flash could capture the essence of your soul
Your face shone like the sun
All that saw you were in awe; Such beauty... such grace
"Olachi and Obiora , did this being really come from you?" all asked
Obiola my son, the fruit of my womb
My handsome son..
..You were so beautiful, so much that God kept you for himself.
God loves beautiful things too, my friend said to me
"That's okay..." I said
"He can have him... he is the Maker and Taker of life."
I give you freely to God , a sacrifice of love
Like Abraham did his son.

Obiola my son...
Born on March 19th, Feast of St. Joseph
Baptized on March 21st, and
Passed on March 25th, 2007

Laid to rest in the Lord on March 28th, the day God chose
Your life and passing have brought souls together
It's brought family and friends all over the world together
It's brought enemies and foes back together in peace
It's brought straying souls back to God repentant
It's solidified our faith in all that is pure and true

Obiola my son,
I was looking forward to seeing you grow up
A strapping young lad playing basketball with Daddy,
being Mummy's little boy
A life so full of promise
A life so well fulfilled, 26 weeks and 2 days in my womb
You kept me from the death claims of pre-eclampsia
You saved your sister from fetal demise
She had no chance of survival, it was thought,
with no placental blood flow or nutrition for 6 weeks
But you kept her warm, with your body
And whenever she would stop breathing,
you would thump on her little chest
And it would rise up and down and she breathes again,
as we watched on the ultrasound.
Your heart beat always in synchrony with hers
Urging her on, giving her strength, giving her life till it stopped
And you gave the sign that it was time
 for you both to be born into the world

Obiola my heart, My very own soul, my very own OBI.....Ola's heart.
For seven full days you lived, a life like Christ in suffering and bravery
My silent hero, six days you worked to give
your sister and I back our life and health,
Just like in the creation story, said Aunty Ngozi
On the seventh day you rested in the Lord,
Just as God rested after the creation
Your destiny is truly fulfilled, Obiola my son.
Seven days I was your mummy,
I loved you, sang to you and prayed for you, and dedicated you to God
Seven days that will live with me forever

Obiola my son, My God-given saint
Save a place in heaven for us your family
Take care of your twin sister OlaRose
Whose life you bought with your own
She became healthy and stronger each day
while your breath slowly failed you
Her heartbeat dropped as you passed away in my arms
And I knew she felt you leaving
You were kissing her goodbye
I tell her you are always in the incubator with her, holding her hand,
I tell her you have recruited all the heavenly hosts
for her as her friends and they are watching over her too.

Obiola my son, you will forever live in our hearts
Pray for Mummy, Daddy, OlaRose, your grandparents,
your uncles, aunties, cousins, and all who weep for you and miss you
Pray for all unborn babies and premature babies
who fight for their lives
Pray for all expectant mothers suffering any illness
and mothers who long for fruits of the womb
Obiola Julian Anthony, Patron of unborn babies,
premature babies, and expectant mothers, Pray for us

Obiola my angel
You've joined the choir of angels
Like your uncle Obinna Julian Mezu
Who died at barely over a year of age, 35 years ago
Your Daddy and I named you Julian after him
Praying for his guidance and protection
Out of fear, I felt a little voice tell me often,
"That's the name of an angel... who did not stay on earth..change it."
But I could not do it, no matter how much I tried
Because that was the name God had chosen for you
It was your destiny from the moment of conception
You bore the name of an angel and your mission was crystal clear
So stick the name did, and you were baptized in a hurry in 2 days
When you started to get weaker from your immature lungs
So Obiola Julian Anthony Ndubuisi you were baptized,
an angel of God.

Obiola my son.... My beautiful son...
I put some items with you in your casket
The second time it was opened
The picture of your patron saint, St. Anthony
That I had pasted inside your incubator
My wrist band with my name and the label Twin B for you
That I had worn on my wrist, next to my skin, the week you lived,
for I wanted a part of me to be physically with you forever
And your zebra teddy bear given by your nurses,
That had kept you company while you lay in your incubator
These things will connect us forever on earth
While your spirit lives forever in my heart
Till our souls are reunited again in God's presence.

It was hard to say goodbye
And I kept trying to see your beautiful face again
"One more time.... One more time," I cried over and over again
As I was pulled away from your golden casket
I could not let go
But let go I have to of your earthly body
But never of your spirit
This will live on forever

Soar to the skies, my sweet
Soar to the skies, our little one
Spread your wings and fly.
Life eternal is Yours, our little one
Luminous and pure, your soul flies high.
You live in our hearts forever to glow,
Your light of love and peace to flow

Mummy loves you; Daddy loves you;OlaRose loves you
But Jesus loves you more
Obiola, my son

March 30, 2007 , *Westminster, MD*

Part Four:

The NICU Diary of OlaRose

Foreword

I started to write down today, March 26th 2007, a diary for OlaRose, a day to day account of her life in the neonatal intensive care unit (NICU), so I would not miss any second or struggle to remember any precious minute. Obiola's passing left a deep painful void in my heart; and I found myself re-living every moment I spent in the NICU with him, trying to remember every gentle touch with my finger, trying to remember the sweet feel of him the first time I held him in my arms as he died. After my emotional journey in the labor and delivery, I had stopped my writings due to exhaustion and part relief that the ordeal was over when my twins were born. Soon, came the shock of Obiola's brief illness and passing, and I was consumed with being there for him and living each moment with him, and had no thought to document my time with him. I guess part of me hoped and prayed he would pull through. It would not happen with OlaRose, I told myself, the next day after Obiola died. I will write something down every day so that no matter what happens to her, whether she lives or not, I will have a piece of her journey with me. ... March 26, 2007

"...I never imagined I would be sharing this with the world as a testimony of God's love and divine mercy..."

Monday, March 26th, 2007:
I had visitors: family and friends and well-wishers coming to console me all day due to the passing of Obiola Julian Anthony, my son, yesterday. NdaNina had been there by his death bed with Mum and Dad; and she had come home with Obi and me. That was a great comfort, for Obi and I were devastated from the whole experience. My sisters, Nina and Ngozi, stayed the whole day in my home cooking, cleaning and helping out. Kelechi and Chigozie, Obiola's God-parents,

came bright and early to console me. It was so painful for me to remember how my son passed. I would cry intermittently as I remembered every single moment with him. I called several times a day to talk to OlaRose and let her know Mummy loves her, but Mummy could not come just yet to see her. The NICU staff had sent a memory box of Obiola's belongings and clothes he had worn after he died: his zebra skinned teddy bear, the holy pictures I had on his crib, and pictures taken after his death. The NICU had made a mold of his little hands and feet. It was so beautiful. I cried till the tears would not flow anymore. The anguish and hurt in my soul is inexplicable. I literally feel like my heart is breaking into two or indeed, a thousand pieces. All I could keep saying was: Obiola my son, Obiola my son, Obiola my son, my beautiful boy,... my handsome son... my baby boy...

Tuesday, March 27th: At 11pm, Obi and I went with Okey to see OlaRose. This was my first time laying eyes on her since the 25th when Obiola died. For a couple of minutes, I just stared at her and my heart broke... I loved her, but it reminded me too much of what I had lost. I could not yet touch her, and I started to cry softly. Suddenly, she started crying, grimacing her face since no sound could come out of her due to the ET tube, and her oxygen saturations suddenly started to drop to 80%. I cried, "It's happening again," as my NICU fellow friend and Obi tried to console me, telling me she could sense my sadness. I stopped crying and her oxygen saturations increased to 95%. I now sat by her side, touched her and started softly speaking, then singing and praying for her. She responded by grabbing my finger and moving her hands and feet with excitement. I love my baby girl....She is mummy's little princess... Mummy's miracle baby. I promised her I would see her every day and would never leave her again.

Wednesday, March 28th: Obiola was laid to rest today. The funeral service was beautiful. The family and most friends wore white to signify his innocent purity; and that he was an angel of God. The second time the coffin was opened before mass, I kissed his soft, lips and touched his hair and hands. I then placed some items in his coffin with him: the St .Anthony picture and prayer mum had given me while in the labor and delivery ward, which I had pasted on his crib; the little zebra stuffed animal given by the NICU nurses when he was born, that had stayed the whole time in the crib with him, and my wrist name band that had my full name and the inscription: Twin B - it had touched my skin, and I wanted a part of me, always with him. After the funeral, I went to the NICU to visit with OlaRose with Obi and his two siblings, Adanze and Francis, who had come for the funeral. I told OlaRose how her brother was laid to rest in a beautiful ceremony, and how mummy loved her so.

Thursday, March 29th: Obi, Ngozi and I went to see OlaRose in the evening. I sang to her, prayed with her and told her about Obiola and how he gave his life for her. I told her that he was always in the crib with her, holding her hand and watching over her. I told her that he had recruited all the heavenly hosts for her as her friends to pray for her. Her second head ultrasound was normal. Glory be to God.

Friday, March 30th: I dropped off the digital recorder with a 20 minute recording of my voice saying prayers and singing to my babies, Obiola and OlaRose. It was the same words and prayers I had said to her and Obiola the whole week of his life and while they were in my womb. She got her first feeding in the evening. A nasogastric (NG) tube was placed by Alex, her attending, and she was started on gut priming of 0.2cc/hr over 11hrs with 1hr of rest. with a check for residuals/aspirates before resuming feeds the rest of the 11hrs. Obi and I went to dinner at Olive Garden with Ngozi and Ure, and we had a nice time. We were desperately looking for some normalcy in our surreal life.

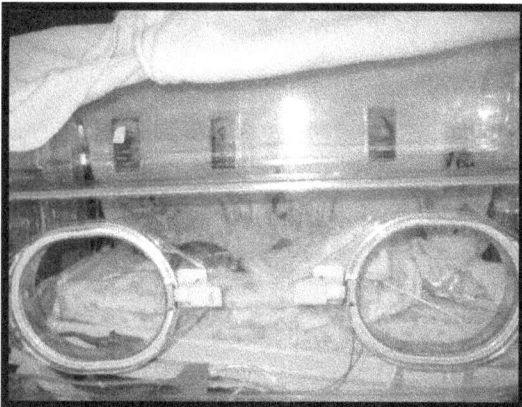

****

OlaRose, my Miracle Baby

OlaRose my first daughter from God
Twin A to Obiola, our God-sent angel
Who gave his life to save you and Mummy
When all thought you were dead
When you would not gain any ounce of weight
For three weeks or more.
And Mummy prayed to God
To give you life, strength, and breathe for you
All our family, friends, even strangers prayed for us three
Our prayers were answered when you were born
On March 19th, 2007, feast of St. Joseph
My one pound miracle baby, 11 and half inches long
All marveled as you took your first breath all on your own
With Apgars of 7 and 8.
My beautiful princess,
Your limbs all long and dangly, your skin translucent and dainty
A marvel that one so tiny was in our midst, My brave little angel

OlaRose my darling, Mummy's *warrior princess*
The name is so fitting for one so feisty
That's what your grandma Rose called me as I fought for your lives
But it reminds me more of you.
You fought hard against all odds
You kept breathing through immature lungs
Surviving pulmonary hypertension, systemic hypotension,
Hypoxemia, PDA, respiratory distress syndrome
All the hazards and dangers of severe prematurity
All the risks for being born at 26weeks and 2days
With a very low birth weight
But you exceeded all expectations
As you lay active, and pink
Grimacing impatiently, tugging at your endotracheal tube constantly,
hands and legs flailing wildly
as if trying to free yourself of the annoying gadgets
Each day you improved, your twin brother grew weaker
as he was overcome by the same ails that you had
Even though he was 7 ozs. bigger with Apgars of 9 and 9

Alas, Little did we know he was giving up his life for you

OlaRose my baby girl, my beautiful girl
You were baptized on March 21st, along with your brother
As we feared he would not make it that night
He was christened Obiola Julian Anthony, and
We called you OlaRose Adaobi Rita
And our hearts were at peace knowing
You were both now with the mark of Christ
He did survive that night
And I continued my work,
Of Daily visiting with you both,
Singing, praying and touching you lovingly
Enjoying the bitter-sweet moments of being your mummy.
Bitter, since I could not hold you or kiss you
All secured in your incubator, embowered by lines and tubes.
Sweet, since it was the best moments of my life
Filling my soul like nectar that lasts a lifetime..
You looked so fragile, so unassuming, so brave
Unaware of your tiny frame,
you looked like you could conquer the world
My brave little girl.
And when your brother was called to the Lord,
You had severe bradycardia
As your heart rate dropped in panic and sadness
And he came to your incubator and seemingly kissed you goodbye
"Don't be sad my sister," he must have said,
I'll be with you in spirit
To protect you and keep you safe like when in the womb."
Then suddenly your heart rate rose back to normal,
as you must have felt reassured.
OlaRose my angel..... Mummy's own angel

OlaRose my darling,
Mummy's little princess
I looked forward to every minute with you
You knew my voice straight from the womb
And would response with excitement
At the familiar sound of my voice,

singing, whispering and praying through the incubator door.
My heart always skips a beat when you reach out your hands
searching for the voice as if to grab and hold on
My soul flutters each time your tiny hand
Grips firmly at my finger as I touch you so softly.
My spirit is lifted and I shed tears of joy
whenever you open those big dark eyes
Gazing intently at me
as if trying to capture every curve on my face
Your nurses marvel at how your oxygen saturations always rise
and your eyes open widely anytime you hear my voice
on the phone or through the digital recorder.
OlaRose my angel, my baby girl.

OlaRose my darling, my bejeweled Rose flower
I can't wait to hold you and kiss your face
I can't wait to feed you day and night
I can't wait to take you home with me forever
I can't wait to watch you grow big and strong
I can't wait to teach you the way of Christ
I can't wait to tell the heroic tales
of your twin brother, Obiola Julian Anthony
And how He was an angel sent from God
To see you safely into this world
and save your life and mine.
I can't wait to dress you up in pretty pink and blues
Bathe you and adorn your hair with flowers and ribbons
I can't wait to see you crawl, walk and run
And hop onto your Daddy's knee, while we read you a story
I can't wait for you to know
your grandparents, uncles, aunties, and cousins
For they've prayed and prayed daily for your survival.
I can't wait for you to know your Grandma Rose
A woman of virtue, a steadfast spirit
For you were named after her and she knows you so.
You also come from a great lineage of Roses
like your grandpa's mother, a matriarch of note
and your dearest aunt, Kelechi Rosemary

OlaRose my darling, don't ever be scared
Mummy loves you,
Daddy loves you,
Obiola, Twin B Loves you
But Jesus loves you more
Obiola has recruited all the heavenly hosts for you
To watch over you and guide you from any danger
He's now an angel in heaven, your personal angel
He holds your hand and comforts you with baby Jesus
So never be afraid for you are safe
Your life will be one of praises to God
Who has marked you with his graces forever and ever.

OlaRose my baby girl, I love you so,
You are my strength, my hope, my daily joy
You keep me going
You feel the void in my soul created by your brother's departure.
We are all still connected, I feel in my spirit
You, me and Obiola just as when you were in my womb
I feel his presence sometimes around me often
and I know he watches over us with love.
OlaRose my darling, mummy loves you so.

Saturday, March 31st, 2007,
Westminster, MD

****

Saturday March 31st: I wrote a poem for OlaRose, my beautiful angel and brave little princess. As I wrote it, I kept perceiving a familiar scent of embalming oil...the same scent that I had smelt on Obiola as I bent over him and kissed his lips on the day of his funeral. I smiled, knowing he was right there with me, reading the poem and comforting me. "Obiola, my son....I love you so much," I said. I went to visit my baby girl at 7.30pm with her daddy. She opened her big black eyes at the sound of my voice, and gazed at me as I sang and spoke softly to her. "She knows your voice indeed," the nurses said laughing. Each time I spoke, her oxygen saturations keep rising higher to 97-100%. "You have a lot of breast milk," the nurse practitioner said, and "it looks so rich and nutritious. OlaRose will enjoy it." I changed her diaper for the evening for the first time and moistened her lips, which were dry and applied aquaphor to it. It felt good to take care of her like her mummy should.

Sunday, April 1ˢᵗ: OlaRose had her first large bowel movement since feeding and some gas, indicating that she had tolerated the feeding so far. Thanks be to God. She is my miracle baby. Her Grandparents Rose and Sebastian went to visit with her after noon mass. I went with sis Nina to visit OlaRose. I was a little emotional as this was Obiola's one week anniversary of his passing away. OlaRose seemed to have a bad day. Her PCO_2 in her blood gas had been 81mmHg and so her ventilator rate was increased to 40, and her feedings held for most of the day. By the time I got there and sang to her, she felt much better and her O_2 sats increased to 96% from 83%. I kept reminding her Obiola purchased life for her with his own life... Hold on to life, baby girl it is yours...O God, please, I cried... his death cannot be in vain. "Your will be done in our lives O Lord," I remembered to add.

Monday, April 2ⁿᵈ: Ngozi escorted me to buy pretty pink and cream blankets and other items for my baby girl. Mom gave me St. Anthony and Rita holy pictures which I put in her crib. OlaRose was happy to see me today. Her face is now more distinct and mature. I believe she looks more like me and Obiola now; but she definitely has her Daddy's ears and long limbs. She's so beautiful. I sang to her and talked softly to her. Her vent rate was still 40 and her FiO_2 or oxygen level was 33%. She had another bowel movement after a glycerin suppository. It hurt me to leave her. The next few months are going to be long and hard. God give me strength. When we got home, the birth certificate confirmation for both Obiola and OlaRose arrived, and it made me cry all over again. That was evidence of his birth. It's amazing how God made it possible for us to fill out the birth certificate a couple days after their birth.

Tuesday, April 3ʳᵈ: I'm still pumping breast milk several times a day and getting a good volume about 50 to 100 cc total each time. I had an appointment with my obstetrician to follow-up my blood pressure and look at my stitches. She said the stitches were healing well, and my blood pressure was 134/86 and so I should stay on the 90mg of Procardia for now. My urine dipstick still had 4+ protein, so the plan was to follow up in 6 weeks, and if proteinuria persists, then I would do a home 24 hour urine collection for protein. If high, then, I would be referred to a nephrologist. Today OlaRose was noted to have a high white blood cell count (WBC) and bandemia (9) on complete blood count (CBC) with a high c-reactive protein 8.36. So a septic workup was done, and she was empirically started on ampicillin and gentamycin. Her cerebrospinal fluid (CSF) was clear and normal. Otherwise, she looked fine and active, and not sick at all. Her vent rate was reduced to 36 from 40 and her fi02 ranged from 30 to 33% with sats above 90%. Her weight was 560g. She really is a strong girl. I sat with her for a while, and she would open her eyes and gaze at my face. I was there for a blood gas, and it broke my heart to see her wince and cry silently in pain as she was pricked, but no sound came out due to her ET tube. I had gone to visit with my mother that day. She drove me home afterwards. Obi also went to visit her from work, and picked me up from Mezuville, America. When we got home, the social security cards for Obiola and OlaRose had arrived and I gazed at them numbly for a while wishing I could turn time back and Obiola would be alive as the card signified. There is no end to the pain, is there, I thought?

Wednesday, April 4th: I decided to stay home all day and relax a little. It was so painful to see her yesterday, I could not bear to go today. I cleaned the kitchen a little bit and cooked ogbono soup, rice and beef stew. I called several times a day to speak to her nurses and see how she was doing. I could no longer talk to her over the phone in order to prevent infections, her attending suggested. So, they would be playing the voice recorder for her as often as they could. Ngozi and Bobby came over in the evening to hang out. I got two Easter bunnies for OlaRose and a camera to take pictures of her in the NICU. Her FiO2 was reduced to 25%, and I was glad. Her vent rate was still at 36. Her weight was 530g and she was still gut priming. Her ET tube grew Enterobacter, likely a contaminant, but the decision was made to keep her on antibiotics for a week.

Thursday, April 05, 2007: Her FiO2 or oxygen need improved today and ranged from 21% (room air) to 26%. She was still active and fine.

My strong little girl... my miracle baby. She was placed on caffeine for apnea of prematurity and to facilitate extubation, whenever they thought she was ready. Today was my first time driving in over 4 months. I drove to the church to see Obiola's grave.

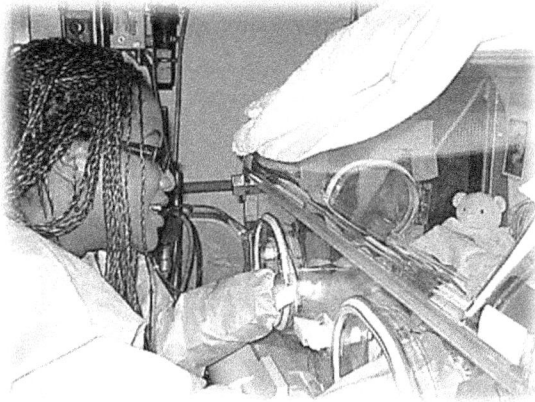

I was very emotional. I love you baby. Mummy loves you... I kept whispering. From there, I drove to the hospital to see OlaRose. For the first time since my ordeal, I was quite relaxed at today's visit. She was looking really good and active, still loving her tape. I talked to her through the incubator door, sang and prayed for her. Her vent rate had been reduced to 32, her oxygen saturations were great, and she was still feeding. According to her neonatologist, by Monday, they hoped to extubate her and tomorrow, they planned to increase her feeds slowly. Her weight was 540g (up 10g). I'm happy with her progress.

Friday, April 6, 2007: Good Friday. About 11am, I was at home writing a poem "Life Is yours, Claim It" for OlaRose and I wrote about how strong and resilient she was, and how it was a marvel to everyone she remained active and well, tugging constantly at her ET tube, though the smallest baby in the NICU. I wrote about how Obiola's death cannot be in vain, and how the Holy Spirit should breathe for her, ending each verse with thy will be done O Lord. Just as I wrote the last verse, I felt compelled to call the NICU and check on her. Her nurse answered and told me that she had just self-extubated - her ET tube was out from her constantly tugging at it and shaking her head. The doctors were at her bedside watching her breathe on her own, and not knowing what to do with her. They had just left me a voicemail letting me know she had self-extubated and they didn't know what to do with her, as she was so tiny but really doing well breathing on her own. After half hour or so, they decided to put her on CPAP and later Sipap where she stayed at 26% FiO2 and a PEEP of 6 and rate of 20. It was amazing. I was so excited, I bought cookies for the nursing staff and doctors on my way to see her. God is great! He was in control of everything. My daughter will live by his mercy, as a testimony to his power and glory. Nda Nina took me to the hospital and I spent time with OlaRose and labeled her name on all the blankets I had bought earlier. I love her so much... She is so brave and beautiful. Her weight was 540 grams, and her feeds were held when she extubated and restarted later in the evening at a higher rate of 0.5cc/hr. Her O2 sats remained great 91 to 97% all day. That evening, we all watched "The Passion of Christ" and Jesus of Nazareth with Mum and Dad at Mezuville, America.

****

This Week of Your Passion

Help me Lord
To turn my sorrow into joy
To turn my anguish into bliss
To smile through my tears
To hope and trust even when all seems bleak
Help me Lord, this week of your passion

Teach me how to Lord,
Make someone else smile though my soul weeps
Help others in need, despite my needs
Tell people of your love, even when I feel so far from you
Give others a shoulder to cry on, though I want to be consoled
Teach me how to love others Lord, this week of your passion.

Show me the way Lord,
To grow from this pain I feel
To find the light at the end of the tunnel
To trust in your divine will and plan for me
To testify to your goodness in my life
To glorify your name in all I do
Show me the way Lord, this week of your passion.

May we Lord,
Love you more each passing day
Thank you for your daily graces and blessings
Die to sin this Good Friday, and
All Rise from the dead with you this Easter Sunday, and
Live a life renewed in your Holy Spirit
May we Lord, be born again this week of your passion.

Holy Thursday, April 5th , 2007
Westminster, MD

Life is Yours, Claim It

Give her life Lord

Give her strength, Jesus
Breathe for her, Holy Spirit, You sustained her in the womb
When she was given up for dead
You brought her back to Life, and heralded her birth
Obiola purchased her life with his death
Let his death not be in vain, I pray
Life is hers, Let her claim it Lord
But as always, Your divine will be done O Lord.

As we watch her daily grow bigger
All marvel at her strength, spirit and will
Smallest baby in the NICU at 1 pound
But clearly the most active and strong
Eyes flickering open always
Hands and feet moving constantly, about to fly
Fingers tugging at her endotracheal tube
From the first day of life
Resilient, bold, purposeful.
Life truly is hers, Let her claim it Lord
But as always, Your divine will be done O Lord.

My darling princess, angel and brave little girl..
OlaRose Adaobi Rita, You are a chosen one
You've communed with the heavenly hosts
You share a spirit with an angel from God
Your twin brother, Obiola Julian Anthony
Who bought your life with his
Life is yours, Claim it my daughter
But as always, Your Divine Will be done, O Lord

Good Friday, April 6th, 2007
In the middle of writing the last verse of this poem, the author called the hospital to check on her daughter and was notified that OlaRose had pulled out her endotracheal tube connected to the ventilator and was breathing on her own.

Saturday, April 7th, 2007: Obi and I after breakfast, watched the story of Jesus, "The greatest story ever told" - a 1965 version. It was very moving and real for me: the true passion of Christ that I had indeed witnessed personally these past few weeks. We cleaned our home together afterwards. This whole experience has brought us together, given us a new perspective and made us appreciate each other more. I prayed, it would continue this way. OlaRose is 29 weeks corrected gestational age today and 550g. I went to see OlaRose with Mummy. She was sleeping peacefully, but of course moving her limbs with every opportunity. Occasionally, she'd open her eyes at the sound of my voice. I love her so much, it scares me.

Sunday, April 8th, 2007: It was a lovely Easter day. Obi and I went to mass at St. John's in Westminster and then drove to see OlaRose. We brought her a lovely Easter bunny with two baby bunnies and cookies for her nurses. She was peacefully sleeping. Her feeds were increased to 1cc/hr. She was still on the Sipap device with nasal prongs at a rate of 20 and a peep of 4. Kelly and Chazie met us at the hospital and visited with OlaRose too. We ended up at Mezuville, America, Pikesville for the family Easter lunch/dinner. We had a nice time with the whole family. My wedding band and engagement ring fit into my finger for the first time in over four months. I can't believe that I lost a total of 34 pounds in a little over two weeks. Most of it was fluid from the ascites which diuresed quickly the first week after my C-section.

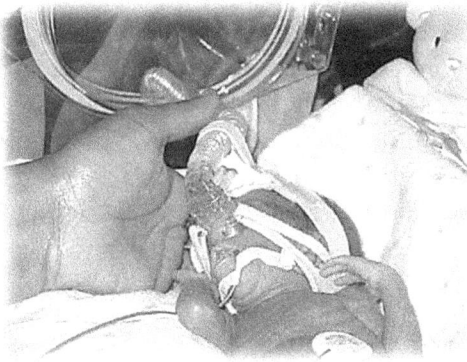

Monday, April 9th , 2007: OlaRose is 3 weeks old today. She gained 20g over 24 hrs and weighs 560g (a little over one pound 4 ozs.) She is getting there. Her FiO2 stayed at 26% on her Sipap with excellent oxygen saturations. Her feeds were increased to 1.5cc/hr. I found time to reply some emails from friends still sending condolences about Obiola's loss. I thanked them and let them know I was well, and thankful to God for Obiola's life and the time I had with him. I laundered some of OlaRose's blankets today so I could take fresh linen to her. My breast milk volume was quite increased up to 250 to 350cc (about 10 to 11 ozs) each pumping

Tuesday, April 10th, 2007: She is 1 lb 4 and half ozs. (580g); and her feeds were increased to 2.0cc/h and her TPN reduced. She also got a blood transfusion for a hematocrit of 36, which signified anemia since she was still getting supplemental oxygen. I drove with Ik to see OlaRose. She was doing really well. Her FiO2 ranged from 21% to 26% with great oxygen saturations. She had gotten her last dose of antibiotics today, and her TPN would be turned off that night or the next. She would then be on full feeds of 150cc/k/day when her feeds increase to 3.2cc/h. I brought her clean laundry and took home her used blankets to launder. Today, for the first time I heard her cry. I had whispered after two hours of visiting that mummy was leaving, and she started crying. It sounded like a kitten, and Ik and I were surprised – so tiny and sweet, but sad music to my ears. This was about 5 days after extubation. It could takes weeks before their trachea recovers enough for premature babies to make noises. I was excited and kept talking to her. She cried for a few minutes till she calmed down and went to sleep, then I left. She made my day… It was such a normal, baby milestone – her first cry. I was on cloud nine after that. My baby would be home soon.

Wednesday, April 11th, 2007: Today, she weighs 620g (1 pound 5 ozs). She sure loves her breast milk. I bought a heart shaped sterling silver locket and had inscribed on the front " *OlaRose & Obiola, My Twin Angels" and inscribed on the back: Mummy loves You but Jesus loves you more."* I would wear that locket next to my heart every day to remember my twin babies. I had Obiola's pictures enlarged and got frames for them. I planned to have a portrait made of his and OlaRose together. I feel sad that I never got a full view picture of them together and of him without tubes except after his death. I visited OlaRose with my brother IK again, and she was very happy to see me…staring as long as she could with those beautiful dark eyes. I held her frame in my hands, and had Ik take a picture. She is so tiny, it's amazing. I thank God each day for the miracle of her life. He is indeed keeping her alive, not just oxygen or breast milk, but by God's grace. Her feeds were increased to 2.5cc/hr and her TPN further reduced. I bought some wash cloths today to be used as a neck roll for her. She seems more comfortable lying on her abdomen. During the visit, I moistened her lips and wiped her eyelids with normal saline drops as they were usually dry. My beautiful baby girl.

Thursday, April 12th, 2007: OlaRose looked well today. Her FiO2 ranged from 26 to 33%. She is on diuril PO for chronic lung disease to reduce edema form her lungs. Her feeds were kept the same so as not to stress her out since she was using a lot of energy to feed and take breaths. I did her laundry today and took fresh blankets to her. I also taped classical music to the second folder of her digital recorder. She really liked the music. Obi met me at the NICU, and visited for a while before we drove home.

Friday, April 13th, 2007: Mom and IK came up to Westminster and we had a nice lunch at Johansson's restaurant in Westminster. After that, Mom and I drove to visit OlaRose. She seemed to be needing higher FiO2 up to 38%. She weighed 600g. I talked gently with the nurses about avoiding frequent fluctuations in the FiO2 to reduce the risk of retinopathy of prematurity (ROP). Obi and I had dinner at Sakura, a Japanese restaurant in Westminster.

Saturday, April 14th, 2007: OlaRose is 30weeks corrected gestational age today. She'll be 4 weeks old on Monday. How time flies. Obi and I did some house cleaning and I did some cooking too. OlaRose weighs 630g (1 pound 6ozs) - praise God! She also got a blood transfusion for a hematocrit of 34, which helped resolve her bradys and desats. Her FiO2 ranged from 21% to 28%. Its emotionally draining to watch her daily, and not hold her to my chest or to watch helplessly as her oxygen level fluctuates. My heart sinks and skips a beat with each bradycardia or low heart rate that alarms on the monitor. I have to trust in the divine protection of Christ that has brought her so far.

Sunday, April 15th, 2007: I pumped breast milk this morning as usual. Today is the celebration of the Divine mercy Sunday. This was my first time of learning about this feast. It is a beautiful celebration and I watched the mass at the divine mercy shrine in Stockbridge, Massachusetts on EWTN. I will not let my suffering be in vain, I thought. I pray that all I am going through may be joined with the passion of Christ, and bring me closer to God and cleanse my sins that

I may rise to holiness in the Lord. Also that the mercy of Christ may flow to my family and all over the world. Obi and I visited OlaRose in the evening. She was doing well, getting bigger each day. She truly enjoys hearing my voice and the classical music.

Monday, April 16th, 2007: She is 4 weeks today. Her weight today was 640g. She is on 3.5cc/h of breast milk and today was her last day of TPN. Her FiO2 ranged from 24 to 26%. Her chest x-ray showed mild edema. She's improved greatly. She was started on daily potassium and sodium supplements and ferrous sulphate (iron) drops since she was off TPN, and is still on the caffeine.

Tuesday, April 17th, 2007: Her weight is 630g; she lost 10grams. Her TPN is off and her feeds are at 3.5cc/h and fortified to 22cal/oz. My baby girl is growing up. She was on room air 21% for most of the day and PICC line was pulled today. I took flowers (beautiful white potted chrysanthemums) to Obiola's grave with Ngozi. My angel is in heaven. OlaRose looked so beautiful today... I still think she looks like me. She also looks more like her brother, Obiola every day. I got to take her temperature, change her diaper and clean/moisten her lips. Ngozi and I took her first pic without the CPAP mask. After visiting, I bought some more blankets and baby bath products so I could give her a bath tomorrow. Thank you God for my baby girl. I prayed for the 33 kids shot at Virginia Tech... their parents must be devastated. At any age, it is painful to lose a child. May their souls rest in peace.

Wednesday, April 18th, 2007: Took fresh blankets to my baby girl. She stayed about 21 at 22% on her oxygen requirement most of the day. Her highest being 26%. Her chest x-ray looked great too. Her head US at 4 weeks was normal...Praise God!. God is truly great. He shows his power through my daughter every day. Her breast milk was fortified to 24cal/oz and if she tolerates it, the plan is to increase her feeds to 4.2cc/hr (full feeds) and pull her PICC line. I gave her a bath or rub down today for the first time...using warm water, a wash cloth, and her Johnson's baby soap. It felt great to be doing mummy things. I can't wait to hold her in my arms. I was a little concerned about the frequent turnover of her nurses. They were all great, but each time there is a new one, I have to explain over again about her recorder needed to be played and how to change from my voice to classical music, her blankets and sheets being hers and not the hospitals" and how she likes lying on her belly... etc. Most nights there is continuity of care, but during the day, she seemed to be getting a new nurse each day. I told myself to relax... I guess I'm just being a mummy...I really have to let go and let God! He's brought her so far and only him has control of her destiny, no one else!!!

Thursday, April 19th, 2007: OlaRose is one month old today!! I'm so happy. She gained 10g and is now 650g (1pound 7ozs.). Hurray!! I bought a beautiful pink cake and Disney princess balloons for her. I took pictures with Kelly, Mum and Dad and then drove to the NICU. My colleagues and friends were there, and also took pics at her bedside before sharing the cake. OlaRose did not get to eat any, though. She was so beautiful on her birthday ... with her pretty pink blankets and sheets and teddy bears. Renee, her night nurse had taken a beautiful picture of her without her mask and left it for me. I brought back a big slice of cake, the part that had her name on it, so everyone at home got a taste of it.

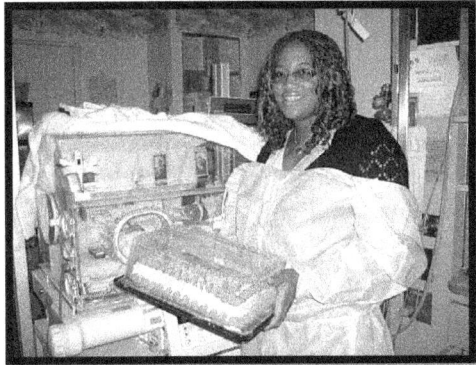

Friday, April 20, 2007: I called as usual at 630am to get a sign-out from her nurse and was happy that she had a good night, a huge bowel movement (heme negative, which meant no blood detected in her stool), and was down to room air (21%) on her oxygen. Her weight was 695g (1 pound 8 and half ozs.) and she was 13 and half inches tall. Can you believe it ? She now weighs more than Obiola did at birth after a whole month. My baby girl is so blessed. Her brother is truly watching over her with all his heavenly friends, who are her friends now. I went to visit OlaRose with IK, Mum and her friend Aunty Meg. OlaRose was excited to see us, very active, arching her back, squirming, stretching and smiling. After a while, I left for a baby shower held for me and two other staff in my department that were expecting. It was really nice and thoughtful of them. When I got back,

Mum informed me that immediately I had left, OlaRose had gone into a fit, crying at the top of the lungs and being agitated and eventually desaturating. Her FiO2 had increased to 30% during her episode. "She really missed your voice... she knew you had gone," they marveled. The nurse then played her the digital recorder and she seemed to calm down a bit. I gave her a bath later that evening for the second time. She does love her bath time - she smiled and gazed wide-eyed at me the whole time. It was a beautiful moment, as I cleansed and dried my baby's tiny frame with such love. It was indeed surreal! I love her sooo much...it scares me. Being a mother is something one can never imagine or fully prepare for until you experience it. I didn't know it was capable to feel so deeply for someone in that way. It was like I hardly knew her, yet I knew her soo well. It is a special, unique, elating, surreal and nostalgic bond. She also had a big bowel movement before her bath and messed up her teddy bears and I cleaned them up. "Princesses don't do that," I chuckled. After her bath, she felt relaxed and refreshed and her nurse placed her on her tummy and she fell fast asleep.

Saturday, April 21st, 2007: OlaRose was 685g (lost 10grams) today. Her FiO2 was the same. I did some house cleaning today and visited at night with Obi. I took some more breast milk to the hospital in a cooler and more clean clothes/blankets. It's harder to leave her each day. I wished I could stay the night by her bedside, but it was an open unit layout with several beds in one room and barely enough chairs to sit at the bedside.

Sunday, April 22nd , 2007: Obi and I went to mass at St. Charles and prayed at Obiola's grave with Mom and the boys. While we were still standing there, Emeka, my brother, said "Isn't the aim of living to get to heaven one day? Obiola is definitely in heaven, but most of us have to do a whole lot of good to get there..." Well spoken, we all thought. But no-one wants their child to get there before them, I said (also remembering my brother Obinna who died at a little over a year old, 35years ago and how my parents were devastated, being a young couple themselves at that time). That is not the natural order of things. Children should bury their parents... that's what we all hope for, but it doesn't always happen that way. Some special little angels like Obiola complete their life's mission in a short time, and he indeed did a whole lot of work and sacrifice in his short 27 weeks of life (most spent in the womb). Obi suggested we all go to Olive garden for lunch, and we all did, including NdaChi, NdaNina and kids; and we all had a nice time. After that, we all stopped by the family eye clinic, Aqua Vision Center, Pikesville, where dad was installing protective glasses over some of the eyeglasses shelves. Obi and I later visited OlaRose with NdaChichi who marveled at how tiny and active OlaRose was.

Monday, April 23rd, 2007: OlaRose weighed 715g (1 pound 9ozs). She is growing so much bigger. Her skin had filled out very nicely. I gave her a bath, and as usual, she enjoys her bath time, smiling, eyes very alert, her mask off and still with O2 sats of 100%. After the bath, I gently massaged the Johnson baby lotion on her skin, and she felt fresh and snuggled contently in her bed. I placed her yellow teddy bear next to her, turned her over on her belly, and she went peacefully to sleep. Her feeds were increased to 5cc/h. I enlarged a picture of OlaRose at one month of age and that of Obiola and placed them in pretty oval frames on my bedroom wall, so they are the first and last things I see every night.

Tuesday, April 24th, 2007: Her weight dropped to 710 (she lost just 5g), which was fine. Her feeds were held at 3pm today because her abdomen was very distended and her abdominal x-ray showed dilated loops. I gave her a bath and she had a huge bowel movement before the bath. She was still very active and well. To rule out Necrotizing Enterocolitis (NEC), they kept her NPO (nothing by mouth) and placed an IV line for fluids. A repeat x-ray at 8pm was unremarkable, but she was still given a bowel rest for the day.

Wednesday, April 25th, 2007: OlaRose had her first eye exam today and her retinal blood vessels were noted to be immature, which was as they should be. No signs of ROP. I thanked God for his goodness. Her feeds were restarted at half (2.5cc/hr) and the rest made up with TPN. I went in after shift change at 7pm to visit, so that Obi could watch me bathe her. Before her bath, we noticed she was a little cool, her temp was 97.5 deg F. She enjoyed her bath; and I just wiped her so she wouldn't be too cold. I wiped her eyelids gently with a wet cloth... poor baby.. they were so swollen and red from the dilating drops and the stress of the eye exam. I massaged her body lotion as usual, and she enjoyed it and settled down to sleep. But after a few minutes, she started crying, and would only stop when I held her in the palms of my hands through the window of the incubator. She wasn't usually so fussy or needy, so I became worried. Also, she had a few desats, bradys and apneic episodes all at the same time. I then realized that her incubator door was not sealed (probably from during the day) and had a draft of cool air coming in, so she was a little cold, and her temp had dropped to 97.3. I sealed it with the clear plastic covering. We turned down her lights, and snuggled her little teddy bear close to her as she went to sleep. Obi and I then left. I called her nurse an hour later, she was till sleeping peacefully with no bradys and desats and her temp had risen to 98.2 deg.

Thursday, April 26th, 2007: OlaRose was 735g. Her FiO2 was 23%, and her feeds were increased back to full feeds of 5cc/hr. I spoke with the attending about the importance I feel of continuity of nurses for the patients, not just OlaRose. It helps the parent have security and feel assured that someone knows their baby very well. So for example, I don't have to remind someone at each shift about her blankets being her own or that she likes her tape being played or that she loves to sleep on her belly.. etc. Also, I mentioned that though I used to work there, I would like to just be OlaRose's mom when I visit, and not be expected to turn her oxygen up or down when the alarms went off because her nurse was busy with another patient, as had happened on numerous occasions. The attending suggested that I share my ideas with the nurse manager as they would appreciate my unique perspective as a mom and physician. I did as delicately as I could, but I am not sure my suggestions were received too well. After that experience, I felt discouraged and hesitant about voicing any concern about her care to the staff anymore. I did not want anyone to feel that I was being critical or judgmental.. I was really just anxious and afraid, and wanted her to be okay as her mother. As a physician, I understood why the staff would be defensive, offended, or sensitive to any parental concern. I was one of them, and should know how it feels. But for the first time, I was experiencing those feelings of anxiety, fear and pain from the other side of the bed – and helplessness of not knowing, and longing for compassion and understanding. I bore these in silence and decided to trust God that she would be okay – He was all I could hope in.

Friday, April 27th, 2006: I visited with Okey and very pregnant Oge; and they marveled at how much bigger she was (almost twice her size literally) from three weeks ago when they had last seen her. I cleaned her, but noticed that she was slightly more alert than yesterday. Her nurse informed me that her breast milk was almost out, so I had to drive back to Westminster to bring more supplies of breast milk and run it to the hospital. When I arrived at 900pm, I was informed by her night nurse that she had a brady to 48 and was stimulated before recovery. I was a little anxious and looked at her sleeping peacefully, still with occasional jerks like she was shivering. She's still cold, I told her nurse... who insisted that her temperature is normal as last checked. But she's acting cold, I insisted. I looked around her incubator and noticed that one of the windows behind her head was open. It had been sealed with a cellophane wrap, but the bottom was flapping freely from where the CPAP wires and cords had been removed. A large cold draft was coming in from there into the incubator. I was a little bit alarmed... but calmly pointed it out to her nurse, explaining that that was probably the reason OlaRose had been acting cold, and she must have had to burn her calories just to maintain her body temperature. This would explain why she hadn't gained any weight for a couple days. I left and said I'd call later that night to check on her. Her nurses were great, but I just needed them to be a little more careful. I wondered about other mothers there who didn't have a clue about neonatal care ... how would they know to check these things? I really do thank God as I had realized while hospitalized with pre-eclampsia that this is the reason for which I am in neonatal-pediatrics - to prepare me for this point in my life. God wanted to give me the heart, strength and understanding to take care of my premature child.

Saturday, April 28th, 2006: OlaRose is 32 weeks corrected gestational age. She lost 5g down to 730g, and I was not too pleased because I related it to the fact that she had burnt her calories trying to maintain her body temperature. I spoke to Dupe, my friend, a neonatology fellow too, and she agreed with me and allayed my fears. I thank God I'm able to detect when something is wrong clinically with her due to my knowledge as a neonatology fellow. Who knows what would have happened if it went on undetected for a few more days? According to

Dupe, I should thank God but also use the knowledge wisely. I decided not to complain to the attendings, but point it out to her nurses and leave it at that, and leave it to God who had been taking care of her from the womb. I visited my princess in the evening. She was more alert and active and smiled for me and enjoyed my visit. Her FiO2 was at 21% most of the day. Ngozi and Bobby returned from New York and we congratulated them on their engagement. I took my niece Amanda home with me for the night.

Sunday, April 29th, 2007: OlaRose is 810g (1pound 12 ozs.), and were we ecstatic or what?? Obi, Amanda and I did the 810 dance quite ecstatic and pleased with OlaRose for her progress. I told her nurse, Susan, to let her know that Mummy is very happy with her. It's amazing how my day and well-being are consumed with my daughter…and how well she is doing or not dictates my emotions by the minute. But it's a feeling I would never trade for anything else in the world. I visited her as usual in the evening and spent some time with my baby. She squeezed my finger and gazed at me for as I cleaned her up. She's grown soo much. Her feeds were still breast milk 24cal/oz at 5.5cc/h.

Monday, April 30th, 2007: Today is Daddy's 66th birthday. Oge, my twin had her precious little baby boy today Ikechi Fortune Mezu-Alabi and like Oge says, I'm sure he and OlaRose will be best of friends. OlaRose, my princess, is 6 weeks today and gained 20g today to become 830g (1 pound 13 and half ozs.). Her nasal cannula flow was 0.9L on room air. Mummy is soo happy with her. A couple more ounces and she'll be 2 pounds. I was there just on time to see Oge push out Ikechi into the world … a beautiful, well-bodied 7lb 15.2 ozs bouncing baby boy indeed. I kept joking that he will not be lying next to OlaRose any time soon, so she doesn't get squashed by him. He was a handsome boy. Oge was so strong; I was proud of her. Immediately her son was born, he was placed into her arms for her to cuddle and kiss him before he was taken to the warmer for assessment. My heart fluttered in joy for her at the sight. I suddenly had an intense longing to hold OlaRose. I couldn't help dwelling on the thought that I had a baby girl that was six weeks old that I had never held in my arms before. I left my sister's bedside later that morning with Kelechi and went straight to the other hospital to see OlaRose in the NICU. "I want to hold OlaRose... I want to hold my baby!" I said persistently to her nurse practitioner and her attending. They thought about it for a second saying... she was still under 1 kg. "But she is stable on nasal cannula," I pointed out. They saw my resolve and gave in. "We were going to let you hold her soon anyway," they said. I was ecstatic as I got ready to hold her. OlaRose according to Allison, her nurse, got two treats today - a new cousin and a well-awaited cuddle from her mummy. Yes, I got to hold my baby girl for the first time since birth today at 6 weeks of age.

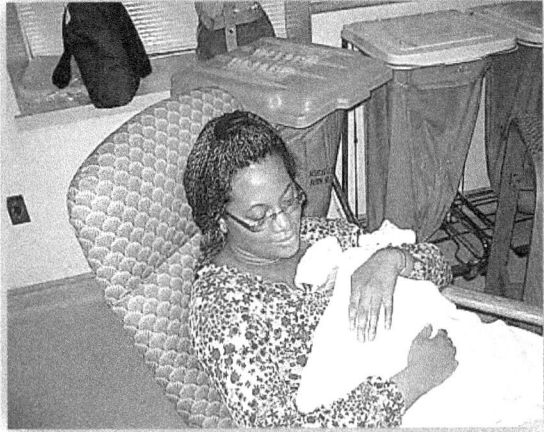

Kelechi had escorted me to visit OlaRose and she took pictures of me holding her. I got to Kangaroo her today since she had gained a lot of weight. I held her next to my bare skin and covered her with her blanket after I cleansed my chest with the sanitizer and rubbed her baby lotion on it. It felt so good and boy did she love it, as she drifted slowly to sleep. I held her for two precious hours. It was nostalgic and memorable.

After I left her bedside, I sat on one of the benches outside the hospital and cried tears of joy. I had held my baby like a mummy for the first time. It seemed as if she was being born today; and I had just been placed into my arms. It was not the same touching her hands with my fingers or wiping her during a bath through the incubator door and holding her in my palms to comfort her. Cuddling her next to my skin was an emotion I could not express. We had bonded instantly as I spoke softly to her, and I think she knew it was me... her mummy. If only I had gotten to hold Obiola like that while he was alive, I thought sadly. I drove from there back to see Oge and met Ngozi there. Soon, Chigozie arrived and Obi too and we had a nice visit with the new mother and father and baby. From there, we went to Mezuville America to celebrate Dad's birthday.

Tuesday, May 1st, 2007: Guess how much she weighed today? 875g (1 pound 15ozs.). My baby girl is getting bigger... She is as much in a hurry to come home as I am to have her home with me. Her nasal cannula flow was weaned to 0.7L/min on 21% FiO2, and her feeds are at 5.7cc/h. Thank you Jesus. I held her close to my heart for about an hour before putting her back in her incubator. She whimpered as I removed her gently from my chest. My poor baby... she was loving her mummy carrying her. It is amazing how my emotions and mood is so dependent on how well she is doing. Any day there is a setback, I'm sad, and my day is ruined and everyone can tell; but any day she makes some progress, I'm radiant and on top of the world. She does keep me going, and helps me endure her brother's loss.

Wednesday, May 02, 2007: OlaRose lost 20g and was back to 855g. Her flow was weaned to 0.6L/min. Her feeds were increased to 6.0cc/h. I have to accept that she will take her time with the weight gain... She's come a long way and has been through a lot. I visited at night, and Obi came by from work. I held her for about an hour and put her back in her incubator when she had a couple desats. Her temperature was a little high because her incubator had slightly overheated when her temp probe fell off so the bed could not read her temp accurately; and that sure didn't make me happy. Obi agreed with me that she does look like Obiola more so now that her face had filled out due to good weight gain.

Thursday, May 03, 2007: OlaRose weighed 875g, she regained 20g. They started compressing her feeds today to 16cc over 2 hours, every 3hours, and she tolerated it well. Good for her. I visited today and gave her a bath. I did not Kangaroo today, because I didn't want her to have both a bath and kangaroo care on the same day.

Friday, May 04, 2007: OlaRose is 2 pounds 0.2 ozs. (915g). Thank God!! I took fresh, pretty linen and clothes to her. Visited the NICU with Fortune, NdaNina, and Ngozi. I held her today and did some

Kangaroo care. She loved it as usual. Her feeds were further compressed to 16cc over 1 hour.

Saturday, May 5th, 2007: I visited OlaRose in the evening, and changed

her diaper. Her weight was 920g (2 pounds 0.6ozs). She had gained 5g. I was happy that she was maintaining the 2 pound mark, and I hoped it would continue that way, so I did not give her a bath or kangaroo care in order to conserve her calories. She is so much bigger. Her nurse, Sue helped me take digital picture of her and printed them out for me.

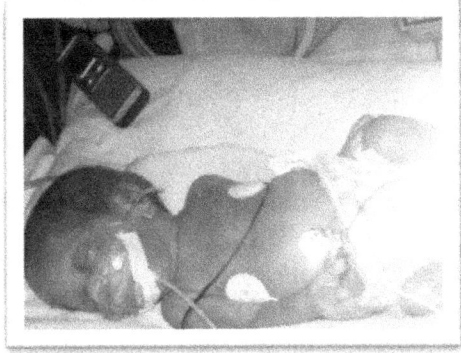

Sunday, May 6th, 2007: Obi and I picked Mummy up and went to see OlaRose late in the afternoon. She weighed 935g (gained 15g) which is 2 pounds 1 oz. Hurray!!! Her feeds became finally compressed over 20mins at every 3 hours like a regular baby, and she has been tolerating it well. So far, she has been having regular bowel movements. We chatted with Dupe at the NICU; and we all prayed by OlaRose's bedside. We reminisced about Obiola's precious coming and going from this world, and how God had used him to give her life. She is really a special girl, and I am proud to be their mummy... both OlaRose and Obiola, the two most beautiful babies in the world.

Monday, May7th, 2007: 7 weeks old. OlaRose weighed 945g as weighed at midnight, but her nurse reweighed her in the evening and she was now 970g (2 pounds 2 ounces!!) . I was really excited and even happier to know that I could start breastfeeding. I visited her in the evening and decided to wait till the next day to breast feed to help her get as close to 1kg as possible because she would burn calories to suck or breastfeed. All day, I tried to drink as much fluid as possible to increase my breast milk volume... I must have had over 3 liters of fluid all together. Her FiO_2 ranged from 21 to 25% on 0.6L oxygen via nasal cannula. She had a good day according to Sue, her nurse, with minimal bradys and desats.

Tuesday, May 8th, 2007: Today is a milestone. She weighed 1025g (2 pounds 3ozs) and I breastfed my baby for the first time, and I was in 7th heaven. I brought cookies for the nurses and doctors to celebrate the milestone. It was the most beautiful experience to hold my baby close to my heart and feel her suck for the first time after seven long weeks. She blew into it at first, quite sleepy, not sure what it was. Then a trickle of milk touched her lips and she smacked and licked eagerly. From there on, she was like a pro. "Good girl,"... "That's my girl, " I thought. We've been practicing all these weeks with a pacifier and she knew how to suck well. "That's the only way I can take you home, " I whispered to her. I would breast feed once a day for now, I decided, till she was able to tolerate more frequent breastfeeds. She took some rest in between sucks and I took to expressing the nipple for her to make it easier. After twenty five minutes, Allison, her nurse helped me put her back in the incubator. She checked aspirates and got back almost 2cc of breast milk. This confirmed that she did get something and she could swallow. I was so proud of her. She had no brady, apnea or desat throughout the whole breastfeeding, which was good. She then got her 20cc bolus feed over 20 mins through gavage. The breastfeeding for now was just to stimulate and get her used to the nipple. That night, I watered my white stem mums still by the kitchen window still in the beautiful vase. Six weeks and they were still fresh mostly, with only a few flowers starting to show signs of wilting. They are amazing plants and symbolized to me the presence of Obiola in our home and our hearts forever.

Wednesday, May 9th, 2007: I visited at shift change in the evening with Obi. I held her for a while and tried to put her to breast. She sucked for a short while. Her weight was 1025g, she had maintained the same weight, and I was happy she didn't lose anything. Her bowel movements are still regular. The eye exam was Stage 0 zone 2; and I thank God for small mercies. I trust and believe she will be fine, and will not develop ROP.

Thursday, May 10th, 2007: Her weight was 1040g (2 pounds 4 and half ozs.) I'm so proud of her. I held her for an hour and didn't really try to breastfeed to give her a break.. so she doesn't burn calories. Drank about 3 L of fluid today.

Friday, May 11th, 2007: Her weight was 1070g (2 pounds 6ozs.). She had gained 35g. I was ecstatic. Her oxygen flow was weaned to 0.5L nasal cannula, and her fi02 still ranged from 21 to 25% with a few desats and brady episodes.

Saturday, May 12th 2007: OlaRose turned 34weeks today. She lost weight down to 1055g. That's ok. I cleaned her up today and she enjoyed it as usual. I took some breast milk to her and requested that she be supplemented half and half with special care 24cal/oz formula. It was a hard decision for me to mix half breast milk and formula, but my flow was very decreased and she was catching up fast to me. Moreover, I would hate to completely run out and then have to do 100% formula all of a sudden. I continued my 2 plus liter consumption of water daily hoping to increase the flow.

Sunday, May 13th, 2007: My first Mother's day. It was an emotional day for me. I started the day crying because my breast milk flow was less than 20cc that morning; and Obi tried to console me. I went to the hospital by noon with Mother's day pastries for the staff. I held my daughter in my arms for a while and then tried to breastfeed her. I missed Obiola especially today, and felt a connection with him through his sister. OlaRose had further dropped to 1025g in her weight. I tried not to be worried. I wondered if the fact that she had been tachypneic the past two days was responsible as that was a sure way to burn calories. I decided not to bring her out of her incubator the next day to give her time to regain her weight. The nurses had made a beautiful card with her footprints.. it was so touching. I love these gestures they do for the mothers, it means a lot. The rest for the day was a relaxing, nice barbecue at my parents' home, Mezuville America with the extended family. It was quite breezy. I got a lot of phone calls and texts from friends and family, and gifts from my family. Obi gave me a card along with mother's day gifts and part of the card read…. "Thank you for giving me two beautiful babies.." and that meant the most to me. I did have two beautiful babies and I still do… one on earth and one in heaven watching over us all. I touched my heart shaped pendant that I wore daily close to heart and fingered the inscription: "OlaRose and Obiola, My Twin Angels... Mummy loves you but Jesus loves you more." Ngozi and Ure, my younger sisters, had gotten me a baby angel statue which I loved. "That's Obiola," I cried with joy when I saw it. "That's why we got it," smiled Ngozi. I decided to take it home and place it on my bedside till his tombstone was ready.

Monday, May 14th, 2007: OlaRose is 8weeks old and weighs 1115g, (2 pounds 7 and half ozs). Well, she had gotten a blood transfusion for a low hematocrit; and a whole bunch of reference labs done to work up her conjugated hyperbilirubinemia of 4.0, including an abdominal ultrasound and head ultrasound which were both normal. Thank Jesus! She looks bigger. I didn't bring her out of the incubator so she could rest after such a stressful day.

Tuesday, May 15th, 2007: I visited my princess at noon after my 2nd post-partum appointment. I still had 3+ protein in the urine. I really need to schedule to see an internist and a nephrologist. She has been stable on 21% FiO2, but got a second blood transfusion for a low hematocrit of 27. I didn't take her out of the incubator today trying to conserve her weight. Her face is getting more mature and she looks so much more like Obiola. They would have made beautiful twin siblings, we thought. Her weight was 1120g (2pounds 7.9 ozs). She is getting there gradually. Late in the afternoon, Ngozi and I drove to Obiola's grave. My beautiful baby boy... I whispered kneeling down and talking to him. "You know he's not there," she said... "I know he is in heaven," I said, "but his body is and it's still a beautiful body. It 'll never decay forever." Ngozi smiled adding, "Because he's a saint." I said "Yes, he's a saint." I now commented on how I am so relieved that we got them both baptized before he died. I would never have forgiven myself if I had missed the chance to by trying to wait till they came out of the NICU like we had originally thought. I then went to visit Oge and little Ikechi and my parents at Mezuville, America. I thank God for the strong presence of my family during this time. Obi and I would not have made it through without them. Obi had gone from work to visit OlaRose too and stopped by Aqua Vision afterward and we drove home together.

Wednesday, May 16th, 2007: OlaRose weighed 1185g today (2 pounds 9 ozs.) and 16 inches long. I was really happy. She had an eye exam today and her fi02 was increased to 30% but she was later weaned down to 23%. She still was a stage 0, zone 2 with no ROP. Thank God!! Her brother is really looking out for her. I requested for her to receive artificial tears after the eye exam and she got it q6 hrs x 24hrs. Those dilating drops hurt and I didn't want my baby to be in discomfort for so long. She is still on 20cc of half breast milk 24cal/oz and half SC24cal/oz.

Thursday, May17th, 2007: OlaRose weighed 1210g (2 pounds 11 ozs.).She was weaned on her flow to 0.4L/min and seemed to tolerate it well and was still on 21% Fi02. I visited in the evening and held my baby for a while before breastfeeding. She sure had missed it since I had not brought her out of the incubator for a couple of days trying to conserve her calories.

Friday, May 18th, 2007: She weighed 1205g. I visited with Ngozi and took her some breast milk and fresh blankets. I bought a beautiful birthday cake for her and took pictures with the family so that in the morning, I could take her cake to her straightaway. Ngozi and I also took fresh flowers to my first born son's grave... my beautiful Obiola. He is truly loved. I know he is happy and I'll keep reminding him that he has a Mummy and Daddy who love him.... Mummy loves you baby boy... I will never forget you.

Saturday May, 19th, 2007: Olarose's birthday. OlaRose is 2 months today and actually 35 weeks. I took her the beautiful pink and white cake and took pictures in the NICU, and shared the cake with her nurses and doctors. She weighed 1190g. The NICU staff found it hilarious that I bring a cake (a pink one) every month on her birthday. I plan to celebrate her birthday every month till she is a year old, I told them... Then it'll be yearly birthdays from then on. "Girl, you have no idea what you're in for," her nurse, Pam chuckled to OlaRose. I laughed. Yeah, I was going to smother her with love and attention.. I couldn't wait to have her home with me. I dressed her in her pretty, pink birthday dress with a bow around her head for pictures.

Sunday May 20th, 2007: She weighed 1225g (2 pounds 11 and half ozs.). She stayed stable on 0.2L oxygen on room air, with just a couple desats and bradys. It looks like she is maturing more. Mummy visited in the afternoon; and I visited with Obi in the evening. I dressed her in one of her preemie shirts for her. She is sooo big. Obi and I talked about how much she looks like Obiola and how they would have made such beautiful twins. OlaRose is grown so much; and it is amazing that she is so healthy and whole like I prayed... untouched by any illness... no chronic lung disease, no intraventricular hemorrhage (IVH), no ROP no sepsis, no necrotizing enterocolitis (NEC). Her brother is truly watching over her and taking care of her. She is a blessed child of God. He must have a special mission for her in this life – for he has preserved her so.

Monday, May 21st, 2007: 9 weeks of age. OlaRose weighed 1240g today (2 pounds 12 ozs.). I visited her in the evening to see that she had been moved to the window sill to make space for a new baby admitted. Her incubator was literally squeezed in between two babies, and to get to her oxygen source one had to squeeze behind the other baby's incubator. Her cardio-respiratory monitor and her basket of clothes were on the window sill behind her incubator, and the monitor was not visible where it was placed. The whole set up looked unsafe to me; and I felt her care would be compromised that way. The NICU was full and closed to admissions, I was told... Yes, have I heard that before... I remember those declarations by the charge nurse as a fellow, and I remember repeating it to the Ob staff as instructed by my attendings a number of times to deter them accepting new transfers for deliveries. However, if full to capacity at 40 beds means squeezing babies on the window sill exposed to cold draft, then maybe we should re-evaluate our bed capacity. Maybe we need to be a 35 or 38 bed unit and not 40 beds. Not only that, her nurse was assigned another baby in another room, such that I was there for over an hour before I met her nurse, who was a new one for OlaRose. Suffice it to say, I was not very happy or comfortable with the situation. The nurse manager at my request, kindly found a desk or nightstand for me and cleaned it so I could arrange OlaRose's belongings. In the process of moving her, her incubator door behind her head had a loose crew and I pointed it out to a nurse, who tightened it. I kept my emotions and thoughts to myself, and bore them in silence, not wanting to offend her caregivers, who had been so dedicated to her.

Tuesday, May 22nd, 2007: My lovely white stem mums on my kitchen window sill which I had placed there in memory of my beautiful son, Obiola since the past six and half weeks finally wilted. It was amazing they lasted sooo long as I watered them often. I took them away and made a note to get new ones. I requested that Olarose's incubator be changed today for a clean one, as she had had the same one for a whole month. Daddy accompanied me to visit today. She was moved to satellite today where the feeders and growers stay. That was the last stop before going home and a huge progress. I later breastfed her for 20minutes and she suckled vigorously. I was really happy... This was the first time she really breastfed well. She has surely grown stronger. Her weight maintained at 1240g and she was weaned to 0.1L NC still on room air (21% FiO2).

Wednesday, May 23rd , 2007: She weighed 1270g (2 pounds 12.5oz.) today. I went to see her at 8am and breastfed her. She sucked for about 15 mins before getting tired and then she got her regular scheduled 22cc. I returned in the evening and fed her again for 10minutes. She was weaned to 75cc nasal cannula, still on room air. I'm really happy with her. I took lots of pictures with the digital camera to enlarge for my home. Her HIDA scan was negative.

Thursday, May 24th, 2007: Ikechi Fortune got christened today at 8.30am in a private beautiful ceremony at St. Charles church. After mass, we all prayed at Obiola's grave. I took breast milk and clean sheets to my baby girl. Mom dropped by to see OlaRose too. Her feeds were increased to 24cc. She weighed 1322g (gained 52g) which is about 2 pounds 14.5ozs. She was on 75cc NC flow at 21% fio2. Her eye exam showed stage 1 zone 2 ROP. I tried not to be worried. She is in God's hands and Obiola is watching her. She will be fine, I said. I enlarged more pics of OlaRose and hung on my stairway. I feels like she's home with us already.

Friday, May 25th, 2007: I went to visit with Nneoma (Obi's sister); and my Daddy had visited earlier in the morning. I cleaned OlaRose and held her for a short while and then dressed her with her beautiful pink dress, hat and socks. She had gained 20g to be 1342 (2pounds 15.5 ozs). I was so happy. I love you baby girl!!!! According to my mum, she is already 3 pounds… we'll give her that. I had asked them to change her feeds to 1/4th breast milk 24cal/oz and ¾ Sc24cal/oz to give me time to rebuild my milk supply. Also her oxygen was completely removed,… so she no longer has a nasal cannula!!! Isn't God great? Nneoma and I dropped by Obiola's grave and I placed beautiful silk flowers in two angel pictured vases.   When I called at 11pm to check on OlaRose, her nurse, Sandra, told me that she had taken all of her 24cc by bottle and still looked like she wanted some more. She then began to suck her thumb. My poor baby…. I am sooo proud of her.

Saturday, May 26th, 2007: I woke up and said good morning to my son, Obiola as usual. Mummy loves you, I smiled at his picture and imagined him smiling back down at me. I think about him daily as I go about my activities and he's usually the last image on my mind after I call the NICU to check on OlaRose and settle down to sleep. Pray for mummy, I said… OlaRose is officially 36 weeks old today. Obi and I went to see our daughter at 3pm and were in for a nice surprise. She was all dressed up in her clothes, bundled up in a blanket with the incubator heat finally turned off… only on air temp. She was able to maintain her own temperature and was still on room air. I fed her the bottle of 24cc; and she took it all in 15minutes. Her weight was 1400g (3 pounds 1.5ozs.). She is such a multi-tasker, just like mummy. I am so proud of her…. She is nippling, on room air and off the incubator heat , and maintain her temp and gain weight at the same time … within 24hours… such stamina. Her desats and bradys have about completely resolved. Oge, my twin sister and her new son Ikechi left for Pittsburgh today escorted my Mum and Dad. I asked Oge for some breast milk for OlaRose and she happily pumped 4 to5 ozs before leaving for Pittsburgh. It was a hard decision for me, but it was better than OlaRose running totally out and going on 100% formula. Breastmilk contained nutrients, immune cells, helps fight infections, and is better tolerated than formula. I continued to pump every 2 to 3 hours, as often as possible to rebuild my supply. Obi and I attended a wedding with Ngo, KC and Chazie; and Nda Nina and Uncle Edward… our first outing together since my ordeal with the pregnancy. It felt good to relax a little.

Sunday, May 27th, 2007: My princess continued to maintain her temperature and wear real clothes. I took new clothes for her... mostly pink of course. It's amazing how she already has a wardrobe full of the prettiest clothes, before even being home. I continued to pump breast milk as often as I can. The supply is increasing slowly up to an ounce each pump....to my relief. Her weight was 1420g (3 pounds 2ozs.). ... Imagine that. She is also still on room air. I gave her a bath, dressed her in pretty pink gown, and then breastfed for 4 minutes before feeding her the bottle. She took the bottle down in 10minutes gulping all the way. I was really ecstatic. Obi, Nneoma, Emeka and I drove over to Kelly and Chazie's for dinner and then Emeka treated us to a movie... we watched pirates of the Caribbean. My baby girl will be home soon... I really cannot wait.

Monday, May 28th, 2007: Memorial day. She is 10 weeks old. OlaRose was increased to nippling three times a day. She weighed 1400g. She had lost 20g... and I was concerned she was burning calories with the nipple feeds...even though she was taking them like a champ. I visited my princess in the evening. She was all cute and snuggly in her pink and white overall. I breast fed for 7 minutes before bottle feeding her. She took 21 cc in 12 minutes and seemed sleepy, so we gavaged the remaining 5cc. I burped her, held her for a while and then laid her to sleep in her isolette. She is soo pretty... As I held her I imagined that I was holding Obiola too... my baby boy. I then joined the rest of the family in Kelly and Chazie's home for a nice fun barbecue party. We got home at midnight, and I had just enough time to put OlaRose's blankets and clothes in the washer and pump 50cc of breast milk before passing out to sleep.

Tuesday, May 29th, 2007: I took my baby girl more breastmilk and fed her at 3pm on breast for 5minutes and then her 26cc bottle (breast + Sc24) over 11minutes. Her weight was 1420g (3 pounds 2.1ozs.). I changed her clothes and held her for a while before placing her back in the isolette to sleep. I'm glad she's been stable with her temp and saturation on room air. The isolette is still switched to air temp with the heat off. Her caffeine was discontinued today, but she is still on potassium, sodium, iron supplements and diuril. Mum and Dad returned from Pittsburgh in the evening with some cute preemie clothes from Oge and about 9 ozs of breast milk. I bought a Disney paint "pretty in pink" for OlaRose's room with Disney princess borders and lamp. Obi and Emy or Ik could start painting her room over the weekend.

Wednesday, May 30th, 2007: OlaRose gained 40g to be 1460g today (3pounds 3.5ozs.). I held her and fed her, and just as I was about to lay her back in her isolette, Mum and Dad walked in to visit her. Mom held her and we took pictures, and Dad said a prayer for her. It's amazing how much she's grown, they said. Ikechukwu's graduation was at 7pm and we all attended after which we went to dinner at Olive garden.

Thursday, May 31st, 2007: OlaRose weighed 1490g (3pounds 4.5ozs) today. I did her daily laundry early in the morning and pumped breast milk 3x before heading to the hospital with fresh clothes and breastmilk. I visited with Ngozi and later K.C joined us. I cleaned her up, changed her diaper and dressed her warmly in clean pretty pink overalls before feeding. She took all of her 26cc in 5minutes and also breastfed for 6 minutes. She's a true survivor. I so enjoy being with her and can't wait to take her home with me.

Friday, June 1st, 2007: Today, I pumped close to 2 to 3 ozs each time and I was really relieved that I was flowing well, back up to 70% of previous capacity. I put on my pendant with my twin babies pictures as I do every morning after a shower; and I was ready for the day. OlaRose was 1510g (3pounds 5.2 ozs.). My baby is getting there, slowly but surely. I took fresh laundry as usual, cleaned her, changed her diaper, dressed her in her pretty pink and fed her at 3pm. She is now taking 28cc and her bottle feeding are now every other feed. Also, her pulse ox was discontinued today. I got some colorful rattles and musical toys to stimulate her eye movements and brain and also keep her from being bored. I'm truly counting down the days...and right now I am guessing it would be about 14 days before she can come home, all she needs to do is keep up with the weight gain as we slowly make all her feeds nipple feeds. "Please baby, give mummy a good birthday present and come home by June 16th", I whispered as I held her after her feeds. Ngo, Mum, Ik and I watched Shrek, the third in the evening. I checked on OlaRose at 11.30pm and was told by Gladys, her nurse that she took all her 28cc feed very well by mouth.

My baby girl... I then pumped breastmilk, filled her daily diary and went to bed.

Saturday, June 2nd, 2007: OlaRose is officially 37 weeks today. I visited her in the evening and took her fresh linen and breast milk; and changed her blanket over the incubator to a new pink and white one. She maintained her weight at 1510g... and I'm glad she didn't lose any weight. Her bowel movement are still daily and regular. She was started on actigall for her high direct bilirubin, which should resolve on its' own since there is no biliary atresia on the HIDA scan. Friends and family called as usual to check on her progress. I thank God for all the prayers being showered on her. It sure is working because she has so far being untouched by any of the neonatal diseases I so feared.

Sunday, June 3rd, 2007 : Obi and Ik painted OlaRose's room pink today, truly pretty in pink. It was soooo beautiful. We planned to paint a heart-shaped blue symbol on the wall in memory of Obiola... because they were supposed to share the room together if he had lived. Now instead, he would always be there in spirit to watch over her like he's been doing. I cooked pepper soup for Kelechi who was sick, and we all enjoyed some of it. We went back to half and half with the breast milk and special care 24 calorie milk since my breast milk supply is much better. I spent 5 hours with my baby today. She's gotten so used to me carrying her, and knows when I am there. She whimpered whenever I tried to move or get up, and when I finally laid her down, she started crying; and I had to pick her up again. She was starving for more human touch. I can't wait to take her home. She took all 28cc and wanted more smacking her lips and sucking thin air...poor baby. I had to hold her till she finally went to sleep. She weighed 1530g (3 pounds 5.8ozs.) Her nurse, Joanna, took out her feeding tube so I could take pictures without the tube and then later replaced it with a new, bigger one. Ben, one of the NICU fellows and my friend came by and we chatted as I held OlaRose. He marveled at how big she was and what a miracle indeed that she was going home without oxygen. A miracle indeed!

Monday, June 4th , 2007: OlaRose is 11 weeks old and weighed 1540g (3pounds 6 ozs.). She was allowed to nipple as tolerated and seemed to be eager about it. She nippled all of her 9am, 12noon, 3pm and

6pm feeds like a champ, but by 9pm she was worn out and would not wake up to feed. Poor baby! She got gavage feeds for 9 and 12midnight; and woke up at 3am to feed again. I thought maybe we had been too excited at her nippling and should let her rest a bit. When I visited she was quite sleepy and could barely open her eyes. I brought fresh clothes and bedsheets, and held her for a while before putting her down to sleep. Her sodium and potassium oral supplements were discontinued as her electrolytes normalized with her maturity and PO feeds. Her only meds now are actigall to help reduce her conjugated hyperbilirubinemia and iron supplements, which she would take for a while since she would be at risk for anemia for some time due to prematurity.

Tuesday, June 5th, 2007: OlaRose got gavage feeds in the morning so I was to nipple her at 3pm. I got up at 6am as usual to pump breast milk. Now we are back to half and half, she was catching up to me again, so I was pumping earnestly every 3 hours. Her room borders (Barbie) and her Disney princess nightlight arrived and look sooo pretty and pink and complement her room well. According to the nurses and my family, she will probably rebel against pink when she grows up. Well, like I say, till she is able to tell me her favorite color, it stays "pink" because she is a princess. Ha! Ha! I spent the whole morning calling around finding doctors for OlaRose in anticipation for her discharge. I found a pediatrician in Carroll county 0.8 miles from our home in Westminster; and a pediatric ophthalmologist to follow her eyes after discharge till she was no longer at risk for ROP or its' sequelae; and a Pediatric GI specialist to follow her conjugated hyperbilirubinemia. Whew! It was a lot of work, but I was satisfied after it was done. I took the list to the hospital and gave it to her NNP, Linda, who was impressed at the foresight and organization. I guess from working at the NICU, I knew what to anticipate for discharge. I gave her a bath and weighed her before dressing her up and feeding her. She finished her 28cc and still breast fed for 6minutes. She latched on very well with a strong suck and I was really happy with her progress. She really feels my presence and yearns for my touch. It was hard to leave her later on. Her weight remained stable at 1540g despite the fact that she nippled all but one feed that day.

Wednesday, June 6, 2007: I visited her in the evening and spent a few hours with her. Her follow-up eye exam was done today and was to my joy, a stage 0 zone 3 showing maturity of her retinal vessels. My baby did not have ROP. They, however, noticed that she had small optic nerves which is really inconsequential for her. She had nippled all her feeds that day and they had finally removed the NG tube. I was ecstatic to see my baby's beautiful face finally free of tape or tube. She was relieved too. I feed her half and half 28cc bottle and also breastfed for 6minutes before she snuggled on my shoulder to sleep peacefully as I rocked her to sleep on the rocking chair. I look forward to days and nights of her falling asleep on my shoulder and body in my huge king-sized bed. "You are my world, OlaRose,." I whispered as I kissed her. "You've kept me going all these months and you keep me going every day. I can't wait to have you home with me." She seemed to smile cozily as I spoke softly. I marveled as I gazed at her. She really had my nose, eyes, lips and light skin color, but her Daddy's head, shape of face, ears, and smile... she was a perfect combination of the best of us... My beautiful princess.

Thursday, June 7th, 2007: She weighed 1600g (3pounds 8.2 ozs). Imagine that!! And she is still nippling all her feeds well. After feeding her, she began to cry and would only stop when I rocked her gently to sleep. My baby is getting so used to the feel of my skin. I can't wait to have her home so I can rock her to sleep any time she wants. I bought some slow flow preemie nipples for her today as some of the ones she was using in the NICU either were too big and flowed too much or the right size and did not flow too well.

Friday June 8th, 2007: I did some cooking in the morning: made delectable egusi soup and rich stew for the weekend. I visited OlaRose for the 3 pm feed and spent a few hours with my baby girl. After feeding, I burped her and she left for a while on my shoulder. She started crying an hour and half later, and I realized she was hungry again. I breastfed for 20 minutes and then fed her the bottle of 35cc which she took in 10minutes. She really was hungry and 30cc was not enough for her. She was now taken up to a maximum of 40cc and a minimum of 30cc. She was started on the fat- soluble vitamin supplements to ensure absorption by her liver since her bilirubin was still high.

Saturday June 9ᵗʰ, 2007: Today was my baby shower organized by our family and friends. It was a huge occasion and all our friends and family were there. It was a lot of fun with lots of food and drinks and a good DJ. Guests were asked to wear a touch of pink for OlaRose or a touch of blue for Obiola. I drove to visit my daughter for a couple hours before the baby shower and spent some time cuddling her. Her weight was 1630g (3 pounds 9.5 ozs.). I'm so proud of you, I whispered to her.

Sunday, June 10ᵗʰ, 2007 : We spent the morning opening up her numerous gifts from the baby shower. She got a lot of nice presents. Her weight was 1680g (3 pounds 11ozs.). She was placed on open crib for the first time, and I was very excited. She maintained her temp and continued nippling all her feeds. Obi and his siblings, Chichi, Chijioke and Francis, one of her godfathers, came to visit her. She was glad to see her aunty and uncles. They marveled at how beautiful and cute she was. Francis who had seen her at a week old, could not believe how big she had gotten.

Monday, June 11ᵗʰ, 2007 : I decided to see OlaRose first in order to take her long sleeved overalls, so she would not be cold. On getting there she was soo cute and beautiful, I couldn't leave her. They debated trying to put in an NG tube saying she was feeding a little bit slower over 30minutes. I decided to stay and feed her myself. She fed well for me, and we found out using the slow flow nipple was difficult for her to suck with. Her weight was 1700g (3pounds 12 ozs.) and she still maintained her temp on open crib. I'm literally counting the days till she comes home. Ngozi and I drove to Babies R Us to exchange some gifts and buy more items. Chijioke was admitted to the hospital from the airport in sickle cell pain crises. Poor boy, I went to visit him and Mom and Dad came later with some food and clothes.

Tuesday, June 12ᵗʰ, 2007: I did more shopping for OlaRose and visited Chijioke in the evening. She weighed 1720g (3 pounds 12.5ozs.). I bought a musical mobile for her bassinet and a little music box with shooting stars to keep her occupied because she looked so bored staring up at the ceiling in her bassinet. Her eye exam was repeated and still confirmed no ROP (Stage 0, zone 3) with mature vessels and fully vascularized retina. Her optic nerve was noted to be small but not hypoplastic, so an MRI was ordered to visualize structures better . Her follow-up eye exam is in 3 weeks. She is really being watched from heaven because she is still perfect with no major issues. Adaora, her neonatologist and my friend, thought she was getting tired because she had done a lot in the past few days nippling all and open crib and wanted to have the NG tube placed. I was sad because it seemed like a setback for her since she had been progressing so well. The NG was placed after her six pm feed.

Wednesday, June 13th, 2007: The NG tube was removed in the morning because she began to brady with a feed. She didn't like the tube at all. The steam cleaners came and pre-cleaned, degreased, deep-scrubbed and dry-foamed our berber carpets in all the rooms and later sanitized and deodorized the whole house and cleaned out all the air ducts/vents. That cost a lot, but anything to keep my daughter safe and healthy when she comes home. I'm relieved that the house will be sterile, clean, and sanitized while she was there. I visited her in the evening with my mummy, and her weight was 1730g (3 pounds 13.2ozs.). She got an MRI of the brain to check her optic nerves and ear canal, and was quite sleepy and tired when we visited, but I cleaned her, dressed her in comfortable pink overalls and rocked her gently with mummy. My beautiful baby girl.

Thursday, June 14th, 2007: Obi's birthday. I got a beautiful cake for our breakfast together before he went to work. I asked him to take the cake to work and share with his co-workers. I did OlaRose's laundry as usual early in the morning and started to put her room together. She is still on room air, open crib and nippling all. I visited her in the evening and held her for two hours, cleaned her up, changed her and fed her. She is so soft and cuddly. She had gained 20g to be 1750g. Good news! She passed her developmental exam and was at newborn level for all her skills. I am very pleased and thank God for his mercies. Obi and I went to dinner at Johansson's restaurant in Westminster for his birthday. It was very nice.

Friday, June 15th, 2007:I visited her in the afternoon and spent time with her. Her MRI results were normal and I was so happy. She weighed 1770g (3 pounds 14.5 ozs.). I was informed that OlaRose could come home tomorrow. I was suddenly taken aback! I wasn't quite ready for her, I thought. I had dreamt of her coming home on my birthday, but when it became a reality, I was in shock. I asked her attending to keep her a couple days more till Monday, so that the house could dry well from the carpet cleaning just done and I could get fully ready for her. Well, that was not a medical reason to remain hospitalized, but I was in a little panic. I never thought I would ever ask for her to stay in the hospital one more day. They decided to keep her to monitor the few self-resolved bradys she was still having. I asked them if she needed a home apnea monitor for the bradys but they said she wouldn't need them. I knew I may not sleep at all when she came home. I could see myself staying up and watch her all night, to observe for a brady. She was scheduled to be discharged on Monday and I spent the day doing last minute shopping for her. I can't believe my baby is almost home. Okey, my younger brother (and the first son) arrived today. Edward Junior, my nephew and my youngest brother, IK spent the night at Westminster to help set up OlaRose's stuff. She has so many toys and gadgets, its' amazing.

Saturday June 16th, 2007: More shopping for OlaRose trying to get almost everything we would need because I didn't plan to go anywhere with her for a few months except to her doctor's appointments. I visited her in the evening with Okey. She weighed 1820g (4 pounds 0.5ozs.). Our family held a party for the June birthdays at Mezuville, America for Okey and Obi, Oge and I.

Sunday, June 17th, 2007: Father's day. She weighed 1830g (4 pounds 1oz.) I visited her and dressed her in her cute pink and white outfit for her first baby picture. Emy, Ngo, Daddy and Mummy came by to help us set up for OlaRose. We worked hard and finally got all her gadgets put together. Her room is a beautiful pink paradise. "You know, this is more for you than OlaRose," my mum teased. "She is not going to need half of these gadgets." I smiled. I just couldn't wait for my baby to come home and I'll give all her all the love she deserves and more.

Monday, June 18th, 2007: OlaRose came home today. When the almost one pound security bracelet was removed from her ankle, she weighed 3 pound 15 ounces. It was a nostalgic, memorable event for me. My parents, Obi and Ngozi came to the NICU to help bring her home. It was like a fanfare bringing her home and my family was overjoyed.

I felt like a **real mummy** for the first time as I wheeled my baby out of the NICU; and I recalled 3 months earlier when I was discharged home from post-partum and went home empty-handed without my babies. The joy I felt today made up for that previous anguishing evening. God is great and forever will be praised. She was coming home without oxygen, on room air on full oral breast /bottle feeds and healthy with all her senses intact. We thanked the NICU staff for their outstanding job of nurturing her and in appreciation for their efforts catered a lovely lunch from *Olive Garden* with a huge thank you cake, and gave the head of the department a $1,000 check for the needs of the NICU from the ObiolaRose Twin Angels Foundation set up by the family in memory of our angel and hero Obiola, who was OlaRose's personal guardian angel in the womb and in the NICU, and who had given his life for his twin sister and me. Today, I believe is one of the happiest days of my life. Alone with her, at home, I held her to my chest and wouldn't let go. I can't believe I would wake up to her beautiful face every day from now on. A new chapter in our lives is about to begin and I happily end the NICU Diary OlaRose.

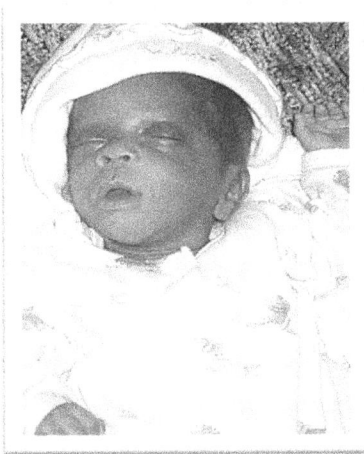

Welcome OlaRose by Dr. Ure Laura Rita Mezu

Anyone in need of a miracle
Should look at OlaRose.
Anyone who just wants to believe
should look at OlaRose

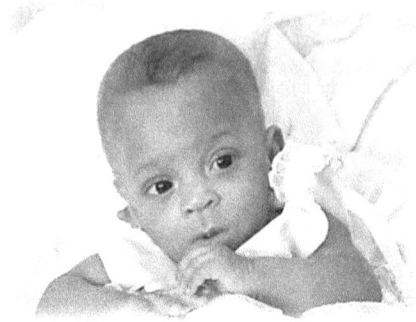

If you ever feel hopeless
Look at OlaRose
If you ever doubt the Lord's
presence
Look at OlaRose

Should you want to see a living testament of the Lord's love
See our little miracle
Should you doubt that the impossible can happen
See our little miracle

Our darling daughter is home
Our beautiful angel is here
You have shown us why we have to love always
You have shown us why we have to believe again
You have shown why we always have to trust the Lord
You have shown us the face of the Lord by just simply being you
We love you OlaRose.
Welcome home.

Aunty Ure Laura Mezu
June 20, 2007

Book Three
A Divine Mercy Experience

Jesus I Trust in You!

Mummy Dearest

Hold on to your faith
Hold on to your trust
Believe as always that the God you worship
Will be faithful to His words.
He shall see you through all trials
He shall never leave you
Even though you walk through death's shadows
Life is yours, my mama, claim it.
Healing is yours, mummy, possess it.
It surely is well with your soul.

Waters from the side of Christ, will cleanse you
Blood of Christ, will inebriate you
Spirit of Christ, will strengthen you
Soul of Christ, will sanctify you
Body of Christ, will save you
Not a hair on your body will be touched.
Your organs will be preserved by Christ's spirit
No blood vessel, nerve, or tissue shall be harmed
Because you are Christ's highly favored one, His very own Rose

Mummy dearest, our family's strong matriarch
We dare not imagine life without you
It is not time; God has not deemed it so
This is only a trial, a test for you
A cross for you to bear with God's grace.
You shall arise from it victorious in Jesus' name.
He wants to use you as a messenger
A testimony of His love and power
You will testify and speak from the rooftops of God's mercy and might.
Endure for a little longer mummy, this passion of yours nears its' end.
Endure the pain, the thirst, the hunger, the anguish of the unknown
For you shall bear witness to all that there is a God
And only He is the giver of Life.

Your work here on earth remains
Your spirit must fight to hold on

You are not done teaching us your virtues
You are not done teaching us to love God
You have more grandchildren to pamper
You have your aging mother to tend to
Your dear chum awaits for the promise
To grow old in beloved Akwuosa.

Don't worry mummy
Though your strength is weakened, your spirit is as strong as ever.
Though you cannot speak, oyur prayer resounds from your heart
Showers of blessings surround you from friends, family and strangers
Whose hearts and lives you have touched
With your kindness, gentle heart and cheer.
They all are witnesses to your virtue.
Doctors consulting from across the globe,
heeding to the pleas of your loved ones
as they puzzle and debate your condition.

Don't worry loved one
If you cannot pray out loud as you lay there
Even though I'm sure your lips are sealed in silent prayers
Don't worry for He has stored a basket full of prayers
you have offered all your life
A basket full of masses attended, rosaries said, good deeds done
Stored for use at this time when you need it most
To be reborn and given the gift of Life.

Mummy dearest, do not be afraid
You are a legionary, a soldier of Mary
With a faith firm and immovable as a rock
And she will not abandon you in your hour of need.
She will visit you with graces like she did to her cousin Elizabeth
She embraces you to her bosom
For you are her child, her sister, her friend, her very own Rose.
She remembers your faithfulness to her
For you have dedicated your life to her
You have honored her in all you do
You have been a champion of her course
With "our Lady's Food Kitchen" which you founded to help the needy.

Mary our mother remembers, she will intercede to the Father for you
Her graces she gives to whom she pleases
And you are her chosen one, mummy dearest.

Your patron saints are praying for you
It is not by chance that you lay now in St. Joseph's Hospital
Under the wings of St. Joseph, your beloved one.
Your beloved departed are interceding for you:
John Ogugua, your beloved father,
Rose and Clement Mezu, your cherished parents-in-law,
Obinna Julian Mezu, your innocent first son taken at the age of 2;
Obiola Julian Anthony Ndubuisi, your grandson, precious twin to
OlaRose; John Paul the great; St. Phillip Obinna Aguh,
our beloved friend and priest - we have called upon all of them.
Choirs of angel hover around you
Your guardian angels are guiding the hands that tend to you
When all hope seemed to be lost,God manifested his power to all
When all thought your heart had failed, God renewed it with His love
" She has a beautiful heart," the cardiologist said, as he marveled,
 for no artery or muscle was harmed like they had seen on tests.
"Her heart is perfect and beautiful," he said. If only he knew,
 just how perfect and beautiful indeed you are to us:
Our precious mother, wife, sister and friend...

Mummy dearest, give thanks to God for his healing
Thank you Jesus, you should say over and over
Like your mother, Mama Bessie would say.
You should bear witness to God's love
You should testify to God's mercy
Claim healing, mummy dearest; Claim life, mummy dearest
We love you so much and will be at your side night and day
Till you come back home to us at Mezuville, your very own home.

*February 8, 2008 written at my mother's bedside while she was on the
ventilator in the ICU for 2 weeks. She did miraculously recover
completely with no deficits.*

Ode to My Parents on their 40th Wedding Anniversary: September 6, 2008

ABOUT MY FATHER, DR. S. OKECHUKWU MEZU:

Dr. S. Okechukwu Mezu is the third son and child of 10 children (seven boys and 3 girls) was born on April 30, 1941 to Clement Ugwuezeonu Mezu of Ezeogba, Emekuku, Owerri LGA and Rose Nlemdiuwaoma Mezu nee Akuta of Ihitta Ogada, Owerrri. He left for the United States in 1961 for further studies receiving in 1964 a B.A. in French and German from Georgetown Univeristy, an LL.B. in 1966 from La Salle Extension University (Chicago) and a Ph.D. in Romance Languages from the Johns Hopkins University in 1967. He also did research as a UNESCO Fellow at the *Ecole Pratique des Hautes Etudes (Sorbonne, Paris).* He was a Professor at the State University of New York at Buffalo where he taught French and was the Founder and Director of African Studies. He is also a renowned writer and publisher, establishing Black Academy Press, Inc, a publishing Company which he founded in the 1960's as a young scholar. It remains one of the longest standing historic black publishing companies, where he published some of his great works including, *Behind the Rising Sun*, (a novel on Biafra) *Igbo Market Literature, The poetry of Leopold Sedar Senghor, Black leaders of the Centuries, The Tropical Dawn, Black Academy Review* and many others.

Our Father is one of the few great minds and pioneers in the world that come once in a lifetime; and there is no-one like him. He has great foresight and seems to always give the right advice and have the perfect solution and answer to every problem. When in doubt ask him, because most of the time, he is right; and I've come to realize this through my life. I've always thought that this was a gift from God indeed, that I believe he nurtured through a lifetime of experience, purposeful living, hard work, perseverance, driven innovation, and exceptional self-discipline.

He is a perfectionist, and there is no task too much for him or any goal too far for him to reach. Growing up, he would tell us, "You are the master of your own destiny and architect of your own future," as he would urge us on to reach for our dreams no matter the challenges. And when things seemed bleak he would encourage us never to give up. The word "No" or "Can't" were not in his vocabulary at all. That is not surprising as he excelled at everything he touched accomplishing all the goals he set for himself in his life. He was the best student in his class, achieving distinctions in his academic endeavors through Holy Ghost Juniorate, Ihiala and going to higher education in Europe and the united States.

He married his true love, a young girl named "Rose". A Straight "A" student he had met, and followed her progress over the years as he studied abroad in France and U.S. He came back for her when he was 27 and she was 20 in worn-torn Biafra and like a romance plot they were married on September 6, 1968, and he whisked her away from danger as he accepted an appointment as Ambassador from General Chukwuemeka Odumegwu Ojukwu as the Biafran Ambassador to Cote d'Ivoire. He showed his great love for his country by embarking on several dangerous missions on behalf of the defunct Republic of Biafra. and served in several capacities as a young scholar in the 1960's during the civil war between Nigeria and Biafra representing the new Republic in the Peace Conferences in Niamey, Niger Republic and Addis Ababa in Ethiopia. In the 1978-1980 as a prominent politician and Secretary of the Nigerian Peoples Party (NPP), he helped elect notable names including Governor Samuel Mbakwe to office. He was the Chairman of the renowned Imo Newspapers in the 1980's and the Golden Breweries Limited, after which, he focused on building and expanding his numerous businesses and spending time with his family ensuring his children had a bright future.

A philanthropist, not only did he provide employment for numerous people in the community for decades in his several businesses: Mezu Plastics, Foundation Insurance Co. Inc; Mezu Construction Company, Mezu International Limited and Black Academy Press (a publishing company). He was instrumental in bringing progress to the Owerri, Emekuku and surrounding communities of Eastern Nigeria by constructing solid, good quality roads that withstood the weather elements for years; and helped bring electricity, water and telecommunication to Emekuku Autonomous Community.

Truly respected by his peers and community at large, he is known by all to be a man of his word, honest, a man of great ideas, a champion of any good cause, a formidable force to be reckoned with and you wanted to be on his camp, not the opposite camp. Despite his achievements, our Dad is truly a humble man refusing repeated requests from the community to accept a traditional title of honor. The only honor he wanted was that of seeing a progressive community.

In a bid to secure the best educational future for his children in the face of political, social and economic instability in the 1990's Nigeria, he and my mother made the decision to relocate the family to the United States leaving behind their life's work, social network, friends, extended family, businesses, and their beautiful home, Mezuville Akwuosa. It was not just enough to send all 10 children to the U.S, they wanted to be there with us to guide us and provide the same stable, family unit we had in Nigeria. For this sacrifice, we are eternally grateful.

Our Father pushes us to be the best we can be, even when we feel like giving up or all hope seems to be lost, he is our ever unwavering champion. He is firm in his direction, gentle in his counseling, witty and funny when we desperately need to laugh, our strongest critique when we fail to see our error, and the proudest Dad when we accomplish those goals we set for ourselves. His direction is not pushy, also letting us make our decisions in our lives and work, learn from our mistakes, but always kind with a ready shoulder to console when we stumble or fall.

He seems perfect; but one of his weaknesses I must say, is that he does not know when to stop working. Even now at 67 years old, he is the most hardworking man even more than people half his age. If there is a roof leaking, he climbs the house to fix it . If a pipe is broken, he bends for hours to mend it. If the house needs remodeling, his hammer and nail are working before you know it. He ignores our pleas to slow down but we believe that the disciplined physical and mental work he engages in like constantly producing new written works, running Black Academy Press, publishing, editing, keep him as healthy and strong as ever.

He only seemed to stop when my mother, his wife, was critically ill in February this year. His world seemed to come to a halt. He said little but was slumped for the first time, looking really alone, refusing to eat, sleep or rest while the love of his life lay there with little or no hope for recovery. When the doctors informed us that there was nothing else they can do. He went to her bedside, and I heard him say, "My Rose... My Chum, you cannot leave me... My God, please... . " We realized she had to get better, even if just for his sake. God did listen and healed her miraculously because that love story was not over. There are more chapters to be written.

These two are chums indeed... dear friends and soulmates. Even at their age, they hold hands as they walk, making us smile. They do not have any secrets between them and are each other's best supporter. They do everything together and even write literary works together. My mother has implicit trust in my father's opinion and he keeps encouraging her to reach out to even greater heights in her career. They finish each other's sentences and think alike, its uncanny ... but amazing. Looking at them, one realizes the meaning of a love that stands the test of time.

Dearest Dad, you are truly one in a million. Of all the roles you have played in life: a Scholar, a Statesman, a Politician, a Businessman, a Philantropist, a Lawyer, an Engineer, a Husband, your most rewarding and important role is that of being our Father .

ABOUT OUR MOTHER, DR. ROSE .U. MEZU

Dr. Rose Ure Mezu is the First daughter and child of 5 children born on November 12, 1947 to late John Ogugua Okeke and Bessie Chiege Okeke of Ihitteafoukwu, in Ahaizu Mbaise LGA. She received her early education in Port-Harcourt and later studied in Abidjan, Cote d'Ivoire and obtained a Diplome d'Etudes from Sorbonne, Paris, France. She got her B. A (magna cum laude) and Masters (M.A)in French from the State University of New York at Buffalo in 1972.

She served as principal of Emekuku Girls Secondary School and later was appointed the First Woman Commissioner for Social Welfare in the Greater Imo State (Imo, Abia and part of Ebonyi state) from 1979 to 1983 when the Army took over the government. She was the only political office holder not sent to prison following the Military tribunals as the then Colonel A. Adisa joingly asked her "Abi, you no wan chop or you no sabi chop," attesting to her probity and incorruptibiity She later obtained her Ph.D in Comparative Literature in 1993, specializing in Francophone and Anglophone Feminist Literature from the University of Port-Harcourt, Nigeria setting off a new example and trend that you can be a mother of eleven kids and a renowned academic, that age, marriage and motherhood should be mo barriers to continued academic progress, development and nururing.

She is presently an Associate Professor of English, Women Studies and Comparative literature at Morgan State University, Baltimore, Maryland. Dr Mezu is the founder and coordinator of WADS INSITUTE International and Interdisciplinary Black Creativity Conference. She has written and published many books, some of which are *Women in Chains: Abandonment in Love Relationships in the Fiction of Selected West African writers*, *Songs of the Hearth, Homage to my People, A History of Africana Women's Literature*. She has also co-authored and edited several books with her husband, Dr S. Okechukwu Mezu.

Her romance with a young man named Sebastian seemed like a love story from the medieval times, about a Knight and his lady that would make any young girl's heart flutter.

Our Mum is an epitome of grace and beauty. Growing up, she was the most brilliant student in her class scoring the highest in West Africa in the School Certificate Exams. It is no wonder that she and my Dad fell in love because genius knows genius. Fresh from Holy Family College Higher School, Abak, Nigeria the young, fair, handsome teacher had taught our Mum at high school and seemed to be quite encouraging and supportive about her excellent school work, but she paid no attention as the other girls in the class wrote secret love notes to him, which he refused to take saying famously, "I am not your mail man." He seemed to have no time for girls or so it seemed. After six months as a teacher at Holy Rosary College, Diobu, Port-Harcourt, he left with a full American ASPAU scholarship for Georgetown University in the United States. He maintained cordial mail relationship with her and her parents encouraging her to study hard and avoid distractions, urging her father not to marry her off young like other fathers were in those days but to let this brilliant girl continue to higher education. Now we know he had an ulterior motive, he meant, "Wait for me... while you grow up to be the best you can." And after several years, his intentions became clear, and the letters became more poetic, romantic and dazzling to any young girl's mind. She refused to commit to anyone over the mail. It had been years and she was just a young girl when he had come to teach briefly in her secondary school. The romance was nurtured and grew by mail. She fell in love with the writer, and the vibrant young scholar who seemed to have excelled in all his endeavors. She was anxious that she was in love with a phantom by mail till one day, a knock in the middle of the night in war torn Biafra revealed the most dashing, handsome young man she had ever seen. "It is Sebastian," he said. He had come for his Rose. They looked into each other's eyes and that was it. **Thus began the Romance of a lifetime.**

My Mummy's life is one to be emulated. She spends every waking moment and thought caring for her kids... all ten of us remaining. We had all we could ask for growing up, but taught us never to take anything for granted, instituting our daily chores cleaning inside and outside our home. In addition, some weekends we would visit our various farms to assist the laborers in planting , harvesting crops and fruits. She taught us to love God, daily teaching us psalms from the bible, church hymns and making us memorize prayers from St.

Anthony's Treasury, our family's favorite prayer handbook. She also taught us be each other's best-friends and always look out for each-other and to share everything together. That motto made the challenge of having ten kids in the house a fun time for us all.

Our mother is a terrific cook, and always had a new menu of the dish each meal. She would wake up daily by 5am to prepare breakfast such that when we got up the sweet aroma of home-baked muffins or croissants would energize us to get our chores done faster. She would walk on foot the three miles to the church, Our Lady of Mt. Carmel to attend daily morning mass and be back after an hour for breakfast.

I remember the Sunday family visits to places of interest in Nigeria, for example, Oguta Lake, and how my parents would make us write an essay after each trip. Even visiting Grandma Bessie at Mbaise, 30 mins away, required an essay. They would make us keep a vocabulary book of every new word we encountered and had a library filled with books for us to soak in the world around us.

After staying home for over 10 years to take care of us and my mother felt we had the tools we needed to guide us, she decided to return to obtain her Ph.D in Comparative Literature teaching us that at any age and at any time we can achieve whatever we wanted; and that the mind should be continually nurtured.

Our mother's inspiration is her own mother the formidable Mama Bessie Chiege Okeke whose live is a story of strength, perseverance and Faith in God. She lives today in her 90's, blind, aged but still strong in spirit and faith.

Even though we are all grown, some with their own new families, my mother's words of wisdom resound in our minds and her model of motherhood shapes our lives. She still send us, her kids, emails weekly with words of inspiration and encouragement or reminding us which saints feast day it is or with the liturgy of the day. We treasure the precious values you instilled in us, which we will pass on to our children.

As we live our own lives, she is always there to guide us; patient to listen to our troubles calmly, ready to rebuke and point our faults to us, but always there for us no matter what. I remember my favorite quotes from her are, "Let Go and Let God."... she always had a special relationship with God and always had a cheerful , positive spin on life's issues. "He gives the best to those who Let Him make the choice," she tells us, urging us to always do our best and leave the rest in God's hands. In the face of our difficulties she always told us, " All shall be well and all shall be well and all manner of things shall be well."

Our mother cares deeply for the sick, homeless and less privileged. As a Commissioner of Social welfare, she would frequent hospitals and rural areas to give food and aid to the poor and sick; and would take us along during Christmas to give lots of gifts and toys to sick children in the hospital. Even here in the US, she has continued to participate in charitable acts like cooking for and feeding the homeless. Not forgetting her community in Emekuku, she instituted "Our Lady's Food Kitchen" a means where by which the women and families in the villages are given food items to sustain them on a regular basis and have inspired many to care for the less fortunate. Our Lady's Food Kitchen is now being inaugurated in different communities in Imo State.

So when in February 2008, she fell suddenly ill on return from her trip to Nigeria, we were devastated. It seemed our whole world had come to a halt. It had started as a case of exhaustion with a little bit of dehydration and within 24 hours of going to the hospital, she was laying intubated in the intensive care unit on a ventilator, sedated, unable to speak or see us. We called out to everyone we knew in the medical field to help... the best doctors in the country were consulted but no-one knew what was wrong. It seemed like an unnatural force was trying to take her away. It made no sense. The doctors tried every drug, test and procedure they could think of but it only got worse. Suddenly, she had accumulated fluid all over her body threatening a multi-system failure. Huge amount of fluid accumulated in her heart requiring drainage. One procedure after another was performed and no one had answers. When we heard the dreaded statement, "I'm sorry we've tried everything. There is nothing else we can do," our hearts sank. We were faced with the possibility of never seeing her eyes open again or have her beautiful face light up as usual in a smile or hear the infectious cheery laughter again. All hope was lost or so it seemed.

Then we remembered the words she would tell us, "Take it to the Lord in prayer,". We had everyone family and friends praying for her healing as bleak as the possibility was. We held vigils by her bedside and in the ICU waiting area day and night despite dismal results and prognosis. We called on God, our patron saints, our beloved ones in heaven *(I called especially on my son, Obiola, to intercede for his grandmother who had prayed fervently for his survival in the womb),* and our Blessed Mother who had promised never to abandon those who honor her in their hour of need.

Our life on earth is finite, we know; but we did not believe that it was her time. We were not ready for a last goodbye... Give us back our mother, Lord, we prayed. She who cried our tears when we were sad; who prayed for us in our times of turmoil when we could not pray for ourselves; she who taught us to love God and do the right thing. She still had a lot to teach us and our children and our children's children.

We prayed for her though all medical evidence had failed. We knew if it were us, she would pray day and night without giving up; so we had to help her since she could not help herself. We read her favorite prayers and psalms aloud to her. I recall Psalm 91: He who dwells in the shelter of the most high, who abides under the shadow of the almighty……. No evil shall befall you; No plague shall approach your dwelling... You shall call upon my name and I will answer you."

God did answer our prayers. After 8 days of hopelessness, he gave us hope. He healed her in a miraculous, clear and all powerful way. As the illness had overcome her, so did it leave her body without any permanent harm. Not a hair on her was harmed. The doctors and nurses marveled when she suddenly recovered and all acknowledged that God had performed a miracle. When she recovered she told us that she had been praying in her mind and her heart; and that she had heard some of our prayers in the darkness that had surrounded her. That was the best miracle of our lives. Having our mother come back to us; and for that we are thankful to God.

That is why today is not only an anniversary celebration, but a thanksgiving to God for his mercies.

By Dr. Olachi Mezu Ndubuisi for the family.

Do Not Cry Mummy… "From Your Little Baby To You"

Do not cry mummy, I can see your tears
Do not cry mummy, for it makes me sad too
I am not gone at all
Instead I will live forever
Safe and sound in your heart,
The closest I can be

Do not cry Mummy, I was not in pain
Do not cry Mummy, I am now at peace
I went into a deep sleep and
Awoke to beautiful music
With lovely clouds all around me
And lots of happy little babies to welcome me

Do not cry mummy, for I am not lost
Do not cry mummy, for now I can find my way
I now have little wings to fly high up the sky
Wings that will guide me back to you when you need me
To watch over you and send God's blessings your way
And take care of you too
Like you took such good care of me

Do not cry mummy, I know you wanted to know me
Do not cry mummy, for now I know you more than ever
You were the vessel that brought me into this world
Even if for so short a time
I am proud that you are my mummy
Thank you for being so brave and
Taking care of me all these months

Do not cry mummy, for I am content and happy
Do not cry mummy, for your tears will make me sad
I loved every minute when you touched or held me
I loved the sound of your voice each time you talked to me
I can see you so much clearer now
your beautiful, kind face
And I am so glad that you are my mummy.

Do not cry mummy, wipe your tears now
Do not cry mummy, for I am happy and resting
It was an honor to be your baby
And that I will be forever more
I treasured every minute I was in your womb
As our hearts beat together
I cherished every second you spent with me
As I fought to hold on a little longer
I wanted to be your brave, little soldier
So you could be proud of me too.

Do not cry Mummy
For I was sent here for a purpose
To know you and love you and that I did
But now, I must go back to God, my Maker
To continue the work of praying for all whom I leave behind
From my family and friends, to those that cared for me

I loved every moment I had with you
Knowing that you were praying and longing for me to get better
Though I could not tell you how much it meant to me
I would like you to know that all the memories of our time together
Will keep me going till we see again in heaven.
Do not cry Mummy, for I love you so
And I know you love me too.

By Olachi Mezu Ndubuisi; Feb 22nd, 2008

….These are words I felt my son, Obiola Julian Anthony Ndubuisi, would want me to hear as I grieved for him, and also inspired by the little ones I am honored to take care of everyday that do not stay with us for long, and the heartbroken loved ones they leave behind….

An Angel of Comfort

"Lord, teach me how to love them the way you would; show me how to care for them like you would..."
~*Olachi Mezu-Ndubuisi March 30th, 2008*

After an emotionally challenging overnight call where a little baby boy had suffered all night with medical complications due to prematurity only to die despite the best efforts of the medical team, I comforted the family compassionately, and somehow found the strength to complete my shift professionally.

I left work that morning on March 25th, 2008 around 8:00am and went straight to Obiola's graveside and wept my heart out, crumbled on my knees. I wept and wept softly in the still, eerie silence of the church graveyard. I missed my son, so much... It had been a very emotional experience that night fighting so hard to save the little baby and then losing him, and watching his family grieve for him. Kneeling by the cold tombstone, I realized that it was exactly a year I laid my son to rest – March 25th, 2007. I felt empty and alone in my grief, longing for love and comfort. I wept and I wept.

Kneeling crumbled by his tombstone, I suddenly felt warm arms around me and peace flooded into my soul. I turned around slowly in awe to see an elderly lady in her seventies. She held me close and stroked my hair as I wept and wept, and she whispered, "it's going to be okay... you are going to be fine... I'm here to tell you it will be okay," She let me cry for a few moments in her arms, and as my tears ebbed, she soon told me that she was widow of many years who lived in apartment building close by. She recounted that she had been woken up early in the morning by a dream and a deep awareness that she needed to get up because somebody needed her. Without understanding why, she felt herself getting up urgently, taking a walk down the street to the cemetery, and as she approached she heard my soft, anguishing sobs.

"I don't know who you are, or whose grave you are visiting; but I am here to let you know that it is going to be okay," she said. She gathered me in her arms and I wept some more.

"Do you mind my asking who this is?" she asked pointing to the grave.
"It's my baby boy. He died a year ago today. "
"How old was he?" she asked.
"7 days old," I said through my tears. "I miss him so much," I cried. I then told her that I knew that God took him because his little life was fulfilled, but it still hurts so much. That day was one year anniversary. She assured me that it would be okay and I believed her. I felt much better and at peace, and my tears dried up almost instantly. I thanked her and she walked away in the mist... I was sure I had encountered an angel of God. I smiled my thanks to God and felt at peace.
 March 25th, 2008

... She turned out to be a real person as I would find out over a year later. I had told my mother the story of that encounter; and a year later, during a church gathering after morning mass, as my mother was telling the story of Obiola and OlaRose and my leap of faith and fight for life as she often did, she mentioned that her little grandson was buried in the church yard and thus she was forever connected to this church. An elderly lady met her after the gathering and told her: "I think I met your daughter," she said, and she went to tell the story of the young lady she had found weeping by her son's grave yard a year ago. My mother instantly remembered the story I had told her. She came home to me excited; and this was in August 2009; "Olachi, I have found your lady... I met your angel; She is Phyllis Blue." I asked my mother to invite her to OlaRose's Christening and Obiolarose foundation inauguration and she did. I got to meet the stately, distinguished woman again and thank her yet again.

Where He Leads

No one can claim to know
The mind of God
So when things happen
Try not to guess or predict
Just take His hand and
Go where He leads

When the world judges you unfairly
Friends turn against you and betray you
Enemies rejoice in your misfortune
Try not to wallow in self-pity
Just take His hand and
Go where He leads

When Life takes unexpected twists and turns
And you get to the crossroads
With no light or sign ahead
Do not plunge or guess your way through
Just take His hand and
Go where He leads

When nothing makes sense
Things do not add up in life
People deny you credit for your hard work
And try to destroy a legacy of truth
Never lose hope or despair
for the future still there is
But surely just take His hand
And go where He leads

May 27, 2008

My Soul is Troubled

My soul is troubled
My heart is saddened
I am misunderstood
I am victimized
The way I am perceived
Is not true at all
and my soul is troubled

I truly care
I may not say much
But what makes one want
To hurt me so when they see me
I am not what they say

They don't know where I'm from
They don't know where I've been
They don't know what I know
They don't know who I am

I know what I am
I know what I can do
I have so much to offer
I have so much to live for
I don't want to give up
But I can't go on like this

I don't want this to change me
From who I know I am
I don't want this to make me
What I know I'm not
I am not what they say I am
So far from that
Why can't they look into my heart and see
I am not what they think I am

Speak to me Lord
Show me the way

Why now, after the path I've walked
You know me better
You know me truly
Why can't they see me
As you do know me

Speak to me Lord
You must have the answer
My soul is heavy
My heart is saddened
It is happening again
There must be a reason
Forces stronger than I can fathom
Are in control, so strong I feel it
It must be more than the eye can see
There is more to it, I believe
I await your word
I seek your way
Speak to me Lord,
My soul is troubled

April 13, 2009

*Written late at night, while at work, demoralized; and my soul was
experiencing a certain deep darkness and weighed heavily on me.*

Divine Mercy Come into My Heart

In the early dawn, at 3am
As I lay on my bed
Awake , I am
Waiting for something, I don't know what
Then it came to me, the answer I seek
I hear your voice in the still of the morn
You speak to me so loudly, I shiver
You speak to me so clearly, like a whisper
Your words came to me through a voice I hear
Truly, the words I hear are meant for me
So clear, it is surreal

"Let go," the voice seems to be saying
"Your heart is heavy
Have mercy," it says
"For God to have mercy on you"
Like the lost sheep, it says
the shepherd will seek you
Till he finds your lost soul
He does not wait for you to find him
For you've lost your way for real
He searches and calls you to him
Through any means He wills
Till you listen to his voice
Till he finds you His chosen one
The one dear to him

Have mercy, let your heart open
For God's divine mercy to reach you
You have to open your heart to accept it
For it is closed to God, as is
The soul in Hades chooses to be there, the voice says
For their heart is hardened to the divine mercy of God

God will use situations to reach out to you, it says
He is calling you to him because he loves you

He is calling you to him because you have gone away from him
You are doing what is right;
but without God close to your heart
None can see it
He is calling to you before it is too late

You must forgive those that err you
You must forgive those you love
You must let go of the wrong others do to you
Only then can God's love be in your heart
Your heart is hardened, and thus your soul is heavy
What they see are the scars of your heavy burden
Let go of your burden, open your heart, the voice said.

"Your time is up, " I heard from within me,
"But the divine mercy of God will save you,
Come back to me, my child, the Lord speaks
You've been lost for a long time
I want to feel close to you again
I want you to know me like before
It is not them; Yes, it is you
It is not what it seems
It was all my way of calling you back to me "

Flow no longer, tears of mine, I say
Tears of joy you now are
For God has spoken
He was calling me to Him
Speak Lord, your servant heareth

Thank you Lord, for not forgetting me
Even though I seem to have forgotten you in my life
I will come back to your love
I will come back to your side
I will forgive with my heart
I will not count ills or wrong
I will not burden my heart with vengeance so there is no room for you

Thank you Lord, this is the answer I seek

I must accept your divine mercy
And be merciful to those that wrong me
Be merciful to those I love
That I may reflect your love and mercy
Like I should and used to

The difference from then and now
Is that I closed my heart to you
I love you but with a heavy heart
I have to open my heart to you
And only then can I be able to
Do your will and spread your word
And all will see the love of God in my eyes
 It is not too late
The time is now
My heart's door I open freely and willingly,
Please flow in divine mercy of God

Divine Mercy, come into my heart
Come to stay, never go away
Soften and melt away ages of wrongs counted
Chase away vengeance and forgiveness
Let your rays brighten the dark corners of my soul
Let your sparks ignite God's fervent Love
Let your mercy flow, renew, refresh, revive, invigorate
My tepid soul; my weak faith
May I be a reflection of God's love and mercy
I will not count ills done to me; I will let them go
I will show mercy, like God has been merciful to me

Come into my heart and stay, O divine mercy of God.
Reawake my spirit
Empower my soul
To be your ambassador
To do God's will in my life
To do God's work as He bids
To be an instrument of healing and peace

Never go away, Divine Mercy of God
Leave drops of Christ saving blood
To cleanse away any stains of worldly vengeance
That tries to creep in from time to time
I am yours; I want to be yours
I choose to be yours; I choose to do your will
I want to be a mirror and ambassador
Of the divine mercy of God
So make your home in my heart forever
O Divine Mercy of God.

April 14th, 2009

Shortly after writing the preceding poem "My Soul is Troubled", I turned on the TV in my on call room, where I was taking a brief break at 3am in the morning, and it was tuned to EWTN, the catholic network and a man was being interviewed about his book analyzing the revelations of the Divine Mercy to St. Faustina by our Lord. His words seemed to speak directly to me and I stood transfixed for 10 minutes listening and my soul was at peace and the heaviness I felt lifted. I had an overwhelming sense that I had just received a divine message and my time was running out. The urgency of the message of divine mercy would weigh heavily on me for months to come. I had heard about the divine mercy message, but at the time I was neither very familiar with the divine mercy devotion nor had I read sister Faustina's diary or any information of divine mercy. I began to read St. Faustina's diary finally on January 11th, 2010.

A Brain and Life renewed: A Miracle of Divine Mercy

August 3rd, 2009. It was like any ordinary Monday morning. The sun did not shine dimmer or blaze stronger. I had planned to take a trip for the day to New York City with my elder sister, Nina and possibly my mother to purchase traditional lace materials for my daughter's Christening celebration on Aug 29th, 2009 and my younger sister, Ure's upcoming church wedding celebration two weeks later on Sept 12th, 2009. The trip had been postponed a couple of times, so I was sure it had to be that day.

That day was a convenient day since I had a day off from work, and my sister Nina too had been able to take off as well. We knew my mother may like to come along for she loves to pick out her own fabric, and she loves New York City. We also thought my Dad may also want to come to take a break, and he was inseparable from my mother; and he would worry incessantly about us till we returned safely, anyways. We were not sure if my dad was coming along and we debated whether we should encourage him to or dissuade him. An all-girl trip would be cool, and he may not be happy with how much we were spending on the fabrics and we wanted to shop at ease; but on the other hand, he would enjoy a trip away from home for a change. I remembered that he actually had been a good bargainer on the fabrics on our last trip to New York last October for my brother's traditional wedding materials: it had been me, mom and him, and he did the drive smoothly with ease too, giving us a break. So I did make a case for him to join us, and asked my mom to find out if he wanted to come along. It was just that morning that she confirmed that he would be joining us.

I remember leaving my home in Westminster around 845am, kissing my daughter goodbye as she slept soundly on the bed, trying not to wake her. I hesitated with that kiss as whenever I did it in the past she would open her eyes, and then leaving her would be a difficult and tearful ordeal. But that morning, I felt compelled to kiss her gently, just for me – I won't see her all day, and she may be asleep by the time I returned, I told her. She stirred but did not wake up and I was glad. I told my middle-aged nanny, "I will be back later.. much later in the evening; but I will be back tonight – I am not working overnight in the hospital. I will call to check up on you guys."

We had a couple of errands to run that delayed us from having an early start. I, for one, had to drop my car at the dealers for servicing and once that was done, we set out around 10am in the morning. NdaNina, as I call my elder sister, myself, my mom, and my Dad. It was a nice, smooth drive three and half hour drive to New York City, my Dad steady and safe behind the wheel. We started our intense shopping and bargaining at the 39th street fabric district and eventually settled at a store where we ended up buying all the materials we needed. I remember at 3pm, halfway through our shopping, noting that my headache began slowly. It was initially a mild, dull frontal headache, non-throbbing. I initially thought it was part of the strain of the trip. I remember thinking: I really need to take a break this month from work as the past few months had been quite busy due to staff shortage. Most of the NICU pediatricians had either being on vacations or sick leave and I had been working 18 to 24 hour shifts every two or three days for a couple months now. I did love my job as a neonatal pediatrician caring for sick or premature babies in a 30 bed neonatal intensive care unit (NICU) and a 60 bed new born nursery, attending deliveries to resuscitate and transition the newborn babies, and performing perinatal consults on mothers expecting premature or sick babies that will require care in the NICU.

Sometime about 5pm, the headache slowly increased in intensity, and I began to get concerned. I just mentioned it once casually while we were finishing our fabric selection, "I have a headache', and someone brought me a chair to sit in. We then started to have lunch, and I hoped I would feel better after eating. It had after all been a long day, and I did not remember eating breakfast that morning. It was just an annoying headache, or so I thought. Eating did not make it better. I sat down through the rest of the shopping and we finally paid for our goods and left the store around 7.30pm. It was a slow drive out of New York City due to heavy traffic. We finally left through the Holland tunnel. My sisters kept calling my phone to ask how our shopping went, and other mundane questions, especially Ure, the bride to be, Kelechi, my ever curious immediate elder sister, and Ngozi, immediately younger than me - who felt New York was her City and wanted to give us the quickest way out of there. With each call, I would speak briefly and hand the phone to my mother muttering: I can't talk right now, I have a headache..." She would take the phone and talk to them joking, "They are calling Olachi, who has a headache and no interest in talking to them instead of calling me who would gladly speak to them."

As we left New York behind and entering New Jersey, we found ourselves on a high bridge overlooking a mass of water underneath it. "This is the Hudson River! " I exclaimed. I wasn't sure, but I just felt strongly that it was and felt compelled to say it aloud.
"What's special about it? " my mother asked.
"This is where they had the miracle on the Hudson, " I said. ""Don't you remember in January when that plane landed on the river? It was right here." I then began to tell them what I had seen on EWTN a week or so after the crash, a man was being interviewed who had been one of the survivors on that plane. He was recounting how he had been introduced to the divine mercy devotion not too long ago and had taken to saying the prayers at 3pm every day or so. That day on the flight, he had said those prayers at 3pm on that flight; and next thing, they were informed by the pilot that they were going to crash land. He recalled remembering the promise of God to anyone who recites the prayers to His divine mercy that He would grant whatever they asked for, if it was according to His will; and he held God to that promise. Their plane landed on water and everyone survived. He believed deep in his heart that they were saved because of his prayer.

In the car, we all recalled the plane crash, and how amazing a story it was at the time. Someone joked, I think my mother said, "What a story to remember, Ola, when we are right on a bridge?" and we laughed. Someone else replied, "Well, there is no plane flying overhead right now. We need to get through the bridge in one piece. " I wondered how terrified drivers on this same bridge must have been to see a plane flying so low. They did think it would crash over them? That must have been scary. We proceeded into the New Jersey turnpike and my headache intensified. It was 9pm or so. I spoke little, and tried not to complain. I did not want them to worry. We just needed to get on with the journey and get home. Maybe I just need to sleep, and I would feel better. The sooner we got home, the better,

I thought. As the conversation continued, and I was asked a question, I muttered softly, "I have a headache."

My mother grew concerned about my headache and asked if anyone had Tylenol or Advil in the car and no-one did, and she said to me, "I don't understand you doctors, why don't you have any medicine, even Tylenol in your bag." I had this huge white bag with everything in it, books, makeup, a stethoscope, pens, food, everything but an analgesic. I remember telling her I am not supposed to carry drugs about in my purse. I don't have headaches routinely, and I did not anticipate I was going to have one today. They asked me to close my eyes and try to relax. My sister Nina and my parents insisted on stopping at the next rest station to buy Tylenol or Advil for me. I tried to resist saying," Let's just go home. I will be fine," but they would not hear any of it.
"No, we must stop at the next gas station for Tylenol" insisted NdaNina, sounding almost mad at me. I ceased to argue. The pain was so much, it hurt to speak... or think... or even open my eyes. I started longing for the Tylenol to bring some relief.

The turnpike exits at that point were over 10 to 15 miles apart. Soon, we came to a rest station and my Dad pulled over. NdaNina and Dad went in to get the medicine and a drink for me, and I stayed with my mother. The frontal headache got worse and a pain settled over and around my right eye. I did not have any aura or scotomas. It fluctuated from sharp to dull, and was almost a 9 out of 10 pain. Really, one of the worst headache of my life! Immediately, this thought came to me, I panicked inward. All through my medical training, the worst headache of your life is the classic description of a subarachnoid hemorrhage. I panicked inwardly and tried not to show it. Was it really the worst headache of my life? I debated. I have had more piercing headaches years ago; but they subsided with time or rest? I recalled. This headache is the most persistent headache of my life, I rationalized. It has gone on for over 6 hours. I suddenly felt the need for fresh air. I got out of the car and my mother followed very worried. My sister and Dad returned with some medicine and a drink. All they had in the convenience store was Advil and NdaNina gave me 3 tablets of it. I drank it, and sat down for a minute on the ground. I shortly felt an overwhelming wave of nausea and that concerned me. I have never felt nauseous in my life except when I was pregnant in 2006 towards the end of my first trimester.

Being a physician, I thought the worse at this point: This was no ordinary headache: nausea and a throbbing headache? Did I have a tumor in my head? Nausea and a headache as I learnt in medicine meant increased intracranial pressure from the brain, either a tumor or something compressing the flow of cerebrospinal fluid. But it is more likely to occur first thing in the morning, I told myself. Was my blood pressure high, I wondered? I have been on anti-hypertensives religiously ever since my pregnancy with severe pre-eclampsia in 2006; and it has been well-controlled. Lately, with my busy work schedule and related stressors, I had been worried about it. Was I having a stroke? Was I having an intracranial hemorrhage or a subarachnoid hemorrhage? Did this qualify as the "worst headache of my life "? If it did, it would be a subarachnoid hemorrhage from a ruptured cerebral blood vessel, as we learnt in medical school. I quickly panicked at the thought, and did a mental and physical assessment of myself: my memory, cognition, speech, strength, gait - were all intact. I felt my arms and legs, and moved them around, and did not feel any weakness, numbness, paresthesia, tingling or neurological deficits. I mentally went over the differential diagnosis of a headache. I don't have a history of migraines, and this headache had no aura with it. Was I having a bleeding in my head? I breathed a sigh of relief: I was not presently having a stroke since I had no neurological deficits from my physical assessment of myself; but why was I nauseous?. I did not communicate my fears to my family trying not to get them worried. What purpose would it serve? I will just pay a visit to the ER or my family physician after my 18 hr work shift tomorrow evening, I said to myself.

I quickly discarded these thoughts and tried not to dwell on them. We were in the middle of nowhere, still 3 hours or more away from home. I did not want them to panic, so I never voiced these fears. But my parents and sister were very worried. They saw my pain and saw my discomfort. They know I don't complain usually to anyone about my health and so for me to even acknowledge a headache, it must be pretty severe.

"Are you nauseous? " they asked me, watching my facial expressions. I nodded silently. I hated feeling this way and making them worry, but I was scared enough deep down that I did not want to hide my true symptoms from them.   Seeing me admit to these symptoms also scared them. For Olachi to answer these questions and not refuse the medicine, it must be very serious, they later told me they were thinking. Soon, the wave of nausea subsided and I didn't vomit. I just needed to get home to Maryland and sleep in my bed, and I will be fine by morning, I kept saying to myself. It was typical of my family to over-react and make a mountain out of a mole hill. Here we are in the middle of nowhere, worrying about a silly headache instead of progressing on our journey; however, a part of me was deeply troubled.

"We need to find a rite aid pharmacy or any pharmacy to check your blood pressure!" Nda Nina insisted, the pharmacist in her alert and astute throughout this ordeal. I took my medication that morning, I knew; but could my blood pressure be high? If it was I hoped it was just a hypertensive crisis, but why would it give me this bad of a headache unless I had a ruptured aneurysm or blood vessel or I was having early symptoms of a stroke? My head was swirling with different worst case scenarios again. I am worried, I admitted to myself; and my family is worried. So it was probably better to just check the blood pressure, and if it was fine, then we would safely travel home. If my symptoms persisted after I've rested, then I will seek medical attention, I told myself. My family later told me that seeing that I did not dissuade them any further from finding a pharmacy got them worried. It was not like me. Nda Nina went to ask strangers around where the nearest pharmacy was. We were directed to take the next exit: exit 8. It seemed quite a drive, and we drove and drove through lonely roads lined with vegetation, but there was no pharmacy in sight.

"I've taken the tylenol. Why don't we just go home. It's late. The sooner we get home, the better. I will be fine." No-one listened to me, they insisted on finding this pharmacy in the middle of nowhere. I was wondering? If the blood pressure was high, then what? I'm not going to take a second dose of my medication. What were we going to do? Start looking for a hospital for them to bring it down with IV meds?

Hopefully it was just a hypertensive crisis? Maybe it would be just that, and we can be on our way. I thought how my daughter must be sad that I was not home all day and how she was going to cry herself to sleep because she didn't see me. I really just wanted to go home, but I knew it was pointless to argue with them. So I remained silent.

Finally we saw a CVS Pharmacy. It was almost closing time for them. We went inside, and I walked straight to the back where the pharmacy is usually located, and asked a lady where their electronic blood pressure monitor was and she pointed to the corner. Let's get this over with, so we could drive on home, I thought. My family followed behind me. I placed my hand into the appropriate slot and sat still while the machine compressed the cuff around my arms. Shortly it read on the screen : 176/120. My heart sank in fear. That was too high, especially the diastolic - lower number. Once NdaNina saw it, she exclaimed : "I'm calling 911!" I didn't say a word to stop her. I put my hand back in there and repeated it. It was even higher 185/120. My parents helped me up to my feet. The male Caucasian pharmacist behind the counter started to tell us rudely to leave the store. "I am closing the pharmacy," he said, "the store is closing."

NdaNina was livid, "Her blood pressure is very high! You should be the one calling 911 for us. I am a pharmacist too. This is wrong of you to chase a sick patient away. We need help. We are just passing through!" He would not listen, vehemently asking us to leave .
"There are seats outside the store. You can stay there and wait for now. I have to close right now. Leave the store!" he insisted.
I was silently in shock and disbelief! I was inwardly alarmed! I am having a stroke, I thought! I am bleeding in my head! I kept thinking of the worst. Maybe it is just a hypertensive emergency. The pharmacist demanded we leave the pharmacy because he wanted to close up. My sister was infuriated at his unethical conduct! "You are a Pharmacist! You just saw her blood pressure! You should be calling 911 for her! She could be having a stroke! I am a pharmacist too. This is very wrong of you!" He would not be bothered, and continued closing out the pharmacy.
"There are seats outside, he said. You can seat out there and call 911. I have to close now," he repeated. We went outside and there were no seats. So, my father opened the car, and I sat on the back seat with

the door open for fresh air. I was in a state of quiet disbelief. What was happening to me? Was I going to be okay? I knew we couldn't continue on our journey home with my blood pressure that high. It was not typically high. I was now convinced that there was something going on in my brain. It may be an impending stroke or hemorrhage from a ruptured blood vessel. I kept checking myself, but I was having no neurologic changes, no visual changes or deficits, no memory loss, no confusion, no aura, no paresthesia, no weakness. I never voiced out my concerns to my parents or NdaNina, afraid doing so would make it true. I told myself not to over-react. I always tend to think the worst in every situation, and I have to remind myself to stay positive. Maybe it was just a hypertensive emergency, I thought; and lowering the blood pressure slowly for a few hours was all that was needed, so we could continue our journey home.

We were in the middle of nowhere. It was late at night, and no one to be seen around. NdaNina was beside herself frantic with worry, going back and forth to the store trying to get an address of our location from someone to give the 911 operator. We had no idea where we were? They could not trace the call because it was on her cell phone. The store was now closed, but she kept knocking on the door, motioning to one of the store clerks and told him about our ordeal and I think he kindly gave her the store address. Within a couple minutes, two police cars surfaced responding to a notification to check out the 911 call, while the ambulance found their way. They were kind and wanted to stay with us to make sure we were safe till the ambulance arrived. Within five minutes, paramedics arrived in a van and manually checked my blood pressure and pulse assessing my vitals. They confirmed the high reading, and we all waited with the police for the ambulance. It arrived shortly and I was quickly helped into the stretcher and into the back of the ambulance. They proceeded to get a quick history of events from me and medical history from me. They allowed NdaNina to ride in the front with the driver, while my parents followed in our car behind them. They drove ten minutes or so to the nearest local community hospital; and my parents drove behind. "Do you have a CT scan?" was one of the first questions I asked as I was wheeled into the ER; and the nurse said yes to my relief. Thank God! I thought. That was the first thing that needed to be done to check if I was having a brain bleed or not. I was quickly connected to the cardio-respiratory monitor, and my blood pressure seemed to be rising by the minute: It fluctuated from 175/110 to 210/125. My ER physician was a young, Asian female in her thirties or so.

I was given several intravenous doses of Lopressor with no effect. I was soon taken to CT-scan and the results were negative.
"You are not bleeding, " she said; and talked about discharging me once the blood pressure was under control.
"But why am I having a headache still??, " I asked her.
"Maybe it's just a really bad headache, ' she said emphatically. She went on to add a clonidine patch, which still had no effect on lowering the blood pressure. It was just about midnight. At this point, NdaNina and my parents were on the phone with family and friends soliciting help and updating them on my condition. My younger sister Ure, a cardiologist in Univ. of Pittsburgh, doing her sub specialization in electrophysiology, called and insisted that a lumbar puncture be done to rule out microscopic bleeding. If the subarachnoid hemorrhage or bleeding in the brain is early, the bleed may not show on CT-scan but may show microscopically in the spinal fluid. The ER physician reluctantly agreed to perform the lumbar puncture and obtained my consent. Relatively clear spinal fluid was obtained from the LP, and as usual the last and clearest tube was sent for cell count. The ER doctor said she believed the LP was negative and tried to reassure us, saying that I could be discharged with analgesics for the pain. My mother and sister insisted we wait for the final lab reports of the cell count, since we were already is the hospital.

The ER doctor came back an hour or so later with the grim diagnosis: "We found 239 red cells microscopically in the last tube." My heart sank as she said that. It indicated that I could be bleeding in my brain. I saw that fluid, I thought, it was clear, as they call it : a champagne tap. It should not have that many red cells in it. 239, though not an exorbitantly high number, could also result from a ruptured capillary or blood vessel encountered during the tap, I reasoned. It was unlikely because the ER doctor had performed that tap effortlessly and had gotten fluid return immediately on first entry.
"Now what?" I asked her. "I can't go home now."

"Well, I don't think there's anything wrong with you. But, if you are still concerned, we can admit you to our telemetry unit because you need monitoring. "

"Do you have an MRI? " I asked her.

" Tomorrow we will get an MRI and then possibly an MRA."

"Do you have a neurosurgeon in house that can come to evaluate me?" I asked. "

"We do," she said, " but he is at home and will not be called until after your MRI and MRA are done."

"Why can't they be done now?"

"They are not in this hospital. It is in the next hospital , a 20mins ambulance ride. They are not open tonight. They will open tomorrow and based on their schedule we will try and fit you in sometime before noon."

I looked at her with disbelief. It felt like I was in a third world country with no access to medical care.

"Could you please transfer me to a hospital in Maryland. We don't live here," I pleaded. "We were on our way home to Maryland from New York. All our family is in Maryland. I work at GBMC and have worked at Univ. of Maryland. You can transfer me to either Johns Hopkins, Univ of Maryland, or GBMC," I said.

The physician refused saying that it was against EMTALA laws. "I cannot transfer you to a facility with the same level of care." she said the all too familiar statement.

"But you do not have the same level of care, " I argued softly. "Your neurosurgeon cannot see me immediately to evaluate me. I believe this qualifies for a neurosurgical emergency. He is not in house. You do not have an MRI or MRA in this hospital. You have to drive me twenty minutes or so to another hospital. How is it the same level of care as a teaching hospital?"

The physician still would not budge, refusing to transfer me.

"If I'm indeed bleeding in my head, you know I could die by morning?"
She looked at me and did not say anything.

I did not even consider signing out against medical advice and having my family drive me 3 hours to Maryland with a subarachnoid hemorrhage – that would be suicide. I imagined myself slowly losing consciousness as the bleeding intensified while waiting for the noon

MRI and MRI and the leisurely consult to the neurosurgeon, who should have been seeing me stat. I felt a sudden sense of urgency. I had to take matters into my own hands.

"How do I get out of here to Maryland by ambulance?" I asked the defiant physician.

"You will have to find a doctor in Maryland to accept you and you will have to make all the arrangements for transport by yourself for an ambulance. They will most likely make you pay out of pocket for the ambulance, since it is the same level of care, " she warned.

"If I find a number or a hospital? Can you make the call for me and give the transfer report?" I asked her softly through my pain. .

"No, she said," "You have to make the call yourself. I'm done with you." she said an exasperation, and she walked away. She had refused to speak to anymore of my family members on the phone, trying to get an update.

During that exchange, my parents had stepped out to the waiting area. I was left in the room with my sister who had heard the whole exchange and started frantically making calls at that 2am to friends and colleagues, trying to find someone who could find a doctor at that hour to accept my transfer and assume responsibility for my care.

Most of my colleagues were in neonatology and pediatrics - what I needed was an adult neurosurgeon. My brain sprang into action. What do I do? I knew a few physicians at Univ of Maryland. Do I call them and ask them to help me find a neurosurgeon? Or do I call the operator and ask for one myself. I thought of Hopkins and GBMC. I could call the GBMC operator and ask for a neurosurgeon. If I needed surgery, I probably wanted to be in the hands of the best possible care and usually from my training experience, you will get the best possible chance of survival at a teaching hospital. I thought of Hopkins and decided to give it a try. Most of the GBMC doctors come from Hopkins anyway. I called my NICU Director at that ungodly hour and told him what was happening and somewhere around the part of needing to find a neurosurgeon, my voice failed me as I became teary eyed so my sister took over the call. I imagined myself dying in the local New Jersey Hospital. I thought about my family and how devastated they would be, and I thought about my daughter and how much anguish she would go through when she never saw me again and could not understand why her mommy never returned.

At this point, my sister had just finished the phone call to my NICU Director, who was going to make some calls and call us back. My parents returned to the room and my sister updated them. At one point, my sister said, " let's say the divine mercy prayer." We all held hands and prayed a decade of the rosary and repeated the words: "Eternal Father, I offer you the body and blood, soul an divinity of your dearly beloved son, our lord Jesus Christ, in atonement for our sins and those of the whole world. For the sake of your sorrowful passion, have mercy on us and all of the whole world." It was 3am. When we were done, they returned to calling my husband and to check on OlaRose who was fast asleep, and my other brothers and sisters to update them. They called on family friends who were physicians to ask for help or referrals, etc. I felt truly helpless and abandoned by my medical provider, as I watched my family make frantic cell phone calls with no help coming. My life was in my hands and I had to take control of it and try to save myself, and get myself the help I needed. I suddenly remembered that I knew the number to the Hopkins phone operator. I found myself automatically picking up my cell phone and dialed the Hopkins operator (410) 955-2000. I had called that number, just three days earlier at work when I transferred a baby from GBMC to Hopkins NICU that needed a life-saving experimental hypothermia treatment in order to save her life.

I knew the words that would get me direct access to a physician: The operator answered at first ring.
"John Hopkins Medical Center operator, how may I help you?" the female voice said.
"Hi, " I began, "This is Dr. Mezu from GBMC. I would like to speak to a neurosurgeon or ICU attending to transfer a patient.' I gave her two options just in case one was unavailable. I recalled how I transferred my mother a year ago when she needed a cardiology evaluation for sudden fluid overload at a local Maryland hospital that put her in cardiac failure. Helpless and desperate in her hospital room with no help also coming from the physicians there; I had randomly called a cardiologist at another hospital, and he had told me to first call the ICU attending to accept her, and they could consult him after they had stabilized her in the ICU. She first needed to be in an ICU monitoring bed. I figured the same applied to me in my current situation .

"Hold please," she said and a minute later a voice came on the line. The operator came back saying "this line is being recorded. I have Dr S on the line. "

I greeted him, "Goodmorning Dr. S. This is Dr. Mezu from GBMC."

"How may I help you, Dr. Mezu?"

"I am calling to transfer a patient with a possible subarachnoid hemorrhage, but negative CT scan and microscopic rbc's on LP. "

"Who is the patient?"

"I am the patient," I answered. The doctor was alarmed as I quickly explained why I was the one calling, and how we were stuck in new Jersey. "It sounds like you have an aneurysm causing the bleed. You need a neurosurgeon. I am a neurologist from the ICU. You should not be talking to me. Operator please connect her to who she needs. Goodluck," and he hung up with further word. My heart sank in panic at his words!

The operator realizing what was happening said kindly, "Hold on doctor, I will get the right person for you. Who do you want?"

"A neurosurgery attending," I said softly choking back tears as a realization of the urgency and severity of my condition sank in; and I thanked her.

Less than a minute later a female voice answered; "This is Dr. Huang," it was a soft, kind, and gentle voice.

"Good morning, this is Dr. Mezu from GBMC. Are you a neurosurgeon?" I asked her

"Yes, I am, "she replied

"I am trying to transfer a patient with a subarachnoid hemorrhage possibly from a ruptured brain aneurysm to you."

"Who is the patient?" she asked.

""I am the patient, " I said.

She sounded shocked, "Why are you the one calling me? Where are you?" she asked softly.

"I am in an ER in New Jersey. I am a NICU pediatrician from GBMC and my family and I went on a day's trip to NewYork. Around 3pm, I had a sudden severe frontal headache that intensified followed by nausea and unrelieved by tylenol, so we stopped on the turnpike to check my blood pressure and it was 176/120 at a CVS and my sister called 911 and I was taken to a local new jersey hospital. A CT scan was negative but an LP shows 239 microscopic red blood cells (rbc's). The headache and my blood pressure cannot be relieved by any meds..." and I went on the recount the meds I had been given in the ER.

"Why is your doctor not the one calling me?" she asked in disbelief.

"She refuses to," I said. "She says it is against EMTALA laws to transfer to the same level of care. Even though the MRI and MRA cannot be done till tomorrow, and are in another hospital. She says the only way I can be transferred back to Maryland is if I find an accepting physician myself and make all the arrangements.."

Dr. Huang expressed her disbelief and shock that I was not being transferred by my doctor .

" What hospital are you in? What is the name?" she asked.

"I don't know the city. But it's XXXState Medical Center.." I stumbled over the name. I had not paid attention to the sign as the ambulance drove in earlier.

"Is someone there that can tell me where you are? The address?"

I looked around. There was no-one. I motioned to my sister, Nina and she went to find help.

"There's no-one in my room," I answered. I was hooked up to monitors and wires. I told her my sister had gone to find someone. Dr. Huang could sense my desperation and helplessness.

"Don't worry, " came the soothing voice. **"I will take care of you,"** she said ever so softly. Tears welled up in my eyes. That was the sweetest voice and most reassuring thing I had heard all evening. Suddenly, I felt confident, at peace, and I had such implicit trust in her. I believed she would definitely make everything okay.

"Thank you soo much, " I said through my tears. "God bless you."

" I will take care of everything, " Dr. Huang said softly , "Let me talk to your doctor."

At that point, the ER physician had wandered back into my room at my sister's prompting. I told her that Dr. Huang a Hopkins neurosurgeon wanted to speak to her, and handed her my cell phone.

Dr. Huang, as she promised, did take care of everything. She asked the ER physician to find out if I preferred an ambulance or helicopter. I was anxious about how unsafe it may be to take a helicopter in the dark, but knew it would be the quickest way to Maryland. It would be 45 mins by chopper or 3 to 4 hours by ambulance because of the early morning I-95 traffic we would meet.

"The quickest, safest way she recommends, based on the urgency, " I said.

"She says she will send a helicopter for you, " said the ER doctor, Dr. L. She was sending a helicopter with a paramedic team for me from Johns Hopkins, without seeing me, knowing who I was or seeing any of my lab work or medical history.

My parents returned to the room and got updated at the turn of events. I was been transferred to Maryland. I was overwhelmed with anticipation and fear of the unknown. What was happening to me? How was this going to end? My family was being so supportive and brave. Siblings were on the phone looking for updates. Everyone had been consulting with physicians they knew all night, trying to make suggestions to help control my still skyrocketing blood pressure.

"I'm soo sorry Mommy and Daddy," I said with tears in my eyes. I hated to be the one putting them through this anguish again, just two years after my emotional and traumatic ordeal with my twin pregnancy. They assured me that I would be alright. We all prayed together.

Daddy told me he had a premonition about the previous night, that something would happen during the New York trip, but that everything would turn out okay – the reason he had decided to come to New York with us. Mommy reminded me to trust in God who never fails us. Her ever unwavering faith in God even in the face of impossibilities always amazed me. "Believe you have been healed. Claim your healing," she repeated. "Imagine those divine rays from Christ washing away all that ails you. ... renewing, reviving your blood pressure," she continued to speak softly to me.

"I want to see OlaRose... I want to see my daughter," I said to my family. They assured me that I would see her in Maryland and arrangements would be made to bring her to Hopkins when I got there. The helicopter did arrive in a couple of hours after circling for a while trying to find a landing spot in the small community hospital parking lot. I was soon placed on the gurney, and into the tight space on the aircraft. I held onto my rosary my mother had placed in my hands, and prayed softly the whole trip. My family got into their car and began the long trip to Maryland by road.

The flight was a little over an hour, and I lay strapped on the gurney holding on to my rosary and praying silently. The transport team were kind and kept trying to make me comfortable in the tiny space. Once we arrived at Hopkins, I was wheeled to the NCCU: Neurosurgical Critical Care Unit; and into the room all the way in the back: Room 9. Everyone was courteous, gentle and kind to me. The nurses were quick, efficient, and really gentle as they moved me from gurney to the bed, helped me into my hospital gown, assessed vital signs and connected me to the monitors and placed another intravenous (IV) line. My husband who works at Hopkins IT department was already there waiting for me. Shortly after my arrival, just after my IV was placed, I was almost immediately taken straight to the neuroradiology department for a cerebral angiogram that had been pre-ordered by my neurosurgeon even before I arrived. She believed the suspicion of an aneurysm and did not want to take any chances or waste time with MRI or MRA. Everything had been well coordinated before I arrived: the unit was expecting me, my bed was ready; the social worker and charge nurse were in to speak to me.

When I got to the neuroradiology department on my transport bed, I was met by the neuroradiology fellow: a young, pretty lady about my age, I guessed. She was very soft-spoken. She told me the purpose of the angiogram; but also informed me of the risks too. "There is a chance of a stroke during the procedure," she said softly.
"Is this the only way to confirm it? What about other less invasive tests?" I asked.
"If you are concerned about an aneurysm, this is the best way to confirm it?"
I had to sign something saying I am aware that I could have a stroke and was consenting to it regardless. I was mortified. What was happening to me? How was this going to end? "What year are you?" I asked slowly. I think she told me she was PGY 7 or so: her last years of neuroradiology sub-fellowship training. That's a lot of training, I knew. I knew she was a fellow in training and I 've been there as a resident or fellow when parents or patients doubt your ability and want or prefer an attending instead, when you know you are quite capable. But hello, this was my brain or my life here? I get only one shot at this, I

reasoned. So, I wanted to ask her politely being sensitive to her feelings without being scared of expressing my fears or concerns.

With tears in my eyes, I signed the consent form. "Please be gentle, " I whispered. She held my hand gently, "I will. I understand how you feel. I want to assure you that I have done lots and lots of these. I will be very careful. My attending will be there with me all through the procedure." I smiled gratefully at her for her understanding.

I asked her if we could delay the procedure for a few minutes so my sisters and daughter could arrive. They were already in the building; and I wanted to see my family and my daughter before going into this procedure that may give me a stroke. My sister, Kelechi, on the phone assured me she was on her way with our family priest father Maurice. Within a few minutes, my twin sister, Oge appeared with my daughter and my husband followed by my elder sister, Kelechi and a priest, Fr. Maurice, a good friend of the family. I embraced my daughter and held her tight. She was sad to see mommy on a bed looking sad; but she was so brave. She wiped my tears with her hands and that made them flow even more. She leaned over and kissed me on the lips so softly twice, and said, "Sorry, mommy." My heart bled for her. Please God, I prayed. Let me be okay for my daughter. She needs me. Father Maurice read a scripture passage and we all prayed together. He then anointed me and gave me holy communion.

My husband and sisters all kissed me goodbye, wishing me luck. I was wheeled into the radiology procedure room and the procedure started. Throughout the procedure: placing the femoral line, instilling the contrast and taking the images of my brain vasculature, the neuro-radiology fellow and her attending were courteous and efficient, performing the procedure skillfully and effortlessly, giving me directions in rhythmic synchrony: take a deep breath, hold it.... breathe out... turn left ... right," as they took their pictures.

Soon my worst fears were realized. As the contrast was instilled through my femoral artery and it made the journey through the aorta to the internal carotids and circle of Willis, the left side was tolerable; but when the dye was spilled into the right internal carotids and its branches, I felt the most fiery excruciating pain and sensation of an explosion in my brain as if a ball of fire had lit up on my right brain. I knew something bad was there. I have aneurysm, I feared!!

As she finished the procedure and came around to check on me, I asked her, "I have something there, don't I?"
She nodded sadly.
"Is it an aneurysm?" I asked. She nodded silently, holding my hand.
"Am I going to die?" I asked.
She looked at me for a moment before saying softly, "I don't know. You have options. We need to look at the pictures, and we will discuss the options with you."

I got wheeled back to my room and my mood was quiet, contemplative. Within minutes my family all filled the room. My parents and NdaNina had arrived from New Jersey, Kelechi, Oge were there too. Then, a kind-looking Asian lady walked into the room,
"Hello, I'm Dr. Huang" came a soft, kind voice from the doorway. I looked up as she approached the bed. I smiled warmly as I recognized the voice.
"I spoke to you on the phone. You're my neurosurgeon," I said. She nodded with a smile.
"Thank you for accepting me, " I said with sincere gratitude.
"You're welcome, she said.
"This is my family, " I said and began to introduce everyone in the room. My parents, husband and siblings. She was delighted to meet everyone and remarked what a large family we were.
She said slowly, "The angiogram shows that you have an aneurysm." My family had not heard, and they were all silent. She began to explain to them, using the visual angiogram picture just taken.
"It has already ruptured from below, " she began,
"Why did it not show on CT scan ?" I asked.
"Because the bleeding is contained within your brain tissue, and is hidden, so it's not visible on CT, "she said.
"You are very lucky, " she said. "This is usually fatal. Any headaches, blurry vision? Numbness, tingling? Weakness," she asked and I shook my head. She went on to do a neurological exam to confirm that I was intact with no neurological deficits. She asked me if I had had any warning symptoms before the headache in New York. I told her that I had a sudden, throbbing headache in the morning of Saturday august 1st, as I was working in the newborn nursery for which I had to lay my head on the table and one of the nurses gave me two tablets of Advil and the headache subsided till the New York trip on monday, 3rd. My

surgeon was amazed. "It probably ruptured first on that day at work, " she said. "It's amazing that you are alive," she said. "I have never known anyone with an aneurysm that transfers them self for surgery…You chose the best location and place for this aneurysm. Someone must be watching over you, " she said.

"God is watching over me, " I said. She smiled and nodded.

She explained that there were two surgical options for an aneurysm : coiling and clipping. Coiling was less invasive, but was not an option in my case because my aneurysm was already ruptured. She explained that it was a very wide based aneurysm and was dangerous in that it was bridging two main branches of the middle cerebral artery. It will have to be clipped and still stood a high chance of fully rupturing from the top.

"When do I have to have this surgery?" I asked slowly; hoping weeks, days, hours??

"Now, " she said calmly but firmly. "We are already prepping the OR. We cannot waste any time. The aneurysm could rupture at any time. It may be too late. I just came to get your consent."

"Am I going to have a craniotomy?" I asked and she nodded showing me what part of my head was going to be shaved off to make the incision to cut my skull open. Shivers went down my spine. She then showed me the titanium clip: this shiny, tiny metal that was going to save my life and be the bridge between life and death for me forever, if I survived. It was the best quality, she said.

"Ok, let's do the surgery now, please," I heard my Dad say frantically. For a minute I started to panic. I had no time to reflect on what was happening and the possible consequences.

"I need a priest!" I cried. "Find me a priest. I want my last confession and communion and extreme unction." Extreme unction was the last blessings and rites given by the catholic church to people on their death beds or critically ill with little hope of survival.

"No," my mother said, ""You are not going to get your last communion or extreme unction. You will be okay. Nothing is going to happen to you."

"We don't know that, " I cried. I could not understand my mom's confidence. Was she not listening to the neurosurgeon? I could die from this procedure or it could rupture again before we actually get there. "I want a priest. Don't let me go to surgery without my anointing. It can give you strength and healing and courage. I received my last rites every day when I was in labor and delivery pregnant with OlaRose and Obiola, remember?" The nurse was then sent to quickly call for a priest, informing me that there was no guarantee they would find one on time, or at all. Is any man of prayer or chaplain okay if they don't find a priest, she asked? I nodded, saying that was fine, but I would really love to have a priest. She would hurriedly come back into the room in excitement saying that a priest just walked out of the elevator in front of the ICU and had been told about me and he would come shortly.

"I want OlaRose, please... I want my daughter, " I cried and OlaRose was quickly allowed into the unit. She had been in the waiting area because kids were not allowed into the ICU. She was asleep and was laid on my chest. I held her close to my heart and my tears flowed down softly. She was all I could think of at that moment, not death, not the surgery. My beautiful baby girl.. I might never see her grow up... I may never hear her lovely voice speak full sentences... She may never have her mommy. I was leaving her. I knew my family would love her and take care of her, but it hurt sooo much. It was as if a sword had pierced my soul. I was not scared of dying. I was petrified of the pain my daughter would feel if she never saw me again; and it hurt to think I would never see her again. Last night, I was told she stood at the door all night waiting for me to come home crying "mommy! mommy! mommy! "and I didn't come home. She had cried herself to sleep. I kissed her head and face and hugged her tight and would not let go. My family around were overwhelmed, tearful, and confused. My sisters started to cry.

Dr. Huang stood there at my bedside the whole time. I took her hand and she held it gently, firmly in silent reassurance. She informed us that the surgery would last for seven hours or so. She then began to tell us the risks of surgery. It sounded painful to hear but she was required to tell us by law. They needed my informed consent.
"There is a high risk it could rupture even as we clip it, and that could be fatal.." she began in a soft, gentle voice with great equanimity. "If the surgery is successful, there is a risk of blindness in your right eye because the aneurysm is located close to the optic nerve in that eye. You could have a stroke, become paralyzed, lose your speech and

memory, have permanent weakness in your arms or legs..." and the list went on... I closed my eyes silently as I listened. I was either going to die or my life was going to be changed forever. I had no choice but to have the surgery if I wanted a chance at survival, no matter how slim. I took the pen and signed consenting to the surgery.

My mother was dry-eyed and she kept praying and saying, "She will be fine. I believe you will be fine... But what are the positives? Could she also survive this intact? Is there any hope it could happen, even the slightest?,"

Dr Huang nodded, "There is a slim chance, it could happen."'

"Good," my mother said, "That is what we will cling to. She will be okay. She will come out intact." How could she have so much faith at a time like this? I wondered. I had ceased to guess at God's will after my son's death in 2006. Who knows God's will?

Dr. Huang let us know the seriousness of the situation.

"Very few neurosurgeons would have accepted this case, even in this state or region " she informed us because of the poor prognosis.

"But why did you? " I asked her.

"Because you called me in the middle of the night, " She heard my plea for help and it touched her. "And now I have met you, your family, and your beautiful little daughter... " she told us softly with emotion, looking at me clutching to my daughter in tears. She believed, she told me later, she had to do her best as she was my only chance at survival. I really didn't have time to seek a second opinion or go elsewhere... and seeing how young I was, my daughter and how close my family was, made her realize that it could be her lying there in my shoes...

"Thank you very much, " I said softly.

"You 're welcome, " she said.

"Please be careful, "

"I will," she said kindly.

"Will you be doing the surgery yourself?" I asked.

"Yes, "she said squeezing my hand gently. I suddenly had this implicit trust in this stranger. She held the key to my life right then; and I trusted that she would do her very best. I didn't know her... I had never heard of her. Unlike most patients before a major surgery who could research and select the best surgeons for their condition; I did not have that liberty because of the dire urgency. I trusted in God to select the best person for me, and I believed he had... Dr. Huang. I actually forgot she was Asian and I had come from a hospital where I had been neglected by a young, female, Asian doctor. But there was something in her demeanor, her kind face, her soft, gentle voice and the way she appeared to genuinely care about me and my family, the way she patiently took time to explain this technical, scary procedure that was comforting, and made her all so familiar. I didn't know what her experience or track record was, but I trusted her... with my life. She had heard my cry for help and came to my aid when no one would. She had to be God-sent.

"What time is it mommy? I asked looking over at my Mommy.
"It's 3pm, " she said glancing at the wall clock
"Can we say the divine mercy prayer?" I asked automatically, not thinking about it or realizing that it was 3pm, the hour of divine mercy. We all then recited the prayers "Eternal Father, I offer you the body and blood, soul and divinity of your dearly beloved son, our Lord Jesus Christ in atonement for our sins and those of the whole world. ...For the sake of his sorrowful passion, have mercy on us and all of the whole world..." and at that moment I asked God to save me for my daughter's sake and guide my surgeon successfully through the surgery, so nothing would happen to me. The priest arrived at that time and wanted to pray with the family first.
"What is your religion?" I asked Dr. Huang
"I am a Christian, : she said.
"Will you pray with us?" I asked her.
"Definitely, " she said with a smile and she held hands with me, my family and the priest and he prayed over me, her and about the surgery asking for God's mercy and protection and for God to guide her during the surgery. After he was done, Dr. Huang left to prepare for surgery and my family came and hugged me one by one and then stepped out of the room so I could be alone with the priest for a moment. My family soon returned into the room, most in tears, some got on the phone trying to update others not present. I asked my family to call my other siblings not present that I may say goodbye on the phone sister Chichi in California, Okey in Cleveland, Ure in Pittsburgh, and Ngozi in NewYork. I told everyone I loved them: my husband, Obi and my family. I asked Obi to call his mother on the phone (she was in Delaware visiting) so I could say goodbye and he

did. I made my family promise to go ahead with OlaRose's Christening even if I did not make it back from the surgery alive. I gave them all the information on bills and documents to take care of. They tried to dissuade me saying, "You can take care of them when you return," "No," I said, "write them down." Kelechi started to write through her tears, and my father wrote too.

I looked around at my family all around me as I lay on a bed with a white sheet covering me. A cool shiver went through my spine as I remembered the dream I had two nights earlier. I had seen this scene before…. *It was Sunday morning on august 2nd, after I returned home from my 24 hour shift in the neonatal intensive care unit (NICU). The previous morning, saturday august 1st, I had had an excruciatingly bad headache when I got to work, and had to lay my head down for about five to ten minutes. One of the nurses offered me advil and it relieved the headache so I resumed working my 24 hr shift. So, after I got off the next morning, I went home and took a nap. I woke up suddenly in a sweat and confusedue to a weird dream. In the dream, I was lying in a white bed covered by white sheets in a room surrounded by lots of people, most were my family: parents, siblings, but I could not remember everyone in the room. All I remembered vividly was that on my left at the head of my bed was my little deceased son, Obiola, a vision in white, and on my right was my paternal grandfather, long deceased since 1983 wearing white too. They were stationed one on each side of the bed looking ahead firmly as if guarding me, but not looking at me. But the rest of the people in the room seemed to be looking on at me. I could not remember if their expression was of fear, sadness or joy but all the gazes were focused intently on me as I lay on the bed…* I had woken up confused at the dream, as I had never dreamt of my son before. I soon thought nothing of it; and I wasn't scared.

Suddenly, in that hospital Rm 9 at Johns Hopkins it looked like déjà vu, for I lay in a white bed, covered by white sheets surrounded by my family, all looking at me, this time with sadness and unspoken fear and visible grief. It seemed as if my life began to flash in front of me. I realized that I had had premonitions of something happening to me, for the past few months but could not explain it. Several memories flashed through my mind, I began to realize that God was preparing me for that day august 4th, 2009. I may be dying in the OR that day, I thought.

"It is my time, " I said slowly and solemnly to my family.

"No, "my mommy said, "It is not your time. You have to be strong. You have to believe and have faith that you will pull through, Olachi. You can't give up. "

I nodded in tears. I couldn't give up! I had to fight for my daughter's sake. I could have died a work or at home, but God could have placed all these circumstances at each point in the past 24 hours for a reason... maybe to save me.. or maybe, ... so I could have my family around me and be prepared before my last moments?? I shrugged the last thought away. I would not give up! "I believe! I believe! I believe!" I spoke softly . I summoned up mental strength reminding myself that if my will and courage failed, that my body and spirit would give up too. I had to will myself to survive this with God's grace.

OlaRose started to wake up and I hugged her and kissed her. She held me tight, still sleepy and stroked my back and patted it gently as if consoling me. She could see I was sad. "I love you OlaRose," I whispered in tears. I turned to my family, "Tell OlaRose I love her and will always love. Tell her mommy loves her," I choked back tears. "I love you all," I said. My family said they loved me too through their tears. What do I pray? I wondered in my hour of need; in the possible hour of my death.. Who do I call to in heaven for help! Who could reach God the quickest for me, right now? I thought. I asked for Mary, our mother's protection. I thought of some saints and my guardian angels. I was mentally looking for a short cut to God's merciful heart because I was running out of time. I could only remember to say softly ; Jesus I love you.... Jesus I love you... Jesus I love you..." then I started to recite quietly: "Jesus, I love you ... all I have is thine . Yours I am, yours I want to be. Do with me what thou wilt. .." I said it three times and then suddenly stopped before I finished the third time. Why am I saying that prayer? What if His will was to take me today? No, I did not really want Him to do with me as he willed? I thought in fear. I tried to think of another prayer and began the Lord is my shepherd. My family were all praying out loud too. Next I said psalm 91: "He who dwells in the shelter of the most high..."

"Please I need Obiola's relics. They are in my house. Can someone bring them to me," I said and turned to Oge, who nodded in tears. I then realized there was no time for anyone to drive home and bring them. I was going to surgery immediately. I kept my son's clothes, lock of hair, and holy items that touched his body on the top shelf of the wardrobe in OlaRose's room. When my mother was sick on her deathbed last year and the doctors told us that there was nothing more they could do, I brought his relics to my mother unconscious and on the ventilator and touched it to her whole body. I prayed and called onto him to intercede for her to the Father as she was wheeled to the cardiac lab to rule out a myocardial infarction. I asked him to escort her there with choirs of angels and guide the cardiologists hands that as he touched her, he would not find any blockage in her arteries or anything wrong with her heart. The cardiologist found no evidence of heart attack as showed diagnostically and from that moment on, her complete healing and miraculous recovery began. I believe my son was instrumental in her recovery for his grandmother prayed for his survival when his life and OlaRose's were endangered in the womb.

 "You do not need his relics, " my mother said in the Hopkins ICU room. "He is within you." She gave me a second rosary and a picture of Pope John Paul II, which she placed on my heart and I clutched to it with my hands.
At that point, the anesthesiologists entered the room to assess me for surgery, and my family had to step out. I gave my mother the fancier rosary back and kept the simple one. "I only need one. I don't want to lose it, " I said.

The anesthesiologists started to wheel me out of the room. I saw my family hugging each other tearfully as they walked ahead. I thought of OlaRose and my heart bled tearfully. "My baby girl... Mommy is soo sorry. " I thought of never seeing her grow up or have her first real conversation or start school or get married and wondered if she would ever remember her mommy. The pain of knowing I may never see my daughter again was inexplicable. How could I leave her behind with such grief?

I looked straight ahead into space, looking beyond my surroundings, and saw nothing but light. I thought: Mommy is right. Obiola lives in my heart always. I am his mother. I will call him, and he will answer me. "Obiola, my son " I called out to him softly. Suddenly, his beautiful, angelic face appeared to me, luminous, filled with light. He was wearing the clothes he had on him when I last held him a pretty blue overall with white collars. He was dressed in those shortly after he died in my arms, and they brought him to me to hold him as long as I could in a room. He smiled at me and my heart felt such joy as I gazed at him. I didn't want to tear my eyes away from him, else the vision fade would away.

"Obiola, " I said silently smiling through my painful pounding headache, "Mommy loves you, but I cannot come just yet. You are there at the foot of God's throne; go and cradle yourself in His arms. He will not refuse your pure soul. Tell God to leave me here to take care of OlaRose. You sacrificed your life that she may live. Tell God to leave your mommy alone to take care of your sister. OlaRose needs me. I have only asked two things of you : First to take care of OlaRose in the NICU that she will come out unharmed and healthy and bring your angel friends to surround her incubator that no ill shall befall her, and you did; next I asked you to ask God to save your grandma Rose who prayed life into you and your sister while you were in the womb; and you did. This is the first time I am asking you for myself. I am your mommy. I don't know God's plan.. but you are there with Him. Beg God to give me my life back, intact, without deficits. He will listen to your pure soul. I love you, baby," I said. He smiled sweetly at me and faded away.

At this point, I was exuding with joy, anticipation, slight anxiety; but the encounter with my son whether it real or imagined, calmed my soul. He had come to me in my hour of need. I suddenly continued to speak softly to myself, "All you souls in the NICU whom I saved by the grace of God. All you souls whom I have held in my arms as you took your last breaths waiting for your mommies to come. All you souls that I ensured were baptized as you took your last breaths. Today, I ask you to go to God and testify on my behalf. Tell him there are more of you to be saved. Tell him to give me my life back."

I started to talk to God from the depths of my heart. I made promises to him if He saved me from this surgery. "If there is any chance that I have any good to do on this earth, Lord, give me my life back. Let me do your will. I will praise you with all my heart for the rest of my life. I will give glory to you in all I do. I dedicate my work as a neonatal pediatrician to you. If you give me my life back, you can use me for whatever you will. "

At that point, I was filled with calm and serene peace. I started to smile as I was wheeled past my family: they waved, they cheered and blew kisses and told me they will see me soon. I did not look at them anymore I was looking ahead at a light ahead of me. It shone bright and straight at me. I heard my mother's voice following me: "Imagine the divine rays of Christ. Imagine his divine mercy cleansing your brain, your body. Drown yourself in His divine mercy. Claim your healing, ..believe Ola…. …" I imagined the rays as I looked into the light. The light enveloped me. "For the sake of his sorrowful passion, have mercy on us and on the whole world, "I recited "I am healed! I am healed!" I whispered into the light. I was no longer afraid, "Thank you Jesus! Thank Jesus!..." I kept saying over and over. I thought of OlaRose and hope and joy filled my soul. I remembered her last kiss on my lips; I remember how warm and sweet she felt as I held her. I remembered her laughter, her spirit, her beautiful face as she sings her favorite song. I started to sing as I was wheeled into the OR: "I love Jesus… I love Jesus. He is my friend.. He is my friend. He will never leave me. He will never leave me. He is my friend, He is my friend, Amen!" As I sang it, I hugged both my hands around my chest the way I thought her to when she sang "he is my friend"; and I wagged my finger and shook my head gently the way I taught her to when she sang " he will never leave me.."; and I put my hands together to say " Amen". I knew my family was going to bombard heaven with prayers and requests for my life. They would call everyone they knew to pray for me. They would call on every priest, religious and stranger they meet to pray for me. I knew it. I didn't need to be told. I felt so embowered by love, not just from my family, but by God's love. I was suddenly filled with the intense awareness of God's presence and His Love. He loves me soo much, I said to myself. He has surrounded me with such peace, calm, and kind gentle people in this hospital; and I had my family and daughter around me; and gave me the grace of confession, his anointing and his presence in the communion. Even if these were my last moments on earth; they were beautiful and I was thankful for the opportunity to make my peace with God.

As if God wanted to assure me of his grace or confirm my thoughts, something happened as we arrived at the OR. I was still clutching the pope's picture and holding my rosary. There was a certain calm in the OR. The head anesthesiologist as they wheeled me in turned to his team and said, "This is a young lady with a ruptured brain aneurysm. We are going to be calm, we are going to be gentle, and we are going to be safe ." Those words touched my soul. I remember thinking... Ooh how God loves me so. Even at my hour of death, he is kind to me. He has surrounded me with wonderful, kind, gentle people from my doctor who prayed with me to the nurses and the anesthesiologists, to letting me receive his blessed sacrament of his body and anointing twice in one day. Ooh how kind he is to me.

"Thank you, " I whispered to them. I was placed on the operating table, and I handed my anesthesiologist the Pope's picture.

"Can you hold this for me? " I asked gently

"I will put it in my pocket," he said.

I remember asking for the intercession of Pope John Paul II ; and telling him if I recovered intact, that I would give a testimony for his canonization.

"Can I please hold on to my rosary till you put me to sleep?" I asked.

He smiled, "Yes, you can. When you sleep, I will put it in my pocket too."

"Thank you," I said softly. I felt at peace. I was not scared. I had resigned myself to God's will and I trusted Him with all my heart. I refused to think beyond the moment: death or life? I wanted to dwell in the now!... at peace in my body and soul... picturing the face of my beautiful daughter... picturing the angelic face in my soul.. knowing all my family in heaven and earth were wishing me the best. Knowing that God would give me the best, if I let Him make the choice for me. I did not want to die yet because I had so much to offer the world and my daughter; and I did not want to be a vegetable if I survived; I wanted a meaningful life; but I was letting God make that choice for me. He has never failed me.

I was strapped with belts across my legs and body to hold me in place. In a moment of mental weakness, I suddenly recalled the horror stories of anesthesia that wears off during a procedure and you are in unbearable pain but unable to speak or yell because you are intubated and paralyzed. I had never known anyone that had a ruptured brain aneurysm and survived a brain surgery. The ruptured aneurysms of young people I had heard about had been fatal, and discovered during autopsy.

The anesthesiologist was now sitting down beside me, staring at me. I held out my right hand and he took it gently with both hands. I smiled through little tears " Please don't let me feel it... even if it is my last," I whispered so softly

"I won't," he promised. "You will need a femoral line in your right thigh, a subclavian line on your chest; You will need a Foley, another IV; and you will need to be intubated and placed on the ventilator before the surgery starts. But we are not going to do any of that to you until you fall asleep. Dr. Mezu, give me a thumbs up." I gave him a thumbs up with my right hand. As he spoke he covered my face with a mask, and I knew he was giving me general anesthesia. I felt my eyes closing.... I felt my consciousness fading and darkness coming but the light I had seen earlier persisted shining on me in the midst of the surrounding darkness... I continued to whisper "Thank you Jesus...Jesus I love you... Thank you Jesus...Jesus I love you... Jesus I love you.... All I have is thine...Yours I am... Yours I want to be.... Do with me what you will... Jesus I love you.....Jesus I love you..," I trusted His will for ne now – life or death, because I knew He loved me. My eyes closed to the void....the darkness and I was immediately completely enveloped by the light... that light was so bright... I wanted to exist only in it... as the anesthesia took over my body and consciousness, I continued to mutter softly the words" Thank you, Jesus... Jesus I love you.. thank you Jesus.... Jesus I love you," .

"Dr. Mezu, give me a thumbs up, " came a female voice in the midst of the darkness. I gave a thumbs up. My eyes opened slowly, blinking to the bright lights. I looked to my right towards the voice. I believe it was Dr. Huang standing over me. "Have you started the surgery?" I asked in confusion.

"It is over, " she said with a smile. I could not believe it!! I was alive! I was alive! Thank you Jesus! Thank you Jesus! Thank you Jesus! I whispered over and over and over again. Ooh! God loves me. Ooh! How he loves me soo. I was so overwhelmed by the sudden deep awareness of God's love for me, so undeserving of His love. Tears welled into my eyes. I just was suddenly aware like I have never been before that God loves me... Not for anything I did or could do... Just because... he is love and mercy itself. He loved me soo much, he sent his only son to die for my sins. Oh, How He loves me. The value and immensity of Christ' sacrifice on the cross dawned on me. He died for my sake ..that I might live. My heart was overflowing with inexplicable joy and gratitude to God. He saved me yet again from the hands of death. Ooh ! How He loves me! I said this over and over and over for days and weeks to come. I wanted to thank him in every tongue and language I knew or could imagine. How many ways can you say thank you? Suddenly all the worries and troubles of my previous life seemed unimportant and unnecessary. All that mattered was living to do God's will in my life. I truly felt like I was born again in spirit and in flesh. This was my new life, I believed.

I was wheeled back to my room; and my family came in shortly. They were overjoyed. All I could tell them initially was: "Thank God for me! God is merciful and He is kind. It is a miracle! I feel so loved by God... Please thank God for me." I knew I was intact, I was healed, with no deficits. It was nothing short of a miracle and all I could say for hours and days were, " Thank you Jesus... Oh, how God loves me.. God loves me... Thank you Jesus.," I felt beloved by God and thankful to him for calling me to share in his passion and giving me his graces and blessing to see me through it.

The neurosurgeon came in and performed a neurological exam and all my senses were intact; no loss of vision or strength or sensation or memory.
"This is amazing! You are neurologically intact!" she said.
"It is a miracle!" I said
"Yes, it is a miracle, " she agreed. "The surgery was successful. The aneurysm has been clipped."
"You are my angel. God sent you to me," I told her. "Thank you so much,"
She told me to expect to be in the ICU for another three weeks as I was still in danger of having vasospasm of my brain blood vessels which could cause strokes and feared neurological deficits. After that I will be transferred to the regular floor to be observed for weeks and may need rehab for a few more weeks or even months.

Dr. Huang marveled at the speed of my recovery day by day. She came daily to see me regardless of how late or early it was; or how long of a day she had busy in surgery all day. She would come at late at night, midnight after a long day of surgeries or early hours of the morning on her way to work, sometimes before six am. I was so impressed by her dedication. She was always calm, relaxed, never rushed; always good mannered and positive. She made your day brighter each time she showed up. I looked forward to her visits.

Daily, cranial Doppler tests were done to check for vasospasm. I developed a great relationship with my nurses. They were young and very skilled; well-informed about my condition, genuinely cared about my well-being and took interest in getting to know me and my family. They were able to anticipate my needs and were very empathic and sensitive to me and my family. I had a huge family and everyone wanted to see me but they kept to the visiting schedule understanding that I needed my rest; and the nurse managers and nurses were accommodating as much as possible . The nurses joked by the second day that their patients do not usually have conversations with them like I do as they are too sick, weak, or usually unconscious. They were amused and delighted to see me taking my daily physical therapy walks starting from day 2 with support down the hallway or around the unit as most of their patients do not walk as they are confined to a bed due to their critical condition. I felt lucky, blessed, and thankful to God for my healing. I still was not fully accepting of my recovery and tried to dissuade them from sending me to the regular floor, discounting meds, cranial doppler checks and physical therapy or sending me home so soon. I was expecting a long, hard recovery. It was not supposed to be so easy. Everyone marveled at my amazingly quick recovery. Dr. Huang assured me I was doing excellently and well above expectation. It was safe to go to the regular floor, she said; and I believed her. I had such great faith in her. She saved my life. After 5 days in the ICU, they transferred me to the regular floor and after three days on the floor, they stopped all the medications for vasospasm precaution and discharged me to home to recuperate with my loved ones.
"Go home, you are healed, " she said. "Even I cannot find a reason to keep you in the hospital. This is a miracle." My total hospital stay was 9 days.

I thanked her immensely." "You saved my life. You have no idea what you've done for me and my family," I told her softly fighting back tears.

"I think I do," she said softly and kindly.

Reflections: *I now realize that I was not saved because of any wondrous work of mine or promise of what I could do for God, but I was saved by the grace of God. I was saved by the Divine Mercy of God because he loves me so and died on the cross for my sins. His mercy is free, seeks no reward, and cannot be earned. What greater love is that? Despite the cross; God never abandoned me. He was always there; and His divine mercy enveloped me all the way through my suffering (emotional and physical). Praise be to God!*

Laying in the hospital after my surgery, as people prayed and sent their good wishes, I heard a lot of sympathy words like" "Poor you! why you again! You can't get a break…. Why did God let this happen to you again, maybe because he knew you could overcome it!" I thought to myself, "Why not me?" I wondered. If God allowed this to happen, then it must be for my good. He has a plan for me that needed this particular experience. It happened to me precisely because God loved me, and wanted me to share in His passion. In my suffering, He is closest to me.

We are all called in our daily lives to share in Christ's passion on the cross, and as a result grow in our faith. God calls to us each day to pick up our crosses big or small and follow him, keeping our focus on him to strengthen us. If our cross is too heavy or weighs us down, it is because we never even tried to pick it up or we lost focus on Christ crucified on the cross ahead. He will never give us a cross we cannot carry; and He will always give us the means to overcome them. So that in the end, when death comes – as it will for each and every one of us mortals, we will be willing and ready to say, "Here I am Lord! Jesus, I love you. All I have is thine, yours I am, Yours I want to be. Do with me what thou wilt."

August 27, 2009

A Miracle of Life – Saved by Divine Mercy

Thank you Jesus, Thank you Jesus
It's a miracle! I'm alive!
My soul is filled with thanks to you Lord
For saving me from the hands of death

I am a lowly sinner, but you did not forsake me
I called to you in the hour of my need,
And you heard my voice
In my darkness, I saw your saving light
You let your rays of divine mercy fill my brain, body and soul
And brought me back to life, a life renewed.

My soul is overwhelmed with joy
At the goodness of the Lord.
I feel so beloved by you God,
My heart is elated with thanks

God Loves me so, ooh how he loves me so
He did not let me despair in the hour of darkness
but surrounded me with his angels
to protect me from the fangs of evil.
He surrounded me with love, filling my heart with hope.
He gave me the blessing of his sacrament, of his anointing
To give me strength and renewed faith.
Who am I to deserve your love, O Lord
How you love me so, my poor soul is humbled.

Thank you Jesus! Thank you Jesus!
My lips will never tire to say it
For the rest of my earthly life
That you have loaned me to do your will
My mouth will sing your praises forever
For you have raised me from the dead
And given me a life renewed.

Here I am my God

Renew my spirit and strengthen it
Pour the light of your divine mercy into my heart
and chase away all the shadows of darkness
Fill my soul with your divine presence
Consume my heart with your divine love
Let your light shine forth from mine
That all may see, "not me", but only "your light"

When I hurt, let your light heal it
When I feel lonely, let your presence comfort me
When I am impatient, let your patience guide me
When I am angry, let your love soothe me
When I am weak, let your spirit strengthen me
When I am discouraged, let your fire revive me
When I am scared, let your arms shield me
When I am proud, let your heart humble me
When I bear grudges, let your divine mercy free me
When I suffer, let your passion strengthen me

O Lord, make a home in my heart and never leave
Mend its broken walls of faith, seal its holes with love
You are all I want, you are all I need
Bless my life, that it may be a reflection of yours
Bless my eyes, that I may see you in all I meet
Bless my lips, that I may speak your word and truth always
Bless my voice, that I may sing your praises all my life
Bless my ears, that I may hear your voice in the silence of my heart
Bless my silence, that I may listen to your word
Bless my hands, that I may do your will in my work and life
Bless my legs, that I may follow where you lead
and never stray from you
Bless my thoughts, that I may think of your goodness and never evil
Bless my work, that I may offer it in praise to you.

Teach me to love like you would
Show me to care the way you would
Let me die to self and live for you alone
In the depths of darkness, shine your light that I may see
Like a blind man, I will follow where you lead

and trust in your divine will
For you will never forsake your child
You hold true to your promises
Show me the way Lord, that I may do your will
Help me care for the sick and dying: unborn, newborn,, young and old

Teach me to love them like you would
 Show me how to care for them, the way you would
Preserve and protect the lives of your unborn children
while in the wombs of their mothers like you protected mine
Renew, revive, heal and restore
the lives of your servants at death's door
Like you did my mother and me
At death's door, I asked you Lord,
 if there was any good left for me to do on earth
To save my life that I may do your will
If there is any little soul left to be saved
from the dangers of prematurity
To give me back my life that I may save them with your grace
But by your divine mercy and grace ,
I was brought back to life
Teach me to love like you would
Show me how to care, the way you would
You saved me, not for anything I could do
But because You are love and mercy itself

For the sake of your sorrowful passion
Have mercy on us, and on the whole world
When others seek to harm us, help us to bless them
When others mock us, help us to pray for them
When others are mean and speak ill of us, help us to be kind to them
When others persecute us and accuse us falsely,
help us to forgive them
When others hate us, help us to show them love
When others quarrel with us,
hold our tongues and help us speak peace
When others take unjustly from us,
enrich our hearts that we may suffer no loss
When others ask and don't give, help us to still give with all our hearts

When others do not appreciate us, help us to appreciate them
When others judge us harshly or falsely, help us not to judge them
When others do evil to us, help us to always be good to them
When others have wronged us, help us to forgive them
For the sake of your sorrowful passion,
Have mercy on us and on the whole world.

O God the father, bless us and our families
Let the holy family be our model
Joseph, Mary and baby Jesus
Bestow on us your grace and divine love
Teach us to love and appreciate each other,
protect each other, forgive each other
Let us pray daily for your love and protection
That no seeds of discord, selfishness, greed,
hate, dishonesty, envy, deceit, or
unfaithfulness may be sown in our home
May we bring up our children in the teachings of your word
May mothers follow the loving, humble ways of Mary, our mother
May fathers follow the loving, humble example of St. Joseph
And children follow the obedient, meek example of the child Jesus.
May our families on earth give you glory
and unite with in praise with your holy
Church on earth and your family in heaven
till you call us to yourself. Amen!

August 22, 2009

To Ola: For a Complete Recovery from a Sudden Illness
by Dr. Rose Ure Mezu

In my extremity, You prayed fervently for me, my Ola
Now, it is my turn to repay you with a world of prayers
Ours I know is a just God, a merciful God, a tender God
Who has a name - Divine Mercy, His goodness unending
Yours recovery will be quick, complete, unquestioned
And so astonishing as to amaze the world and testify that
Indeed, there is a God Who counts our life minute by minute

You will not be paralyzed; you will
Continue to see with your eyes God's universe –
No tremors, no infections, no encephalitis,
Nor memory loss, no strokes for
The Lord we serve is the Master Surgeon
Who creates and then recreates
Who makes a being perfect and so will God you

Like Bessie Chiege Okeke before you
Your recovery will be so speedy, so complete
That everyone will say, "Now, this is the miracle!"
For you still have your mission of love and mercy
Towards the infant preemies to complete on earth
These newborns' lives you will tend like OlaRose
These are lives that have been despaired of –
Just like OlaRose

Yours is hugely endowed - your mind, that is,
So incisive, methodical and romantic you'll yet produce
Prodigiously for so full of excellences you are.
We plan our thanksgivings when we can but only
The Lord can ordain if it be done then or another day
Only the Blessed Trinity can say when or how or where
Yet, I know Jesus has a long memory and will remember
Those days of youthful ideals when you defended His honor
When together with Kelechi, you led the Legion of Mary Society
And participated in the rosary groups and choir in college
That all youths might sing of the Lord's Goodness

It seemed like a bad, bad dream – your illness
One minute so active, so lively were you, my gem
And the next moment, bravely fighting for life and
Caught in the throes of throbbing head pain
The miracle is that you remained alert to still last the next day
Ah me! It must have been such a confusing and painful time
As we wondered what was in the mind of God to choose
To have this happen at a time of coming festivities, the irony of it!

Is it a rebuke? A Judgment? An Awakening of sorts?
But who can decipher the inscrutable mind of God?
And so the thing to do is follow the Mercy prayer
And not become despondent while we with great
Confidence submit ourselves to the holy will of God.
Through prayer, to bend the Hand of Jesus to
Direct the hands of the surgeons, for He had chosen
This team of Godly physicians and nurses, and so
Guided by the Right Hand of He, Greatest Neurosurgeon
They will bring about the reality of the miracle of survival.

"A special lady, a young lady, a tender lady; so everyone,
Relax, let us be careful so we will not make mistakes," the
Anesthetist says in the operating room, filled with God's aura.
And thus it was that Olachi Joy – God's own gem, full of joy
Came through her surgery with her usual flying colors
And ah! there was no paralysis
And here were no strokes
And she could see well the colors of the earth
And she had no tremors, no memory loss – for
She remembered everything that went before
And everyone; she remembered past, present and future
And I know that Divine Mercy continues to follow her
And us all the days of her life, and ours on God's earth
For Divine Mercy is Jesus and we trust in Him!

These days of convalescence, OlaRose's little friend
Jesus is gently healing you, cradling you, tending you
Obiola and Bessie, John and Clement are busy

Your forebears are pleading before God's throne
Gathering into a festive garland your blessings
From their King and yours and ours too
The babies you saved are busy rooting for you, my Ola
The babies you baptized and prepared for heaven are
Pleading for you, and the weeping parents you consoled
Have sent their prayerful blessings billowing to heaven
And you need not fear, for your job of mercy is still here,
Enhanced and waiting for your mission of mercy to flourish.

Olachi, our family's joy, you will live long and fruitful
And see your children's feet scampering around your hearth
Your dear patron saints – Camillus, Rita, Gerard, Joseph and
Mother Mary, all are around you gathered to ward off evil
And are happy to see the Mercy rays cleanse and dry out all
Foreign irritants, and Tomorrow you will awaken from sleep
Fresh, and serene and free of headaches – not by one year but now.
By your accelerated progress, all will know that the Lord we serve
Is Love and Mercy, is indeed the Only Living and Everlasting God
Who gives life to whomsoever He wishes because He owns life.

Dr. Rose Ure Mezu
August 4-6, 2009

Thorn in My Flesh

How you hurt me so
You thorn in my flesh
Stuck to me you are
Your head buried deep within my tissues
Causing an intense dull ache
Your sharp pointy end sticking out through my skin
Causing a sharp, piercing pain

I cannot get rid of you
You thorn in my flesh
You are part of me it seems
As pulling you out is an impossible feat.
Embedded in my being you are
The very essence of my existence
I feel your sting with each breath I take

How do I live with you
You thorn in my flesh
If I scream out in pain and anguish
At the torture you incessantly cause me?
my lungs will tire, my strength will fail

Do I ignore you and pretend
To be oblivious to the pain you cause me?
Do I curse you and rue the day
I encountered your deceitful countenance
Taking you to me with trust
Not knowing of your cunning guile
To bring only misery and pain
Do I love you as before
With all my heart and soul
And endure the pain as so

I open the word searching for truth
Speak to me Lord, what do I do?
"Forgive those that err you, 70 x 7"
I open the word again and it says

"If your hand or leg causes you to sin, cut it off
For it is better to enter heaven without a limb
Than to be thrown into damnation with both limbs.."
Do I severe you from my body, you thorn in my flesh?
That I may gain eternal life?

But you are just a thorn indeed
You thorn in my flesh
Nothing I feel or suffer
Compares to what my savior did,
who died on the cross for my sins
His crown of thorns, the beating of his divine body,
Nailed to the cross, mocked by all
His side pierced till his blood and water flowed
For his divine mercy to fill the world

You are my cross on earth it seems,
You thorn in my flesh
I will follow my saviors example and
Will accept you humbly and willingly
And follow where he leads
Ignoring your piercing pain
Praying through my agony

I will offer you up in sacrifice
You thorn in my life
In unison with the passion of Christ my savior
For the rest of my life
I will offer my pain, my ache, my anguish all caused by you
So that you are transformed into
A saving grace for me
And no longer will you be
a thorn in my flesh.

August 21, 2009

Your love O Lord

I thirst for your love O Lord
To fill me with your divine mercy
And quench my being from within
Where no human love can reach

I hunger for your love, O Lord
To renew my soul and body
And feed this insatiable need
that no human love can satisfy

I yearn for your love, O Lord
To burn fiery fires of your desire in my soul
And satisfy this hollow longing
That no human love can fill

I trust in your love, O Lord
To wipe away all my doubts and fears
And fill my soul with belief and faith
That no human love can provide

I trust in your will, O Lord
To lead me to my destiny
And bestow on me everlasting life
That no human love can give

I believe in your love;
I trust in your Divine mercy;
and I submit to your Holy will O Lord who Knows tomorrow...
because you give the best to only those
who let you make the choice in their lives.

Tuesday, February 9, 2010

How many times will you Love me, O Lord?

How many times have I rejected you
But you still give your love to me, O Lord?
How many times have I betrayed you
But you still love me, O Lord?
How many times have I closed the door to my heart
But you still knock with your love , O Lord?
How many times have I given in to pride
But you still humbly give your love, O Lord?
How many times have I given in to anger
But you still gently soothe me with love, O Lord?
How many times have I being impatient for your will
But you still patiently show me your love, O Lord
How many times have I lost faith in you
But you still make me believe in your love, O Lord
How many times have I borne grudges and not forgiven
But you still forgive me and show me mercy, O Lord
How many times have I being consumed with fear
But you still give me courage O lord
How many times have I given in to temptation
But you still helped me triumph with your love, O Lord
How many times will I crucify you to death on the cross
But you still rise to life with love for me, O Lord
How many times will you love me, O Lord
As long as there is life in me, now and forever.

Feb 21, 2010

Christ within Us

Kneeling in the church pews, observing the silence of my penance
I looked up at the huge cross hanging above the altar
Focused on the often forgotten shoulder wound of Christ,
and how the cross grated his bone exposed from the torn flesh.
At that instant, I saw people in my mind that I encounter daily
and got a view into their soul to see that Christ lived therein
in different ways due to the different states of their soul

In some, Christ was as if in a cage and frightened
surrounded by darkness, as if helpless
and unable to do anything for that soul;
In some souls Christ was surrounded by darkness and filth
and his light was extinguished in the soul as if it were empty and void.
In some Christ was constantly crucified on the cross
every second of their lives due to their sins;
In some he lay in a dim light as if waiting for the soul to accept him;
In some he lay sad and forlorn in constant agony in gethsemane;
In some he bled profusely from the crown of thorns and flesh wounds
In some he shone like a bright light as if ascending to heaven;
In some he was resurrecting from the dead;
In some he lay in a cradle sound asleep as a baby;
In some he laughed and played happily like a child.

My heart was elated with joy and awe at this sight
but a deep sadness overcame me when I saw Christ
living in miserable conditions in some souls.
I looked away from the cross and saw no more
God had allowed me to know that he was real and lived in all souls
He lived in the people I see each day: friends and foes alike
I should look within and see only Christ within all I encounter
This will help rid me of my sensitivity and self-pride and humble me
so that in persecution, I'll realize God living in the soul allowed it
and Christ in my soul and in that soul is watching over me.
They do not do anything without His permission to me;
and they can bark and howl but they cannot hurt me or touch my soul.
Thank you, Jesus! How many ways can I say thank you!

March 3, 2010

To Love and be Loved ... a sojourn

I have loved so I thought
I've been loved so I thought
From the start to the present
None compares to your love, O Lord

I've loved and been loved
A love so deep, I felt stifled
A love so true, I felt caged
And I let go, hurting the one who loved

I've been loved and I loved with reserve
Not giving of my heart completely
Basking in the thrill of now as the world does
A love so adequate but not consuming
A love true but not fulfilling
And I let go to follow my dreams

I've loved and been loved, or so I thought
A love so real, it could not be true
A love so deep, I must have imagined it
A love that molded itself to my dreams
A mere fathom of my innermost desires
And when the fathom was revealed
And faded into nonexistence, I hurt so much to let go
It drained me of emotion, energy and the will to go on

I've loved fleetingly without a care
As if trying to ignore the pain of love lost
A love not real, it did not matter
A love not deep, it could not consume me
A love without a heart so it could not hurt me
When I let go along the path to my dream

I've loved so deep
Without knowing if I was loved
A love from old awakened that it seemed like my hearts dream
It looked like it was meant to be

Another fathom, beguiling, enchanting
A fairytale romance or so it seemed
A love so real, I did not see if it was real
A love for a lifetime or so I thought
A love that so showed its imperfections
And I still loved for true loves sake
A love so true, I ignored its flaws
A love so shallow, I labored to make it deep
A love that bore fruits so blessed
Then the love revealed its cunning, lies, deceit and true self
A love so selfish, so un giving of time, self, emotion, of its heart
I was hurt beyond emotion; betrayed beyond relief
A love that let go before I could
A love I let go as it tried to hold on
For my eyes opened and
I knew I needed love, much more than was offered

I've loved and been loved through love's sojourns,
I now realize that I did not find true love as I thought I did
For no human and earthly love could fulfil
the desires in the abyss of my soul
Only God can satisfy the longing in my heart
With His love so real, so deep and so true
 it consumes, appreciates, reciprocates and gives of itself
emptying even every drop of life and still keeps on loving
 even when I could not believe he could love much more.

March 7, 2010

I Will love You More

When others mock me
I will love you more
When I am persecuted
I will love you more
When I am misunderstood
I will love you more
When I am denied credit for my hard work
I will love you more
When I am accused unjustly
I will love you more
When my good name is tarnished
I will love you more
When I suffer deeply
I will love you more
When I cannot defend myself
I will love you more
When life's struggles torment me
 I will love you more, O Lord
For you love me so much
You let me share in your passion.

March 7, 2010

My Daily Invocation for God's Will

Here I am Lord... I offer myself up for your will
Teach me to love the way you do
Show me how to care like you would
I believe in your love
I trust in your divine mercy
I submit to your Holy Will, O Lord
You who knows tomorrow
Do with me whatever you will because
You give the best to those
who let you make the choice in their lives.

Nothing happens to me unless God allows it
Good, Bad, Happy or Sad in my life
No event in my life is a coincidence
Nothing happens just by chance
Even decisions I make in a moment of passion
Or seemingly in confusion or indecision
Are all part of God's divine plan for me
I believe , I trust, I submit
To God's will in my life
Because it is part of His plan
To lead my soul to eternal life.

March 7, 2010

Cry of the Soul for Mercy

Out of the depths I cry to you O Lord, Lord hear my voice.
O let your ears be attentive to the voice of my pleading.
If you O Lord, could mark our guilt? Lord who will survive?
I place all my trust in you my Lord,
and I hope in your saving grace.
Lord you know all my iniquities
Lord you know the darkest thoughts of my heart
Lord you know my innermost desires
Lord you know the secret longings of my heart
Lord you know my love is feeble, weak, but true, so true
Consume my soul with the fires of your love,
Burn me with the flames of your divine mercy
And not your justice, O Lord.
I am misery, I am nothingness,
I am unworthy to even be your footstool
Have mercy O Lord...
I give you my sins and the memory of them
Erase them with your precious blood
I place all my trust in you, my Lord
And I hope in your saving grace
Show me your face and
Renew within me a steadfast spirit that I may
live for love of you and die for love of you, Amen!!

April 27, 2010

O Jesus In the most Holy Tabernacle

O Jesus present body and blood, soul and divinity;
 In the most holy tabernacle;
Thank you for loving me, so undeserving;
Thank you for having mercy on me, so undeserving;
Thank you for your blessings on me so undeserving;
Thank you for your goodness to me, so undeserving

O Jesus present body and blood, soul and divinity;
In the most holy tabernacle;
Fill my heart with your light; so deserving;
Ignite my soul with desire to serve you so deserving;
Consume me with trust in you, so deserving;
Inflame my heart with love for you so deserving.

O Jesus present body and blood, soul and divinity;
In the most holy tabernacle; Teach me to love like you do;
Teach me to love my neighbor like you do;
Teach me to be humble like you are;
Teach me to be patient like you are;
Teach me to persevere in my trials like you;
Teach me to live the way of the passion of the cross like you did.

O Jesus present body and blood, soul and divinity;
 In the most holy tabernacle;
Make a home in my heart forever;
Guide my soul through life forever;
May my life be a sacrifice pleasing to your heart forever;
May your light shine through me forever;
May I live for you alone and be dead to the flesh forever.

May 24, 2010

Midday Renewal of Trust in God

I place all my trust in you my God
And hope in your divine mercy
So, let your light shine forth from me

Your divine joy bestow on me O Lord
And wash all my sorrow away from me
And let your light shine forth from me

Your divine mercy bestow me O Lord;
and wash all my sins away from me
And let your light shine forth from me

Your divine wisdom bestow on me O Lord,
And make me an instrument of your peace
And let your light shine forth from me

I believe, I trust and submit to your will
Because you give the best O Lord
To those who let you make the choice

Rearranged May 27, 2010 (originally written by Olachi Mezu in 1993)

My Suffering Love

Knowing and seeing how you suffer my love, hurts me so
Knowing how much you love me,
makes me want to love you even more
Knowing how much you care for your people,
makes me want to care even more
Knowing how much you suffered for me,
makes me want to suffer even more
Knowing how much you forgive of me,
makes me want to forgive even more

Seeing you persecuted Christ,
makes me want to persevere more when persecuted
Seeing you humiliated Christ,
makes me want to remain humble and meek
Seeing you suffering Christ,
makes me want to suffer more for my sins and those of others
Seeing you scorned Christ,
makes me want to endure scorn and derision even more
Seeing you crucified Christ,
makes me want to be nailed at your feet forever
Seeing you sacrificed Christ,
makes me want to offer my life in sacrifice for you
Seeing you dying Christ,
makes me want to die for love of you
Seeing you risen Christ, makes me want to rise to eternal life with you

Does my suffering ease any of your pain, my Love?
Does my agony ease even a second of your agony, my Lord?
Does my pain ease even a pinch of the torture
of one thorn on your head, my Love?
Does my torment ease even a second of pain from your bleeding skin?
May my feeble sacrifice of my weak suffering be pleasing to you Lord
And suffer me to come to you
But never ever leave my side or my heart , O Lord
As I endure all for love of you.
And may no one know or see my suffering, my love
As it is all for you and you alone.   June 9, 2010

Jesus, I Trust in You

Jesus, I trust in you.
 I offer every sad thought, every pain, all my doubts, fears or hopes
To you in reparation for my sins and those of the whole world
I implore you blend my weak and humble offering
with your passion on the cross
That it may make my offering pleasing to God the Father.
I abandon and resign myself to your holy will.
Hide me in your wounds
and no evil arrow or snare shall find me.
Shield me with your love and mercy
and let your justice fall on those that seek my ruin.
As long as my heart is pure and full of love for you,
I will not be afraid
but will always trust in your mercy and goodness.
You alone know the future and
nothing happens to me unless you allow it.
You will only allow what is good for my soul, O Lord.
 I will not worry about dark shadows and gray clouds
 because you are my light and my hope.
 Lead and I will follow you blindly into my future
 because you are all I have and all I need;
and I will be lost without you.
Fill my heart with unshakable faith in you
Embolden me to walk blameless in your light
Because you are my savior and I am your beloved.
Jesus, I trust in you.

June 11, 2010

You Answered

I asked, you answered
I called, you heard
I sought, you found
I knocked, you opened

Sweet Jesus, teach me
To love you even more
More than life itself
More than any creature

Teach me to see
Teach me to hear
Teach me to speak
Teach me to know

Like a child, I am
A babe at heart,
Sweet Mother Mary
Guide and protect me

Wrap me up in your arms
Never let me go
If I fail or falter
Raise me up like your child

I heard your voice in the breeze
In the still of day
In the whisper of the trees
In the blue of the clouds

I heard your voice within me
It's still and calm
It soothes and feels
Like you're always with me

You said you knew me
Through and through
You said you called me
Before I formed in the womb

You said go out
Live the love I give
Give the love I live
And I will give you more

Teach me to love you
Teach me to care
Teach me to live
And die to self

O lord, my God
My God, my all
I'm weak, I'm lacking
But you'll make me whole

I asked, you answered
I called, you heard
I sought, you found
I knocked, you opened

July 17, 2010
During a retreat at Mount St. Mary's Seminary, Emmittsburgh

My Heaven

My Heaven starts today, united with Christ
My heaven starts on earth, suffering with Christ
My heaven starts now, living with Christ

My heaven starts anew, following Christ
My heaven's aglow with love, burning for Christ
My heaven is entombed, buried with Christ

My heaven is forever, risen in Christ
My heaven, O my heaven
Is my soul, entwined with Christ

July 17, 2010
During Retreat at the Mt. St. Mary's Seminary, Emmittsburgh

Adoration and Exposition of the Blessed Sacrament

My Lord Jesus Christ
Present in the Eucharist
Please come, come into heart
When you come inside, my heart will be pure
O good Jesus, please come

Complete what's lacking in me
Save what's lost in me
Heal what's ailing in me
Mend what's broken in me
Ignite what's smothered in me
Raise what's dead in me
Perfect, what's imperfect in me, Lord

Jesus, you are so sweet to me
Jesus you are filled with glory
from the mountains to the valleys
Jesus, you give life unending
Jesus, your love endures forevermore

My Lord Jesus Christ present body and blood,
soul, and divinity in the Blessed sacrament
Please come into my heart, blessed Host
Shine thy face on me, and make my heart pure
O Lord Jesus, please come

July 17, 2010

Where is God? You ask

Look, I found Him
He is in my shadow, following wherever I go
He is in my home, keeping it safe
He is at my work, healing with me
He is in my agony, suffering with me
He is in my worries, soothing my pain
He is in my joy, sharing with me
He is in my hunger, fasting with me
He is in my plenty, feasting with me
He is in my compassion, caring with me
He is in my heart, loving with me
He is in the air, living with me
Where is God? You ask?
I found Him within me.

July 18, 2010
Day 3 of Retreat at Mt St. Mary's Seminary Emmittsburgh

Ascent to Mt. Carmel

God is calling me to Carmel, I thought
Look who He's using to instruct you: the Saints and Patrons of Carmel
"St. Therese of Lisieux, St. Teresa of Avila, St. John of the Cross"
Is it a mere coincidence? Or is it part of God's divine plan
For the salvation of my soul?
Since I have learnt from my life experiences that
Nothing happens to me unless God allows it; so it's not a coincidence

So, to Mt. Carmel, I go; Up to the mountain of the Lord, I ascend
To listen to God in the silence of my heart
He caressed me in the gentle breeze
He enveloped me and hovered with the birds in the air
His majesty blazed in the sun; Igniting my soul with His fire of love

He sends His messenger to speak to my soul
"I cannot say that I discern that which you feel: a call to Carmel.
Your soul is in communion with God
such that your natural and your supernatural are one
You've attained what most seek in years of formation
By using your past to link the puzzles of life and find God at the source
You've found what most come to Carmel to seek -the path to salvation
I cannot say that Carmel is for you."

I believe and trust you, O God's messenger.
God told St. Francis "Repair my church,"
He meant, St. Francis later realized, to repair the spirit of His church
There are indeed no mere coincidences in my life
I herald from Our Lady of Mt. Carmel in the heart of the motherland.
Carmel lives within me and I have been living in Carmel
dedicated to its treasures, now reignited with prior fervor, imbibing
its spirit, charism, and thirst for God's love and evangelization

I came to find Carmel, but Carmel found me
Home I now go with the spirit of Carmel within me
To live and love and Love as I live.   July 17, 2010

Spiritual Adoption: Adopt an Unborn Life – Trust in God's Mercy

"Before I formed you in the womb, I knew you. Before you were born I sanctified you. And I ordained you a prophet to the nations." Jeremiah 1: 5.

This verse refers to you and me, and every unborn child in the mother's womb, whether they are safe and sound through nine months of pregnancy or facing the threat of abortion during the pregnancy from prenatal complications, complications of birth defects or congenital anomalies, threats of premature birth, or even abortion from an unwanted or unplanned pregnancy.

There is no mistake about life. God gives life. Every one of you are special and meant to be here. Every unborn child from conception is special, known by God before conception, and meant to have a right to life.

There is no coincidence in life. Nothing happens to you unless God allows it. Even the mistakes and choices we face are known to God before it happens. They are all part of the plan for our salvation. I was a bonus child... My mother was pregnant with twins without knowing it. There was no ready ultrasound during prenatal checks in the mid to late seventies in Nigeria. I was discovered minutes after my twin sister was born as they were delivering the placenta. I was no mistake or coincidence. He knew me before I was formed in the womb.

An abortion occurs every second in the world. Life is stifled out of an innocent soul every second in the world; a lot of times without the grace of baptism. Mothers are faced daily with difficult, heartbreaking choices.

I am not a pro-life activist. I am not a politician, neither am I a theologian. I am just a mother who has survived the fight for life. I work in a hospital as a neonatal pediatrician, and I witness daily this fight for life as I am called to consult mothers in preterm labor or at risk for premature birth or who have a "non-viable fetus' by medical standards because they are less than 23 weeks of gestation; innocent souls who will not be given the chance to live. I give them the medical statistics, complications, chances of survival, death, or neurodevelopmental ability and prognosis for their baby at the specific gestational age. It brings tears and pain to them; but I also tell them, "all these things don't have to happen to your baby. Every situation is different. Your outcome could be different – no-one knows. You can only have faith and pray." I don't take hope away from them, but let them know of God's mercy and love. I tell them that I've witnessed miracles happen for mothers or parents, and sometimes, things didn't happen as expected. I tell them that through faith and submission to God's will, they will be comforted in knowing that whatever happens is according to God's plan, and not in their hands. Faith works, I know ... because it worked for me.

My story – Miracle of Life: Three years ago, I thought life was good. I had just begun my residency training in pediatrics and started a fellowship in neonatology caring for premature and sick babies. My husband and I had bought our first home, and I was expecting twins: a boy and a girl. I felt complete and thought life couldn't be better. Suddenly, at barely 21 weeks of gestation I was asked to terminate my twin pregnancy due to severe pre-eclampsia that had posed life-threatening complications to me. I was devastated and it seemed my world came crashing down. I was having liver failure, kidney failure, pleural effusions, ascites, at risk of respiratory failure. I could not give up my dreams, my babies, my hopes for the future. I would not give up their lives to save mine.

"Only God gives life. And only him can take life!" I believed that if it was His will to take them, he would have done that in my sleep without my knowledge. "As long as there is life in me," I said," I will not take their lives to save mine." I was told I was unreasonable, and should know better as a physician. These "fetuses" were not viable. They were not getting any placental blood flow and it was impossible for them to survive. I would not give my babies up: I had names for them OlaRose, my daughter and Obiola, my son. OlaRose would die first, I was told. "Let them go, you will have others. If you keep going, you may never have any more babies? Is it worth sacrificing your life for babies you do not know?" Maternal instincts sprung to life in me; and all I could think of was protecting my babies. Against medical advice, I decided to continue the pregnancy and committed my life and theirs to the God of Life. Daily I received his body and blood and my family and friends prayed daily for me.

From my anguish came forth such poignant poetry - me pouring my heart out to God. I stayed on bedrest for about 5 weeks, hoping and praying for a day at a time for them to get bigger and stronger. I talked to them every day, asking them to take care of each other. I asked God to sustain them that whatever trickle of blood they get, is enough for them to sustain their life. My babies were so brave and amazing. Obiola took care of his sister, laying on her for six weeks to keep her warm as she had no blood flow. Twice on the ultrasound at the end of six weeks, when her heart stopped to beat, he was seen kicking her chest, resuscitating her; that I felt was the sign God gave me to know when to have them delivered. OlaRose was declared without a heartbeat, and I was advised to let her die in her sac and keep going another day or two for my son, whose heart rate was already weak and failing. I still refused to choose one baby's life over the other. How does a mother choose her daughter's life over her son's? I committed my life to God's hands believing that the God of life will see them through when born. I chose life! I requested for a C-section. They were both delivered alive and were baptized after three days when Obiola's condition deteriorated; but after 6 days my son died. He was giving up his life for his sister and me. As I held him in my hands in anguish, despite the pain, tears and heartbreak, I felt the real presence of God. I understood in those moments that He knew my pain and all had been done according to His will. I was enveloped with such unimaginable peace in the depths of my sorrow. I believed that God loved me so much, he could not wait to have a part of me with him, so he took my son. I believed God had asked me for the ultimate sacrifice – my son; and through my tears, I freely accepted to offer him that sacrifice and asked our lady to carry him in her bosom and place him eternally in God's arms. God owes me, now, I believed.

The Power of Intercession from souls of Innocence: From that sacrifice I made, God has blessed me abundantly in such an overwhelming degree. My little girl, OlaRose lay one pound in weight, the tiniest baby in the NICU with little or no chance for survival. I was told to expect brain damage, bleeding in her retina that could lead to blindness, infections, etc. I was told she could not hear, and may not walk or talk like other kids if she ever survived. I believed her brother's death was not in vain, and asked him to take care of her, and he did. I asked God for her life, intact with no deficits and my prayers were granted. God gave me my miracle. She came home after 89 days with no oxygen, no surgeries; and she is 3 years old now, vibrant, beautiful, talks up a storm, has no disabilities and is starting Pre-K in two weeks.

I called upon my little angel again when my mother was at the brink of death in February 2008 on a ventilator, in respiratory failure and heart failure. I reminded my son of how his grandmother had prayed for their lives; and asked him for a second miracle from God. I laid his clothes and personal items on my mother and from that day, she was miraculously healed.

On August 4, 2009. I travelled to New York with my parents and sister on a shopping trip to prepare for OlaRose's church Christening when a persistent, throbbing headache stopped our journey home. We ended up at an emergency room seeking help. I had a ruptured brain aneurysm and called upon the mercy of God and aske dmy son, Obiola to intercede for me, his other, as he lay in the arms of God, The Father. I was saved by the divine mercy of God. Through my ordeal, I was overwhelmed with the realization that God loved me. He loved me so much, not because of anything that I had done; but Just because He was love and mercy. He loved me so much that He sent his only son to die for me. That message was so poignant and real in my soul.

Joy of your Gift: I was saved by the divine mercy and through the intercession of my son, Obiola ... my angel in heaven; and all the innocent souls, victims of abortion and prematurity that I had cared for during their very brief lives on earth. My angel in heaven is a constant source of comfort and joy for me. Through that loss, I have gained abundant graces because I fought for his unborn life. Through my pain, I basked in joy. I still suffer with life's daily struggles but I understand now that I suffer because God loves me and wants to raise me to a closer union with him. I let his passion on the cross guide me through life's difficulties.

Spiritual Adoption of the Unborn: Let us adopt an unborn child today in our hearts. Choose any hospital, a city, a state or even any country in the world and visualize your adopted child. Pray for God's divine mercy on that child; pray for that mother in not just physical but emotional pain and suffering that she may find comfort in the knowledge that God loves her. God is merciful and God is near.

God knows all our suffering and pain, let us not suffer in vain: We suffer because God loves us and wants a closer union with us. He allows suffering that we may be purified and sanctified through our suffering; so that in the difficult moments of our life, when we face these life and death choices, we realize our nothingness and turn to Him for help. Let us unite our sufferings to Christ's sacrifice on the cross. Only then can he bestow on us wonderful graces to rise beyond our pain and turn our sorrow into blessings.

It will be done to you according to your faith: Through life's struggles … when we are faced with the fear of death, or abandonment, or lack of material needs such that we think we have no choice but to take an innocent life; let us stop and remember Jesus words:
"Whosoever loses his life for my sake, will gain it!"
"I care for the birds in the air... and the lilies in the field. What more you who mean more to me...?"
Worrying about my babies lives in the womb did not save them? Or mourning the loss of my son, did not bring me comfort? And worrying about my aneurysm and the possibility of dying did not save me. Rather, "Believing in God, trusting in his divine mercy and submitting to His Holy will, did."

Give God your Fear and Trust in Him : As long as your intentions and heart is as pure as these innocent souls, no harm will come to you.
"Lay your burdens on Him.."
"..Even if you walk through the shadow of death, you will not fear...."
"For he has given His angels charge over you to protect you in all your ways"
Even if they kill you, you shall not die... but will have eternal life because: *"he who seeks his life will lose it... and he who loses his life for my sake, shall find it."*

So, do not be afraid of death when making a choice for life because will we all not die one day on this earth? That is for sure. Why not guarantee yourself eternal life by giving God your choices and He will do what is best for your soul. He will fill you with strength to persevere like He did me when you make that choice for life so that even in the face of death, you shall not fear. And that too shall pass, and be a faceless demon, a mere figment of your imagination, part of the memories of yesterdays.

On Thursday July 22, 2010, I was undergoing an intense struggle in my soul and needed to be reminded of God's love and mercy. I knew God was real and I should trust in him, but I was still troubled and decided to pay a visit to my little angel, Obiola; after which I knelt at the altar at St. Charles Borromeo, Pikesville, MD on my way to work one and asked God for a sign of his love to remind me to always trust in Him; and that I should not worry about anything and that this suffering too shall pass.

At 10:15 p.m. that night at work, I was paged to the labor and delivery ward to evaluate a baby born at home. I got there and saw a beautiful full term baby girl. The story I was told was shocking: the young mother did not know she was pregnant, gave birth suddenly in the bathroom, ripped the umbilical cord apart and threw this baby out of a second story window to the hard ground. This baby survived without any bruising, cuts or scratches or broken bones – a true miracle indeed. As I took the baby away to care for her, I felt moved or compelled to speak to the mother even though I really didn't want to. I was mortified at what she had done; but I decided to speak to the mother so I could get some information that may help me care for the baby. Every one of the medical staff was staring at her with venom, disgust, anger, disbelief, and hatred for her. She agreed to speak with me, because I said I was the doctor going to care for her baby. She answered all my questions very honestly. As I spoke to her, I was strongly aware that God loved her too and had shown her mercy. He had saved her life despite her actions because not only the baby could have bled to death, she too could have bled to death. She appeared helpless and emotionally tortured to me. I was moved to be gentle and compassionate with her, despite the horrific act she had committed against this defenseless baby. She had tears in her eyes as she looked at me; and as I talked gently with her.

It was when a nurse in the NICU asked why this baby was brought a whole hour to our hospital from the home instead of other hospitals, in my soul I suddenly had an answer: she came to see me. I suddenly, felt in my heart that God had answered my prayers: "If he could care for this innocent soul who had not even asked for His help? What more me?" God was reminding me to trust in Him ... like this baby girl. As long as your heart and intentions are pure like this innocent child, nothing will happen to you. "Even if they kill you ... you will not die ... I will give my angels charge over you." Imagine one minute safe and sound in your mother's womb and the next flying out the window ... And this baby knew no fear."

Can we trust like this child? Can we give God our fear? Can we adopt an innocent baby spiritually in our hearts each day. When we spiritually adopt a child, let us pray for God to save him or her and for God to bring strength and full realization of His love and mercy to those mothers faced with heartbreaking, terrifying decisions that tempt them to take innocent lives.

"That life could have been another OlaRose, Obiola or this Miracle baby girl – they are all miracle babies (either for being born alive at an extremely low birth weight; surviving prematurity or for surviving abortion). Even if the baby dies, let us pray that our adopted babies are given dignity in their last moments through the grace of baptism that they may enjoy fullness of life with God in heaven and be source of graces to us on earth through their intercessions."

"Before I formed you in the womb... I knew you through and through, and I called you to be mine..." God is real! He will do amazing, beautiful things in your life if only you will let him! So when faced with difficult choices ... Offer it to God because he gives the best to those who let Him make the choice in their lives.

So let us believe, trust and submit to His Holy Will.

August 15, 2010

The Call

I hear it daily, in the depths of my soul
Your voice, Your call, Your musings with my soul
It sounds as clear as day, and persists through the night
I know and feel within me, with every fiber of my being
That you are speaking to me
Yours is that tiny, soft voice deep within my soul
Not the loud rantings of the deceiver lurking outside my soul
It's a daily battle that rages within me
Between the spirit and the flesh

Only God knows my soul,
Only God knows the contents of my heart
Only God understands me;
Only God never tires of listening to the ramblings of my soul;
Only God can heal me;
Only God can strengthen me;
His grace is enough for me;
Only God can satisfy the longings of my soul;
Only God is enough for me;
Only God believes me;
Only God reassures me;
Only God can comfort me;
Only God can protect me.

I am not afraid, even though the evil one is lurking;
I feel his angry breath; I sense his tireless conniving plots;
I will not fear, even though the evil one is howling;
I hear his angry rants; I sense his wicked taunts;
I will put on the whole armor of God in this battle for my soul;
For he has given His angels charge over me, his beloved.
He is all I want and all I need;
He wants an intimate union with my soul;

On earth, I will suffer in small and big things;
In little and mighty things; but I will not tire to seek God's will;
because that is the way to my salvation;
the way of the passion of the cross;

I suffer because He loves me;
He allows suffering my way that I may be purified.
My tears will be turned to joy;
My pain will be turned to bliss;
Even if my body rots and dies; I will live forever
because the spirit of God dwells in me .

You chose me, though I am unworthy
You called me and I answered: here I am, Lord
I've come to do your will
Take my lips and make them thine;
You sent me, and will give me the words to speak;
 I will not fear as I do your work;
You have asked for my hands that you may heal;
My legs that you may go to your people in need;
My lips that you may speak;
My hands that you may write;
My soul that you may love;

Take me Lord and do with me as you please;
My life is not my own; but Christ that lives anew in me.
So, though they kill me, I will not die.
Pain, suffering, humiliations, persecutions will be my lot,
that my soul may not become elated, for my life is not my own;
I am nothing and can do nothing
except through Christ who lives in me.
You have taught me from your lips;
You have instructed my soul with your words;
You have directed me through your servants;
Use me Lord as you please, that all may give glory to your name;
My life is a witness, a testimony of your love and mercy;
I am feeble, weak, lacking in knowledge and courage;
So unworthy of your love and graces I am
but you still chose me Lord, and called me to your side
and You will complete what is lacking in me because you are almighty.
By my faith, it will be done to me.
So, I believe, I trust and I submit to your Holy will, O Lord.

August 20, 2010   @ 3 a.m.

You are Real

Lord, you're real and you are so good (2x)
Don't you know that all I have is yours and you're mine (2x)
Lord, you're real and you're so good (2x)
Lord, I give myself to you (2x)
Never ever leave me (2x)
Never ever leave me, or I will die
You are real and you're so good (2X) *(lyrics written 1994)*

You are real, O God
A real presence in my life
A tangible essence around me
In you I move, breathe and have my being
You are so real, I can feel you
Your breathe is my spirit Lord
You are so close to me, I can touch you
You are no longer invisible to me
You are not a spirit floating around
You are not a figment of my imagination
You are not a hammer of justice
But a father so loving and merciful
Who cares truly for me and provides for my daily needs
A Love so faithful and enduring
Who loves me even more when I go astray
You are the here and the now
You are in the start and end of my day
You are in all I meet
You speak to me through all I meet
You speak to me through all I hear
You are real O God

August 20, 2010

A Sacrifice

I give you my hurt; I give you my pain
I give you my thirst for vengeance
I give you my quest for justice
I give you my broken heart; I give you my unrequited love
I give you my anger; I give you my emotions
I give you my sorrow; I give you my anguish
I give you my fear; I give you my anxieties
I give you my doubts; I give you my worries

I offer it all In unison to Christ's sacrifice on the cross
That you may look upon it with mercy
And let your light of love and salvation, shine down on me
Through my suffering, I will be purified
Bearing my trials patiently, I will be sanctified
Hiding my pain and resisting defending myself against false witnesses
who tarnish my good name, I will gain eternal life
 In my agony, I recall your meekness and patience
through your own agony and passion
So trusting in your divine mercy and your victory over death
I will persevere amidst the fire and brimstone, all for your glory
For as long as my heart is pure, no harm shall come to me
Even if they kill me, I shall not die

No human words can comfort me
No human being can know my pain
No human can know the truth of my life
But you and I O Lord, know
You are my witness; A witness to the truth
A witness to my love; A witness to my sacrifice

I leave vengeance to you; I leave justice to you
I will show mercy, as you have shown me mercy
For what do I profit on earth
If my pain and sorrow is acknowledged by all
If justice is given me over my enemies
What then have I left, for God to bless me with
He only rewards the pain that no one sees

He only blesses the sorrow that no one feels
He only avenges the injustices that no one ends
He only comforts the tears that no one sheds

So my pain, I will hold on to
My cross I will bear
Each lie I will endure
And let God gather my victories
like roses for each thorn in my flesh
To make a crown for me in heaven
For that is the purpose of life
To suffer and die to self
For the sake of Christ
For so did the world treat Him
Why do I want to be different.
If I claim I love Him

I will do whatever you ask of me Lord
I will bear whatever pain you wish me to, lord
If I knew what you want me to do
I will do it and not care if I died, lord
So, speak to me that I may know your will, Lord
I give up my yearning for vengeance and justice, Lord
As long as I know you're with me, Lord
To the truth alone I will cling, Lord
Not caring that arrows fly
Not caring that the path is strewn with thorns
And wait for his saving grace to shield me through the storms of life

So, sweet Jesus, my love and savior
I give you my tears; I give you my broken heart
I give you my thorns; I give you my dark nights
I give you my doubts and fears
A weak and unworthy sacrifice it is
But with your saving blood shed so dear
You will make it eternal and pleasing to God the Father
A sacrifice of Life, Amen!

August 29, 2010

You are my God, in whom I Trust

I am nothing, you are everything
I am helpless, you are almighty
I know nothing, you are all-knowing
I can do nothing, you can do everything
I am full of sin, you are purity
I am a wicked soul, You are my merciful God
You are my God, in whom I trust

Any good in me, comes from you
Any kindness in me, comes from you
Any skill in me, comes from you
Any knowledge I have, comes from you
You are my God, in whom I trust

Take my life, and make it thine
Use me as you will
Use me for your work
Take my lips, and make it thine
Speak through me, what you will
Let your words, touch each heart
You are my God, in whom I trust

Friends and Foe alike plot against me
My hard work is ignored and unseen
My innocent weaknesses amplified and ridiculed
The evil one lurks and seeks my ruin
My sin is always before me; In God I trust and hope
I seek no vengeance, I bear no grudges
Even if they kill me, I will not die
You are my God, in whom I trust

I fear not hurtful words
I fear not humiliations, persecutions
I fear not false witnesses and unfair accusations
I fear not stretched truths and untruths

I fear not heard and unheard evil murmurings
You are my God, in whom I trust

In your wounds Lord, I will hide
Where no flying arrows can reach
With your saving blood, I am purified
As long as my intentions and my heart are pure
I will not fear, but trust in the Lord my God
So this cross I patiently bear
It too shall pass, like the others
You are my God, in whom I trust

I will not defend myself, you shall send a defender
I will not avenge myself, you shall send an avenger
I speak only to uphold the truth and morality
The devil wants to make me despair
He wants to make me abandon
the work of life, healing and mercy you do through me
I will persevere like a soldier and keep my post
For I battle not with flesh and blood
But against principalities and beings in high places
Till you reassign me to another, my post I will keep
You are my God, in whom I trust

I will smile through the tears
I will be brave through the fear
I will be patient through the chaos
because I know you are with me through my daily trials
Giving me strength, giving me hope
Nothing happens to me unless God allows it
So I believe in your love; I trust in your divine mercy
And I submit to your Holy will O Lord
Because you give the best to me
when I let you make the choice in my life.
You are my God, in whom I trust

September 11, 2010

Use your unworthy servant to do your Will

I am so aware of how unworthy I am.
I am going into the midst of people more knowledgeable
People more spiritual and steadfast in the faith than I am;
People more experienced clinically than I am.
Who am I to tell them about compassion or God's divine mercy.

I am an unworthy servant, O Lord;
but you picked me out of Your goodness for your work of mercy.
Not for anything I did or deserved or merited;
but just because you are goodness and mercy itself.
You did not reign your justice on me or my chances run out
I still stray and offend you despite your wondrous works in my life.
But, as long as there is life in me,
I will keep striving for the perfection you wish for your children.

I am a willing servant, O lord; I've come to do your will.
Guide my feet; teach me your words and give me your countenance.
Speak to me Lord, your servant heareth.
I hear your voice in my spirit, and try to act as you have willed.
If my actions are not according to your will;
It's not from pride, but that my feeble mind misunderstood your will

Use then , Almighty Lord, every person or thing at your disposal
to guide me, my feet, thoughts, words and actions back
along the path of your will; the road to salvation.
Be there thorns, suffering, wailing, abandonment or deprivation
I gladly will suffer here on earth, to resemble my crucified Christ
so as to enjoy eternal bliss in heaven with you.

Fill my being with your spirit that I may speak your truth and love
may go forth and bear fruit in the hearts of all listening.
Speak to each soul that all may feel your love and hear your words
For the greater honor and glory of your name.
Use your unworthy servant Lord, to accomplish your will.

September 13, 2010

Invited Speaker - Johns Hopkins Hospital Town Hall:
Mercy and Compassion: The Heart of Medicine –Personified in Dr. Judy Huang

"Don't worry, I'll take care of you." Words of comfort and hope; Words of mercy and compassion - from a total stranger - sight unseen. Dr. Judy Huang embodies the true heart of medicine. She is my hero and has, not only given me a second chance at life, but a chance to live each day as if it were my last.

My ordeal that day, traumatic, but memorable is always before me. After a goodbye kiss to my two year old daughter, OlaRose, a one pound birth weight surviving twin baby; I left Maryland with my father, mother and elder sister on a shopping trip to New York. On our way back, I had the worst headache of my life, and my family stopped at a New Jersey Pharmacy at 10 p.m. at night, to check my blood pressure and it was alarmingly high. The Pharmacist, closed in a hurry and refused to call an ambulance. My sister, Dr. Nina Nwaba, a Pharmacist, then called 911 from her cell phone, and I was rushed to a nearby hospital. A CT scan was normal; and I was being discharged by the ER doctor when my younger sister, Dr. Ure Mezu, a cardiologist, called on the phone requesting a lumbar puncture to rule out brain bleeding. It showed some red cells which concerned me. The ER Physician refused my pleas to transfer to another hospital for neurosurgical consult; but I could not ignore the persistent thought in my mind – **you are bleeding in your head**! My family and I made frantic unsuccessful calls: it was too late at night; the professional liability of a potentially-fatal condition too risky – no one could help us. Scared and in severe pain in the ER at 3 am of August 4th, 2009, we said the "divine mercy" prayer and suddenly I remembered a number to Johns Hopkins Transport Line that I had used to transfer a baby a few days earlier; so I called it with my cell phone asking for a neurosurgeon, trying to transfer myself. Hearing my desperate plea, Dr. Huang spoke those words of comfort and hope.

Dr. Huang was "an angel in human form;" truly God-sent in my time of need. She acted bravely without fear or bias to help a total stranger, breaking the barriers of bureaucracy, making life-saving decisions without delay. Rules are made for people; not people for rules! She immediately sent a helicopter for me and on arrival to Hopkins, had ordered a STAT cerebral angiogram for a quick and accurate diagnosis.

A ruptured brain aneurysm was found, and my only hope for survival was immediate surgical clipping. I was faced with the most terrifying moment of my life. Do I hope in the unknown? or give in to the anxieties of the now? I thought about unfulfilled dreams? I thought about my heartbroken family, I would be leaving behind. I hugged my daughter, OlaRose, close to my heart and she wiped away my tears. I thought about my little angel in heaven, her twin brother, Obiola. "Mummy loves you," I said; 'I would love to see you again but not just yet. I need to take care of your sister. Put your tiny arms around God the Father, and beg Him for my life. I will dedicate my work as a neonatal pediatrician to Him and glorify Him in all I do - There are so many tiny ones like you to be saved in the NICU. He can use me as He pleases, if He grants me my life back, intact." At the 3 p.m. hour, my family and I said the "divine mercy" and made our petitions to God.

My hope in a miracle were strengthened by not only my family's prayers but Dr. Huang's comforting presence, kind and unhurried words. In a professional and empathic way, without diminishing the life-threatening risks I faced, she explained the nature of the aneurysm, surgery and potential complications, including risk of severe neurological deficits, if I survived. Though I was terrified, her honest, calm, and gentle demeanor gave me such confidence in her that it inspired me to be strong and will to live. Her caring non-verbal cues greatly reassured my family: from her warm smile, gentle touch when I reached out, agreeing to pray with me and my family; to a warm hug when I needed one. A stranger no more, I trusted her with my life. Closing my eyes, I thanked God for the compassionate people caring for me.

I woke up from the almost 8 hour surgery, overwhelmed with the knowledge that God loves me...not for anything I did …. just because He is love and mercy itself. I had no neurological deficits, and felt renewed in my body and spirit. Dr. Huang has made God so real to me - He is a compassionate and loving Father who knows our needs and uses everything or person at his disposal to accomplish His will. Through her compassionate heart; the mercy of God flowed to me. Through her skillful hands, the power of God healed me. God allows suffering in our lives to bring us closer to Him, for a greater good we may not see now. Suffering is part of our humanity, through which we see our weaknesses; and see the pain of others. Through suffering, we partake in His divinity, by our ability to show mercy to others.

The neurosurgical team at Johns Hopkins Hospital showed mercy to me through their outstanding, compassionate patient-centered care; astute and quick to anticipate my medical needs: from the kind, swift transport team, to the gentle and precise neuro-radiologists; to the anesthesiologist who reassured me in the operating room that he and his team would be calm, gentle, and safe; to the skillful and efficient neurosurgery physicians; to the dedicated nurse practitioners; to the young neurosurgical critical care unit (NCCU) nursing staff who were efficient and nurturing in their care; to the kind case managers and very patient therapists. The staff were sensitive and accommodating to my family's needs; recognizing that loved ones are essential to the healing process. Discharged after 9 days, my survival and complete recovery was indeed a miracle to the joy of me and my family.

As a physician, I have worked in several hospitals; or been a patient or at the sick bed of loved ones; and I have never seen such an excellent combination of gentle, compassionate and efficient care as I received at the Johns Hopkins Hospital. Leading her team excellently to meet the unique challenges of my case; Dr. Judy Huang has rejuvenated my faith in the medical profession and inspired me to be the best physician I can be.

Dr. Huang was humble and uninhibited by ego: Does pride get in the way of our delivery of healthcare to patients and deprive our patients of life-saving interventions?
Dr. Huang was kind and filled with compassion: Do we when we see a suffering patient, take the time to hold a hand, acknowledge their pain and ask what we can do for them?
Dr. Huang was dedicated and filled with empathy: Do we make our patients feel like the most important people in the world? Seeing me laying helpless and in pain before the surgery, she thought to herself : this could be me? Do we, in our care of patients, think: this could be me, my sister or brother, my mother or father, my son or daughter?

Humility; Compassion, Empathy - can be the difference between life or death. We can't save them all, but our job doesn't end there. Through our compassion, they will feel God's divine mercy. Through our touch, they will feel His arms of love. Through our voice, they will hear His words of comfort and hope, like the uplifting words of Dr. Judy Huang: **"Don't worry, I'll take care of you!"**

Thank you, Dr. Huang; Thank you to the entire Johns Hopkins University Hospital: President Peterson, Dean Miller, Dr. Brem, Chair of Neurosurgery; all Department Chairs; Attending Physicians, Fellows, Residents, Nursing Staff, students and all medical and auxilliary staff. May the good Lord reward you all for your kindness and compassion to those in need. Thank you.

By Dr. Olachi Mezu-Ndubuisi

September 14, 2010

Dr. Olachi Mezu-Ndubuisi was the Invited Speaker at The Johns Hopkins Hospital Town Hall: "Mercy and Compassion: The Heart of Medicine – Personified in Dr. Judy Huang" where she addressed the entire Johns Hopkins University Hospital Community:- President Peterson, Dean Miller, Dr. Brem, Chair of Neurosurgery, Department Chairs, Attending Physicians, Fellows, Residents, Nursing Staff, students and most medical and auxilliary staff. Over 500 people attended the session. There is available on the internet a Johns Hopkins University video on the neuro-surgery.

Ruptured Brain Aneurysm | Video Gallery | **Johns Hopkins** ...
http://www.hopkinsmedicine.org/neurology_neurosurgery/news/videos/judy-huang-olachi-mezu.html

Ruptured Brain Aneurysm | Dr. **Olachi Mezu**'s Story - **YouTube**
https://www.youtube.com/watch?v=G3LetQqBzJ4

My Suffering is turned to Joy

I am suffering so deeply, yet my soul is bursting with joy and delight
I am in severe pain, yet my spirit is overwhelmed with bliss
I am drinking the cup of gall, yet my soul is tasting honey
I am drowning in turbulent waters,
yet my spirit is still and unperturbed
I am blinded by darkness and fog,
yet my soul is illumined, beaming with light
I am surrounded by dark, ominous clouds,
yet my spirit is at peace and clear
I am thrown in the lion's den, yet my soul is brave and calm
I am being chased by a pack of wolves,
yet my spirit glides with tranquility
I am trapped and caught in a snare, yet my soul is free and light
I am weighed down by the cross, yet my spirit feels light as a feather

How can this be that my life seemingly is over,
but my soul is born anew
This can only be because of the love and mercy of God
The assurance of the knowledge that God loves me
I am the beloved of the Father; and whoever suffers for His sake
Though he loses his life, shall gain it
Though he dies, shall live forever.
Thus my suffering is turned into joy
My cross into a blessing
Through my suffering, I am purified
And I offer it up in unison with the sacrifice on the cross
All for the greater honor and glory of God, Amen!

September 19, 2010

My Soul Glorifies You, Lord

My soul glorifies you, O my God
You have loved me so unworthy
You have lifted me up so fallen
You have washed my sins so hateful
You have shown mercy on me so wretched
You have spoken to me, so speechless
You have humbled me, so proud
You have enlightened me so dark
You have strengthened me so weak
You have calmed me so anxious
You have honored me so lowly
By allowing me to share in your passion and sacrifice on the cross
By giving me the strength to bear persecutions and hostility
By giving me the meekness to bear false accusations and witnesses By
giving me the courage to suffer unjustly all for love of you
You have turned my pain and sorrow into joy
Because I accepted your Holy will in my life.
Through my suffering, I am purified
Through my crosses, I am blessed
Through my death to self, I will gain eternal life

Am I so blameless? So when I suffer and the world mocks me
And denies me credit for my hard work
And tarnishes my good name
I accept all humbly and patiently
for my savior suffered same before me and He was truly blameless
With my sinful nature, I deserve even more
But you my Lord only give me a cross as much as I can bear

Thank you Jesus for honoring me
I carry this cross for you willingly through the thorny paths
With your precious blood you bought my salvation
Thank you for loving me so unworthy
And as I suffer, I love you more;
My soul glorifies you, O my God

September 24, 2010

Plea for Protection (Adoration in the Holy Tabernacle)

Wrap your arms around me my Lord;
Though the world is caving in on me, I will not lose heart;
I trust in you with all my heart,
I have such confidence in your love and protection.

They are all more powerful than me.
I am going like a lamb into a den of wolves.
They want to engulf me like flames or drown me like an ocean.
Their snares are set ready to entrap and catch me in a deadly grip.

Save me O lord; Give me courage to persevere as I suffer for you.
Let my silence amongst them, speak loud of your love.
Let my meekness amongst them, show all your might.
Let my compassion melt their mean spirit to ardent love for you.
Lord, take my lips and make them thine
Let all happen to me according to your word and yours alone.

Speak to me my Love, comfort your servant with your words
I open your word seeking comfort
With tears of joy, I hear your voice - the word of my Lord

**Baruch 4: 30 -34: *Take courage, O Jerusalem, for he who named you
will comfort you. Wretched will be those who afflicted you and
rejoiced at your fall…For just as she rejoiced at your fall and was glad
for your ruin,so she will be grieved at her own desolation.***
 **Baruch 5: 1-4: *Take off the garment of your sorrow and affliction, O
Jerusalem, and put on forever the beauty of the glory from God.
…For God will show you splendor everywhere under heaven…***

I close the bible as light and peace flood my heart
O the word of my Lord, deep within my being
Your word is spirit and truth, O Lord.
Your word is steadfact and endures through all the ages
Thank you for your love; Thank you for hearing my plea
I will praise your name forever.

September 30, 2010

Plea for Mercy (Adoration in the Holy Tabernacle)

Kneeling in the presence of my Lord and savior, I pay homage.
I recognize my miserable state; the sinfulness in me
and how I deserved everything that is happening to me and more.
My persecutions as agonizing as they are
are ameliorated because of God's mercy, I realize now.
If they were to know the true state of my soul
How I have not done my duties with the perfect charity and love God
demands of me and with the perfect dedication I should,
They would have more to say about me to add to my deficiencies.
I am saddened and horrified as I get full awareness and knowledge
Of all the hidden places in my heart, known to only me and God
Suppressed by me but now exposed to the light of my soul by God.

O, Jesus; I am a sinful soul and nothing but misery
But you are my savior and Lord.
How can you save , if there is no sinful soul to purify?
I do not commit my sins willfully,
but out of weakness as a human being,
I sometimes lack of vigor, carelessness,
nonchalance, and sometimes ignorance
For I do not know all I should to do my best
But you O lord are all knowing and all powerful.

I hide my sinful self in your wounds
so the wrath of God will not find me
as you shield me in your sacred wounds.
Wash my iniquities away with your saving blood
and accept my feeble offering.
I offer you my tears, my suffering, my pain,
the humiliations and derisions I face now
from men who delight and gloat in my misfortune.
I offer you my fears and doubts as I face
the power and knowledge of these influential people
as they plot and seek my ruin
and do not want to hear or accept the truth about the dignity of life;
The need for compassion in service of the sick
and among those caring for them,

because the sick and dying and helpless are truly you, O God.
As humans we become like you in suffering
and you are closest to us in suffering.

Do not let them laugh at me and say your God has forsaken you?
Where is the God you serve? He has abandon you to the wolves?
I know you have not abandoned me?
You are even closer to me when I suffer
You are in my heart loving and strengthening me through it all
Through the witness of my love in suffering,
they come to know you and live your love in their lives and work
You have chosen me so unworthy to proclaim this message.
What is lacking in me, O God you will complete.

Help me seek knowledge so as to be able to do your work
and only for that reason; not for any earthly purpose or gain
or human respect or accolade. For they are nothing.
As they give it, so do they take it.
But when you O Lord reward my love and efforts
with a crown of thorns on earth, you never take it away,
but transform it into a crown of glory in your honor
in this life and for all eternity.

O Queen of heaven, my mother,
I call on your protection against the evil one.
I implore your intercession and guidance
in knowing the will of your son and following it.
I seek your graces to help me in living out my faith, Amen.

October, 1, 2010.

I Adore You, my Lord

I adore you O my Lord, my Savior, my Love
I adore your sweet crown of thorns, my Lord
I adore your gentle, sorrowful gaze, my Lord
I adore the precious wounds on your hands and feet, my Lord
I adore the brave wound on your side, my Lord
I adore your glorious frail body on the cross, my Lord
I adore your sacred heart filled with mercy, my Lord
I adore every drop of your priceless blood shed so dear, my Lord
I adore your passion, death and resurrection, my Lord
I adore your body, blood, soul and divinity present within me and
in all the tabernacles of the whole world,
through the end of time, my Lord

October 7, 2010
During Holy Hour and Divine Mercy Devotion

I Trust you, Lord

I trust you at sunrise
I trust the path I walk
Cause you laid it out for me

I trust you at noon
I trust the cross I bear
Cause you picked it just for me

I trust you at sunset
I trust the divine mercy I receive
Cause you shed it for my sins

I trust you at my bedtime
I trust my soul in your care
Cause you will bring it to eternal life

I trust you with my thoughts and dreams
I trust you with my joys and suffering
Cause you take away my cares

I trust you with my thorns
I trust you with my trials
Cause you transform them into graces for me

I trust you with my past and present
I trust you with my future and eternity
Cause your divine plan is for the good of my soul

I trust you, Lord with my life
I trust you with my love
Cause you sanctify me with your being

October 7, 2010

Discerning The Will of God in my Life

Where are you Lord? What do you want from me?
I cannot see your face; I cannot hear your voice?
What is your will in my life? What will you have me do now?
My days are filled with thoughts of you
My nights are filled with thoughts of you,
My dreams are filled with thoughts of you,
 I wake up with thoughts of you

I am seemingly lost in a thick forest of darkness.
I am blind and paralyzed;
I do not know the way and cannot see through the dark;
I lay helpless waiting for your word;
I am not afraid and do not despair, but trust in you with all my heart.

I believe in your love Lord; I trust in your divine mercy, Lord.
I know that you are close to me when I suffer;
I know you are right here with me even in the eerie silence

Shine down just a tiny ray of light in my soul and I will follow it blindly
I only need to hear a whisper of your voice to go towards the sound
I only need to feel your breath in the air to strengthen my worn body
I only need to see a crack of opening on the thicket to crawl through
Do not reveal your full majesty, O Lord
For my mortal mind and heart cannot bear it all
But only allow just a little light, thought, path, O lord,
to reveal your will and voice to me.

One day at a time; step by step, I will thread the path
You have destined for me.
If I stray, please close the door shut to block my way
and redirect me yourself through signs, people,
or opening of doors you will.
I want to follow your will because it is good for my soul
and will lead me to eternal life.

October 9, 2010

Do with Me What You Please

Do with me what you please
Deal with me according to your will
Let it be done to me according to your word
I submit to your Holy will
I give you my free will with all my heart
Because I trust you with my life, soul, my eternity

You never change, O Lord
Your word is true and eternal
As the day turns to night
And winter into spring
As childhood turns to youth
And adulthood to old age
You remain the same O Lord

As human praise turns to persecution
As love turns to ingratitude
As good is repaid with evil
As plenty turns to deprivation
As possessions are gained and lost
You are a constant and unchanging O Lord

You my God are true and unchanging
Steadfast in your word and promises.
I believe my sufferings will pass
and my sorrow will be turned to joy
In my toil, I will preserve with love and trust in God
Uniting my cross with yours divine
Seeking to glorify you in all I do
My ever-faithful, unchanging God

This too shall pass, like the others
I will offer it up to God above
For Him to turn my cross into His glory
That it may be done to me according to his word
Because the eternal word lives on forever

I have a mission to fulfil to God
and I also made promises to God to glorify him in my work
To praise Him in all I do;
and He can use me as he pleases.
So if it please Him to send me suffering,
I accept it and welcome it with all my heart.
If it please him to send me pain, I rejoice in it.
If it pleases him to send me joy, plenty and peace,
I accept it with thanks and glorify Him too
and fill my heart with trust knowing that
Even though the suffering is around the corner,
after it also comes relief and peace and joy in God's love.

So I accept both with love and trust from God:
the suffering and joy.
These are the path to my salvation and the way of the cross.
Please do with me whatever you will, Lord
As long as you keep my heart and soul close to yours,
I will not be afraid.
I will never fear mortal pain, suffering or loss
Because you are my everything and
Without you I am nothing
So please do with me as you please.

October 16, 2010

Who Compares To You

Who compares to you, lord?
Who can I say is like you?
No –one on earth or in heaven can compare to your majesty
The heaven is your throne; The earth your footstool
The clouds are your shawl; The grass your slipper

You own all; Human power pales in comparison
You know all; Human knowledge is insignificant
Man in your image is a mere glimpse of your shadow

Why would I fear anyone on earth or in heaven
Why would I fear spirit or human
When you say yes, no one can say No!
So why would I fear evil deeds of mere mortals
If with a breath from you, they cease to exist
Eternity for you is but a second
So I will trust and wait for your word to come to me
Who compares to you, my Lord?
There is none like your majesty

You strengthen the weak and comfort the afflicted
You disenthrone kings and exalt the lowly
I praise you O God with all my heart!
My lips will forever sing your praises O God!
Evil men believe they have all the power and I am nothing
They seek to crush me in my honest defiance of their injustice!
They do not know I am the beloved of the Lord
The cherished daughter of your majesty
But you O God will show them your might
and your name will be glorified across the earth
because He who trusts in the Lord will never be put to shame.
Who compares to you, O lord?
No-one in heaven or on earth.

October 16, 2010

Invocation to the name of Jesus in the Eucharist

My incarnate Jesus, make your cradle in my heart
My baptized Jesus, renew yourself in my heart
My miraculous Jesus, transform your bread into life in my heart
My transfigured Jesus, transform yourself in my heart
My crucified Jesus, suffer with me in my heart
My resurrected Jesus, rise to life in my heart
My ascended Jesus, be glorified eternally in my heart

October 16, 2010

Daily Invocation to Know and do God's Will

I pray for the grace to know God's will
I just need to want to do God's will,
I just need to take a step towards it no matter how daunting, and God
will direct me
and give me the strength to do His will
and complete what is lacking in me
so as to accomplish His work for His honor and glory
and the salvation of my soul.
So help me Lord.

October 20, 2010

OlaRose's Daily Invocation

God is enough for me
I don't need anything
I have Jesus in my heart
Jesus 4 years old, be my friend

October, 2011

Finding the Path : A Dialogue with My Lord and My Mother

No-one knows the mind of Christ
or can boast of knowing God's will:
we can only pray for guidance
in making the right decisions or taking right steps
and if we stray, to be redirected according to God's designs.
That He close the wrong doors
and open the right doors to the path He wants for us.
Even if things do not go our way,
God's way is always the best as only it can lead us to eternal life.

I longed to feel God's presence and hear his voice
and suddenly, it seemed that I did during mass
I was one with the spirit and felt at peace and warm and loved by God.
I felt him speaking to me, saying :

Even if you do not feel me,
I am always with you till the end of time.
Even if you cannot hear me and the world is against you
and everything goes wrong, I am right by your side.
Reach out and touch me ; call and I will answer you.
You are my beloved, my chosen one, my daughter, my spouse.
In you I live and move and will accomplish great things
If you give me your free will
and let me take control of your life.
There will be hardships, you will be mocked and abandoned
and men will lose respect for you
but through it all I will be glorified.

I love you Jesus.
Only God can make the world out of nothing
and make the impossible, possible.
If this is your will Lord, so be it.
If it is not, redirect me Lord.
I want this only so I can do your will
and be an instrument of your love and mercy.

I felt our lady was calling me to her.

She was beckoning to me to lean on her through my trials.
Mary my mother says:
My child come to me… do not be afraid.
I will give you strength. I will protect you and lead you to my son.
Honor me and I will shield you and give you victory over the devil,
the flesh and the world. Let nothing disturb you.
I love you and I am your mother .. come to me my child.

Blessed Mother… pray for me…
I turn to you for help.. make haste to help me.
Lead me to your son and the eternal life He promises.
Show me how best to serve him on earth.
You know his heart, his will is most united to yours.
You were his mother and he has raised you
above all men, angels and saints in heaven or on earth.
Give me the grace to persevere and rejoice in suffering
and trust implicitly in your son and seek His will in my life.
Rid me of pride and inclination to sin and
 make me humble as you were
that the grace of God may reside in me as it did in you.
O Mary conceived without sin, pray for us.

I did not feel abandoned by God, but though I felt I did not know
what he truly wanted for me to do next.
I still trust in Him and will wait patiently as He lingers
 And I will keep on moving and forging ahead
 till he shine His light and I realize
 that the path I have been trudging blindly on,
is the actual path he had made just for me since the beginning of time.
I opened my bible to 2 Maccabees 6: 16-17: …
"Therefore he never withdraws his mercy from us.
Though he disciplines us with calamities,
he does not forsake his own people…"

I smiled and praised God; He would never forsake me.
Discovering that random verse was again
an affirmation of God's presence and providence in my life.
I offer all my trials, joys and suffering, humiliations, anxieties, fears
and uncertainties, disappointments and successes to you Lord

In union with the sacrifice of the mass
That it may be pleasing to you.
I believe, I trust and I submit to your Holy Will.

Do not be afraid my child. Do you not see that I am with you everyday in your soul…In everyone you encounter… in their souls I am physically present in the Eucharist, body, blood, soul and divinity.

Yes, Lord.. you are in my heart everyday
and reinforced through communion.
Help me when I encounter people in my life
to see you in them as you have revealed to me.
When I see the sick, needy, the hurt, anguished by physical, spiritual
or mental needs that I may soothe them, nurture them, care for them,
give them hope and thereby renew their faith in you.
When they look at me, may they see your love and mercy
When they think of me, may they know your goodness and love.
When they speak with kind or hurtful words, may I see your grace,
Allowing me to practice virtues of patience, forgiveness and love
 and grow in faith and sanctity so that when my life is over ,
I will indeed see you face to face my Lord and my God..

Mary, my mother, teach me to love your son
daily more and more Take my troubles to him.
You know them even before I speak of them
like a mother knows her child.
Your son will not refuse anything you ask of him.
Please I entrust my life and my soul to you
that you may safeguard it from the evil one
As you crush the serpent's head with your heel, help me overcome
And the battle of life over, place my soul
 in the bosom of your son for all eternity.
I believe, I trust, I submit to your Holy will, O Lord

December 11, 2010

Ode to Mary, Queen Mother and Mediator with Christ her Child

Sweet Mother, Vessel of grace
Through whom, our savior came into the world,
Through who, our savior humbles himself, teach me humility
You whose womb cradled the child God,
that He may cradle in my heart

Gentle Woman, mother incarnate
Through whom, the word was made flesh
Through who our savior learnt of God, teach me to Love
You, whose body fed the child God,
that He may nourish my soul

Queen of Light, morning star
Through whom, light conquered darkness,
Through who our savior conquered death,
teach me to live for Christ
You. whose blood nourished the child God,
that He may shed it for our sins

Immaculate Mary, conceived without sin
Through whom, God dispenses his love and mercy
Through who our savior purifies our soul,
teach me to seek His will always
You, whose humble sanctity delights the child God,
 that He does her bidding as her will is united to His

Warrior princess, armor of God
Through whom, God bought our salvation
Through who our savior sanctifies his church,
teach me to offer my cross and crowns
You, whose requests pleases the child God, that He may accept our
offerings and lead us to eternal life.

December 14, 2010

The Missing link to Christ - Mary

I realize why my life has been going awry.
I have wandered far from my mother Mary,
my good luck charm, my intercessor with God,
my queen and protector, the overseer of my life.
I had a profound devotion to our lady
I was basking in the face of God's light
and everything went smoothly for me
despite my unworthiness.

Soon, I became lost in the world.
I gradually neglected our holy mother dear
I focused on doing everything myself, creating my own destiny,
disappointments, pride, impatience, sufferings abound, future bleak
I soon hear God's call to a closer union
And retrace my steps to Him on my own
I experience some peace but still discord overcomes it
I am embowered with light, but still it blinks unsteadily
Still I falter, I lose my way, I suffer , the future uncertain
I now know what I had been lacking or missing in my life
I am missing my mother Mary; the salt of the sea;
 the blue in the sky, the fruit of the earth,
the essence of my soul, my mother , Mary.
I do believe that without Mary, the path to Christ is a long, rocky one,
she is the straight short, route to Christ.

I dare to think my sacrifice will be pleasing to God as is?
I dare to imagine that I can approach
 the altar or footstool of the almighty on my own merit?
 I dare to conjure images of crowns won
 through my crosses or sanctification of my good works
 by my imperfect acts?
 I dare to think my love for God and good intentions alone
can soothe His anger and invite His mercy into my soul?
I dare to think I can begin God's work
 with my own strength and resolve?
I dare to think that my prayers, sacrifices, and sufferings offered
in union with the mass are enough to save my soul from Hades?

I dare to think I merely need to believe and trust
 and submit to God's will
for His Holy will to abound in my life?
I dare to think I can get to the savior by himself
and neglect the very vessel through which
he chose to come into the world?
I dare to try to go to God
without going through His blessed virgin mother?

That's why I have been suffering so much
since I departed from my mother, my lifeline my core
That's why I despair so much
since I stopped hoping and flying to her patronage
That's why I feel only God's wrath and justice
 since I stopped imploring her mercy and intercession
That's why my faults and sins have been magnified to all
 since I stopped hiding them under her purifying gaze
That's why I lost my direction and sense of purpose
since I stopped threading the path she creates for me to her son
That's why peace has been so elusive
since I stopped honoring the queen of peace

For when we call on her, she answers always like a devoted mother
For when we ask her for favors, she grants it always if it is for our good
For when we fail or falter, she pardons always like a loving mother
For when we hurt, she soothes our pain like a doting mother
For when we seek, she gives us our hearts desires
cause she knows them
For when we suffer, she makes us feel
only joy as we gaze at her

Did the angel of God not call her full of grace, why would we not?
Did God himself not honor her by creating her without sin
 so she could bare the sinless God man?
Why would we not honor her?
Did Christ not choose her as his mother,
 nursed by her, raised by her, rebuked by her, loved by her?
Why would we ignore her whom he chose among all beings?
Did Christ not obey and submit to her

for thirty years out of thirty three on earth,
why would we not submit to her direction?
Did He not perform His first ever miracle at her bidding,
why not ask her whom he never refuses?
Did Christ not commit mankind to her on the cross as our mother,
why would we disobey him?

As she accompanied him through his passion to his death,
so will she accompany us
As her presence by the cross brought Him strength in his agony,
so will hers bring us
As he listened to her instructions, directions as a child and a man,
so will He listen to her when she pleads on our behalf
For she notices our innermost desires
and brings them to His attention, even without our asking
like she did at the wedding feast when the wine ran out
For her humility pleases him,
and covers up the self-pride marring all our offerings
even the most sincere and noble
For prayers offered through her are like garlands of roses
which he cannot refuse if she presents to him

Dear Mother Mary, I consecrate myself to you today
as your child... A child of Mary.
Take my prayers and petitions to your son, Jesus Christ
as I unite them with his suffering on the cross
Convert them to precious garlands with your mere gaze and offer
them yourself to Him from the foot of the cross where you stand
That he may look on your gentle, humble, and loving face
 as he accepts these gifts
So that my unworthy gift will be pleasing to Him
and all for the greater honor and glory of God.
I believe, I trust and submit to your Holy will through the intercession
of Mary , your mother and queen of heaven and the earth. Amen!

December 15, 2010

Thanksgiving

Thank you God, my Lord!
You hold true to your promises
Your love and mercy knows no bounds
You have answered the prayers of your humble servant
Truly the patient soul that waits for you will always triumph
You give us all our hearts desires, beyond our wildest imagination:
Truly filled up, shaken, pressed down and runeth over
You have vindicated me in the eyes of my afflictors
You have given me a second chance to live my dream
You have given me an opportunity to do your work
You have created a pathway of life,
love and knowledge of truth and justice for me
You have arranged my life perfectly and opened the doors to salvation
I trust in you, O my God; I will glorify you in all I do
You truly do give the best to those who let you make the choice

Even sadness, disappointments, failures, sorrow or pain inflicts our life
are only because you allowed them to purify and bring us closer to you
To lead us to the path of salvation
By mirroring your suffering on the cross
If the devil knew that your death would buy the salvation of mankind,
He would never have influenced your persecution and death
Unknown to him, he was being used by God
to open the gates of heaven to all men
So, when things do not go as I wish or pray for
I will always offer it up in unison with your sacrifice on the cross
And accept your holy will in my life
and trust that nothing happens to me unless you allow it
For all is part of my life's story
which you wrote before I was conceived
All is path of your plan to lead me through life
back to your arms of love in heaven above.
You remember your own O Lord
Your promises are true ,O! so true, and so,
I thank You O God, my Lord!

January 14, 2011

For as You loved me, so should I love

For I am sinful and always prone to sin except for your grace,
I love you lord
For you became man to forgive my sins and reconcile me to God,
I adore you lord
For the judgement you accepted in silent humility for my sins,
I love you Lord
For the cross you bore for my sins,
I adore you Lord
For the women you comforted as they wept for your pain,
I love you Lord
For the anguish of meeting your mother bruised and humiliated,
I adore you Lord
For the times you fell on your wounds,
I love you Lord
For the clothes ripped off your body, riding me of earthly attachment,
I adore you Lord
For the nails piercing through your bones,
I love you Lord
For dying on the cross for my sins,
I adore you lord
For emptying your body of water and blood to wash away my sins,
I love you Lord
For rising from the dead and opening the gates of heaven for me,
I adore you Lord
For through your passion and death you have redeemed me,
I love you Lord
For by your example, I learn daily to forgive and love all that hurt me,
I adore you, Lord.
For as you loved me, so I should try to love my friends and foes,
For as I love them , I show that I love you Lord.

February 1, 2011

Stations of Life: The Way of the Passion through Divine Mercy

I - Through your sorrowful passion as you were condemned to die, help me to practice silence during persecution and trials because of Trust in God's Divine Providence.

II - Through your sorrowful passion, as you carried His cross, teach me obedience to God's laws and those in authority and humility to accept God's will with love.

III - Through your sorrowful passion as you fall the first time, help me always to trust and hope in your mercy.

IV - Through your sorrowful passion as you met your mother, fill me with a burning and steadfast love for your virgin mother, my mother too.

V - Through your sorrowful passion as you as the Cyrene helps you carry his cross, help me embrace my crosses and trials throughout life, accepting God's will despite my desires.

VI - Through your sorrowful passion as Veronica wipes your face, teach me to help all I encounter and see your face in all suffering, sick, and those in need of love and mercy.

VII -Through your sorrowful passion as you fall the second time, strengthen me with faith that I may perseverance in Trials

VIII -Through your sorrowful passion as you meet the women of Jerusalem, help me attain true Contrition for my sins not just for the fear of hell, but because they offend God who loves me so.

IX - Through your sorrowful passion as you fall a third time, give me true courage in trials, armed with prayer, penance, and love for God.

X - Through your sorrowful passion as you are stripped of your garments, help me practice self-denial and detachment from the world so as to conquer the flesh and inclination to evil and sin.

XI - Through your sorrowful passion as you are nailed to the cross, nail me to your feet and forever place me in communion with God.

XII - Through your sorrowful passion as you die on the cross, grant me the grace to die for love of you and Love of God because I Believe, Trust and Submit to His Holy Will.

XIII - Through your sorrowful passion as your body is taken down from the cross and into the arms of your blessed mother Mary, teach me to always embrace her in my life's joys and affliction and seek the intercession of she that nursed and loved you and whom you loved with all your heart.

XIV - Through your sorrowful passion as you are laid in the tomb, grant me the hope of Life-Everlasting and the resurrection of the dead and the joy of seeing God face to face after the journey of Life is over.

February 7, 2011.

Daily Spiritual Communion and Invocation of Love

I see you with the eyes of faith
I hear you with the voice of hope
I feel you with the arms of love
O my sweet Jesus hidden in the form of bread and wine
Come into my heart and chase the dark shadows away
Renew, transform, invigorate
And let your light shine forth from me
I believe in your love, I trust in your divine mercy
and I submit to your Holy will O lord

Jesus, I love you with all my heart above all things
I want to do your will
Weed out all evil from my heart that I may bear only good fruit
Sweet Jesus, teach me to love like you would
Show me how to care the way you would
Do with me whatever you will.
Mary my mother, give me your loving and humble heart
to receive my most gracious majesty
so my heart may be a fitting abode for my Lord.
Eternal Father, I offer up my thoughts, words, and actions today
through the immaculate heart of Mary
so that for the sake of the passion and death of your son,
you will have merciful on me a poor sinner,
the souls in purgatory and the whole world.

July 21, 2011

Angel of Hope

Today, I saw the face of an angel, her eyes were closed in eternal rest
At just 19 weeks of life so short
Her face resplendent in peace and joy
Her ambience gentle, exuding hope
Reminded me so much of my little angel, My Obiola, my heart, my son
An angel like her, pure in heart and soul
A little hero whose sacrifice lives on
That is my baby gone too soon, her mother wept,
Showing me the picture so treasured.
My heart stirred in love and pain
As I listened during my prenatal consult with her, at the close of work
I had asked her to call on her angel gone,
But I was unprepared and in awe of the image of peace
I had just seen... The face of the angel of hope.

And as her mummy clings to new life within
Seemingly in jeopardy of non-existence
At 25 weeks, at the limit of viability with bleak chances of survival
Old fears resurfaced and she looked like all hope was lost.
Though tomorrow is uncertain, I say, miracles do happen..
So cling to hope and faith and look within for succor
Your angel is in eternal bliss, resting in the arms of the God of love
Trust in the divine will and ask of your hearts' desire
He will not refuse a request from your pure, loving advocate
Your little angel will protect and guard and bring graces from above
Receive daily His body and blood - divine food that sustains
And renews the life that moves and breathes within
No-one knows tomorrow, except He who is the divine planner
Then accept all as part of the divine plan whether good or bad
I remember my pain of yesterears, still so fresh, of losing my Obiola
A sacrifice, blessing and a gift that saved my life over and over
My intercessor with God - a beacon of hope and life.
You have that in your little angel who is not gone, but lives forever
I will never forget the beautiful face of her angel of hope.

December 31, 2011

A New Year's Resolution

A new year is upon me; A new chapter in my life
A new chance at life; A new beginning; a fresh start
I will not look back at yesterday
I will leave its mistakes, imperfections behind
I will look to tomorrow , full of hope and promise
I will start anew to live and love

This new year I resolve to forgive all that have wronged me
This new year I resolve to love all that I hold grudges against
This new year I resolve to work like it depends on me
This new year I resolve to pray like it depends on God

As tomorrow dawns, I rise with joy
A joy that not be quenched by sadness, hardship, trials, or suffering
A joy that will not be dampened by failures, mishaps or cruelty
A joy kept alive by the knowledge that Jesus loves me
So much He died on the cross for me

For the rest of my earthly exile, I do not sojourn alone
I invoke the guidance of my patrons and patronesses
The holy servants of my Lord above who riumphed in this vale of tears
They shall be my friends, confidantes and companions as of old
I've gotten closer to old friends and met new friends from above
St. Therese teach me to trust like a child, bearing trials with love
St. Teresa of Avila teach me to persevere and to know God in truth
St. Faustina teach me to immerse myself in God's mercy
St. Giuseppe teach me to care for the souls, not just the body
St John of the cross teach me to seek God's light through dark nights
St. Padre Pio teach me patience and humility in trials
and submission to God's will
St Rita teach me to love even when all is lost
St Catherine of Siena teach me to strive for a closer union with God
Mary, virgin mother of God, teach me to love you as my mother
take my off of my soul to your son that in union with his suffering,
I might obtain God's mercy and eternal life.

December 31, 2011

My Offering of Love

Suffering troubles my soul
Uncertainties of the future plagues my mind
Conflicted emotions for a forsaken love, torments my heart
Guilt from mistakes made, nags my brain
Misgivings for justice sought, eats at my conscience
Fear of the unknown, fills my core
Doubts of my vocation, courses my being

No human words can comfort me
Sincere as they may be,
they perturb my spirit even more
I will retreat within the quiet of my soul
And seek the company of my Lord and savior within
There will I find a listener, comfort, and company for my misery
As He suffered in silence too, innocent victim
Me not so, I deserve all the misery I feel

But his mercy is fathomless like the depths of the sea
Therein will I immerse myself
Cause I'm a miserable sinner, humbled and repentant
and those does He love so much
For us He died a death of shame
That we may obtain God's mercy and eternal glory

Thus Lord of my soul,
I call on you for help and
I hear your words of comfort
I feel your arms of love
I recall your saving grace
I remember your sacrifice on the cross

This is my cross, and I will accept it
I will not reject to accompany you to Calvary
This trial, though trivial or small to some
Weighs heavily on my soul
It will indeed be my path of salvation

This suffering is my road to heaven, I will accept it
I will not dwell on it and be glum or sad
That is what the devil plans and wants
I will accept it with joy of heart and gladness of soul
Even as its thorns pierce deeper and its gall tastes bitter

Its pain and bitterness are my offerings to God
My love for God and my perseverance are like fuel
Igniting my simple and humble offering with fires of love
An offering that pleases God
An offering that I will unite with His sacrifice on the cross
And the sacrifice of the mass in all the tabernacles of the whole world
In this very instant of my suffering.

An offering I will place in the arms of his tender, loving mother mine
Whoever standing at the foot of the cross,
will raise them as garlands to her son
That drops of his saving blood and crumbs of his peeling flesh
may sanctify and turn them into graces for me
to lead me to eternal life

This offering is my road to heaven.
I will not look back; but look ahead at the eternal prize
This suffering is my saving grace
I accept it; I love it ; and I offer it up to you my Lord.
Jesus Mercy, Mary help, All the Saints,
angels and martyrs, ATSAAM, guide me. Amen!

January 5, 2012.

Sacred Altar, where Heaven touches the Earth

Praise God on His altar so sacred
Sacred Altar, where heaven touches the earth
Sacred Altar, Ladder with which God came down to become man
Sacred Altar, cradle of the infant savior
Sacred Altar, anchor of the cross of salvation
Sacred Altar, on which lies the sacrificial lamb of salvation
Sacred Altar, stage of eternal life
Sacred Altar, laden with the nuptial feast of the lamb

Praise and Glory be to you God,
bridegroom of this sacred union with your church
You have invited all heaven and earth to the wedding feast of the lamb
All the angels and saints worship around your sacred altar
With Mary your mother, ark of the covenant at the foot of the altar
Cradling the Holy Spirit in her womb, the word made flesh in her arms
She offers our humble offerings of gold: our joys;
myrrh: our sorrows, frankincense: our praises
At the foot of the cross to her son crucified
And the chalice is overflows with his precious blood
Dripping on our unworthy offerings to sanctify and transform them
to a pure offering pleasing to God to temper His justice with mercy
An offering perfecting Abel's spotless lamb and innocent blood
An offering that completes the bloodless offering of Abraham
Uniting the sacrifice on the cross with the sacrifice of the mass
An offering that opens the gates of heaven that God's love may flow
Like the precious blood poured out for the whole world.

Praise be to you God, Eternal Father
For letting us, mere mortals participate in this heavenly banquet
Eating of the food of angels: manna from heaven , the body of Christ
Drinking of the cup of eternal life, blood shed so dear for our sins
Though such beatific vision is veiled from our mortal eyes,
Increase our faith in you that we may proclaim with all fervor
We believe; We trust; and We submit to your Holy Will, O Lord
As we praise and worship you on your sacred altars over the world.

January 5, 2012, *Old St. Patrick's Church, Chicago, Illinois*

Epiphany in our Hearts

Like you did the Magi of Old
You reveal yourself to us O Lord, an epiphany in our hearts
You are the King of Kings and Lord of Lords
Come to us like a babe, born of flesh from the womb of the virgin

Like the Magi of old,
Let our eyes be opened to see the star of life
Let our mind be opened to accept its glory
Let our hearts be open to seek its guiding light

Like the Magi of old,
Let us follow the star in our lives
The sign in the heavens
The cross of salvation, To lead us to the fountain of life

Like the Magi of old, let us humbly seek the truth
that we do not know but long for
And not like the scribes and wise men
who knew the truth but did not seek it
Abandoning evanities to seek the treasures of our heavenly King

Like the Magi of Old,
 let us bring our offerings of gold, frankincense and myrrh
To Christ the savior dwelling in our hearts
And offer to him and his mother our treasures and suffering
For she blesses with her love, and He sanctifies with his presence

Like the Magi of old,
May this epiphany change our hearts
May this encounter with the light of salvation
Help us redirect our paths back to God,
Not through our old, sinful ways, but through a new path we will walk
To bring this saving light to all we meet the king, the savior, this babe
dwelling meekly in peace, love, and joy within us.

Jan 8, 2012. *Assumption Church, Chicago, IL*

Stay with me Lord

Stay with me Lord, present in the tabernacle
Make your home in my heart
Do not leave me alone
I do not trust myself for a second without you
Without your grace, I can do nothing
Without your presence, I am nothing
So please stay with me

Stay with me Lord,
I am inclined to sin always
Evil only, my mind conjures
The good I do, is from you alone
Promises made today, I break tomorrow
Holy thoughts imagined one second
Evil thoughts envelope the next second
My nature is utterly helpless
I am miserable without you, so stay with me.

Stay with me Lord, I humbly pray
Temper your justice with mercy
You are ever patient with my many faults
Daily I struggle with vices too numerous to count
But as long as there is life in me
I will call on you my savior for help and mercy
And you will wash away my iniquities till
the end of my earthly sojourn
So please stay with me

Stay with me Lord, I cannot live without you
Without your breath, I have no life
Without your words, I have no voice
I need your body to fill my hunger
I need your blood, to quench my thirst
Without your strength, I can do nothing
All is from you by grace alone
I have neither earned nor deserve any merit
Except just punishment for my sins, so stay with me

Stay with my Lord, my love, my all
My heart sadly is always in a sorry state
But please do not leave else I perish
Wash it clean with your blood
Illuminate it with your saving grace
Teach me truth from your lips
Light the path of salvation and guide my feet
That I may walk through the thorns, storms and squalls
Drawing from the graces you bestow
through your church: Eucharist, reconciliation,
succor from your dear mother, ours too.
Thus rejuvenated and renewed,
that I may give hope and joy to all I meet so
They may draw strength to bear their crosses too
As we all journey home to our Father's kingdom
To the very place reserved for each and every child.
So stay with me Lord throughout my journey

January 22, 2012

A Measure of Love

Show me how you love your neighbor,
And I will tell you how much you Love God.

The depth of your love for others
Is a measure of the depth of your love for God

As sincere as your love for your neighbor
Is as sincere as your love is for God

As your love for others increases,
Your distance to God decreases.

When you deny your self-interest for that of others
You obtain divine interest of God for you

The power of your prayers
Is the power of your service of others

Your prayers are answered
As often as you seek to fulfil the needs of others.

Union with God's will is accomplished
By giving up our will for the sake of others' needs.

January 28, 2012

Weep not my Heart

Weep not my heart, for my soul is alight in bliss
For His joy is unending in his blessings
I have not merited anything or deserved any good
But He pours them out like an eternal fountain of graces
Yet He allows my heart to wander into the desert of life
That He may nourish my soul with the unending fountain of love
To quench my thirst for ever
To sustain me through earth's pilgrimage
To lead me to my very own abode,
In His glorious presence I will bask forever,
whether on his bosom, side or feet, my joy is eternal

My Lord allows this suffering of my heart, to mature my soul
He allows the longing of my heart, to fill me with eternal delights
He allows the distance from my love, to draw me closer to His heart
He allows this lingering pain of my past, to heal the scars of my heart
And prepare me for the earthly sojourn rooted in Him
That I may find my way home to Him forever

Weep not my heart, don't you remember?
That nothing happens to you unless He allows it: Good or Bad.
All are for the good of your soul
All are sources of graces, food and drink for this earthly life
I shut the door on the murmurings of the evil one
And walk boldly into the light of salvation
I will pick up my cross willingly, carry it lovingly, live it cheerfully
And offer up my sufferings: big or small, trivial or vital
For the salvation of my soul and those I love and souls in need
Till I learn total dependence on my Lord
Till God is my everything, and I want or lack nothing
Till the enemies' howls don't unnerve me
I remain in this desert with my Lord to fortify my heart,

February 14, 2012

A Sonnet To My True Love

I am drowning in your love
Wash me clean with your blood
Rinse all the doubts, fears, insecurities of my flesh
Cleanse all negativity, sadness, anger, and regret in my soul
Liberate me from the vanity of earthly needs and accolades
Fill my soul like a bottomless crevice
To the brim, overflowing
From my core to my own being
I shake my hair out breathless
Drowning from your blood, so pure, invigorating
Inebriated I am from your love unparalleled
Satisfied I thirst for more, this love insatiable
At the foot of your cross, I will forever lay
Drinking from drops of the fountain of salvation.

February 14, 2012

Free Will Of Mine

I freely, wholly give it to you
This free will of mine
I want you to direct and use it as you please
To do your will and do your work

I give You control of it, this free will of mine
For I do not trust myself
To make any right decision
I do not trust myself
Else I lose my soul

I give you as an offering, this freewill of mine
Bestowed on all men that we may choose
Life eternal and not damnation
By choosing to love you and not the world

I give yo
u to safeguard, this free will of mine
The evil one no matter how fierce or charming
Cannot overcome me without my free consent,
Yet I fall over and over for his cunning guile

I give you to keep forever, this free will of mine
United with Yours on the cross, offered to the Father eternal
Thus our salvation purchased so dearly
Please Lord accept my full consent given humbly to you
My soul's true gift to you, this free will of mine.

February 14, 2012.

Hush, my soul

Hush, my soul
Be still, my spirit
Know that God is ever near
Within the core of my being

Hush, my soul
Listen to the whisper of His voice
Filling my being
Renewing my spirit

Hush, Hush my soul
Drink of His fountain of life
Eat of His bread of salvation
For He now lives within me

Hush , O hush my soul
Unite with the divine will
Abandon all cares to Him
For He will give me rest

Hush... Hush, now my soul
For He will quieten the roaring tempest
Filling me with that sweet, quiet peace
That only He can give

February 20, 2012

Baby Miracle

Sleep in peace, beautiful angel
Rest your weary, brave soul
Your battle is finally won
You've won our hearts, love and admiration

Sleep in peace , beautiful angel
You defied all odds by your birth
Your amazed all by your survival
Your job now is done
The debate has now begun
The conflict of limit of viability?
When life begins or should begin.

You were given no chance to live
Your young parents not offered any resuscitation
at 22 +5 weeks, dates unsure
At 600g, weight disregarded, they were sure you would die
So comfort care was planned.

But born at 518g with obvious signs of life and crying
Your parents asked again. "Can anything be done?"
They were denied and ignored.
Nothing can be done, they were told -she is too young to survive.
For over two hours with no resuscitation at 22 weeks gestation
Giving no chance of survival
You proved all wrong by breathing and crying vigorously
Till hearts were stirred in wonder and compassion.
A miracle indeed –your mummy named you so.

I remember seeing you first in mummy's arms
Pink, active, moving your limbs, a crying with all your might
I was amazed as we watched you breathe without support for another
5 minutes with no distress or retractions or grunting
And 99% oxygen saturations on room air.
The neonatology team decided to offer you additional care
and support with mom's permission
But clearly reiterating the uncertainty of the outcome

Every day all watched while you remained
on minimal respiratory support
Each day all expected you to die
Your only crime being born too early

Each day your breathed, moved, laden with emotion
A living being, God's masterpiece
Each day emotions were stirred
Some of awe, some of rage, some in disbelief, most in conflict
Should she be allowed to live?
Is she still alive?
Why was she given a chance to live?
At what cost and burden to the society and healthcare?
At what cost to the effort of physicians and caregivers?
For what purpose to humanity is her expected handicap?
Mortality or severe neurodevelopmental disability
is her surely her only future, prognosis poor,
So why bother? So why care?

But you exceeded everyone's expectations
No intraventricular bleed for 24 days of your life
Most in disbelief, but the ultrasound remained stable.
Left intubated, all hesitate to let you breathe without support
As you clearly wanted to; and thus
The toll of artificial ventilation began to show
Over inflation, barotrauma, hyperinflation,
till interstitial changes of early chronic lung disease evolved
-all man-made disease processes; All had little faith in you.

In fear of the unknown you were left with no oral nutrition-NPO
No-one brave enough to nourish your gut
Leaving inevitable atrophy to begin
Fluid restricted from birth and maintained so,
You suffered severe dehydration and hypernatremia,
And as fluid was liberalized, you became hyponatremic
Sadly, your needs not anticipated on time
But still you hung in tight.

Your metabolic acidosis worsened each day
due to the existence of a patent ductus arteriosus, PDA.
To treat or not to treat- that was the question?
Your fragile lungs already stressed became flooded with pulmonary
over circulation and edema
The inevitable will happen, all said
But still you had no ventricular bleed.

Your skin fragile and translucent
Inadvertently suffered effects of dehydration
and lack of barrier protection
As well as bronzing from phototherapy
Till it peeled, and wept for pity's sake
Gradually, it was tended and nursed till it healed again

For a week or so, all was calm
Normal electrolytes, normal labs
Minimal vent settings despite BPD and PDA
Sepsis prophylaxis completed,
 your only med Caffeine for apnea of prematurity
Apart from weekly transfusions for anemia of prematurity,
you appeared no different from a stable 30 weeker
Your prognosis good; hearts appeared hopeful
And still no intraventricular bleed.

Then suddenly you became MRSA positive,
on 3rd weekly surveillance
A nosocomial colonization that put you at risk for infection
You tiny system slowly became overwhelmed
And the subtle signs you showed were inadvertently missed
You became increasingly hyperglycemic
and unable to regulate glycemic control
Your breathing became shallow, and in 2 days,
you were less active, lethargic and unable to breathe above the vent

For contact isolation on low respiratory settings,
you were placed in intermediate care
Away from close watchful eyes of majority

Till it was finally noticed that you were pale and "appeared dead",
decreased urine output, in renal failure,
with occult blood indicating GI bleeding.
Immediately, sepsis workup and antibiotics were started
But alas, it was a downward spiral
as within hours you had intractable metabolic acidosis and
cardiovascular dysfunction requiring pressor support.
And went into DIC from overwhelming sepsis,
bleeding from a skin abrasion,
requiring chest compressions and vigorous resuscitation.

Hours earlier there was hesitation
to control your severe metabolic acidosis, even over hours
But later you were now getting bolus infusions
of hyperosmolar base to no end.
Through it all, you remained brave, moving, active,
opening your eyes, trying to raise your arms for succor
Raising our souls to the eternal
and our realities to the mystery of life and death
with the uncertainties of any given hour or second.

But alas your mummy could not get there on time
Conflicted emotions arise
Should resuscitation continue till mummy arrives?
For how long should it go on?
Can she be left on the ventilator without active resuscitation
Till parents can say goodbye
and see her still pink without necrosis occurring?
And give our little angel a dignified exit?
And soon the majority decision made to stop resuscitation
You were baptized and time of death pronounced

Sweet miracle, little angel dear
You stand for all that is good, true and pure
You stand for all the injustice to innocents
That are daily lost to ego, uncertainty, and outcome data
You stand for the inadequacies of our knowledge,
technology and simple faith in humanity
You stand for the proof that life begins in the womb and

You stand as evidence to lower the threshold of the limit of viability
And the ultimate outcome of life is in God's hand,
not man or machine
You stand for the case that compassion needs to be given to all life
No life is futile, unnecessary , or a burden
And even the tiniest human beings have a unique character, emotion,
experience pain and suffering and peace
So it does matter what and how you do it
Who decided who lives or dies?
You can only do you best and leave the rest to God.

You looked resplendent in purity, peaceful and delicate
I closed your gentle eyes in eternal peace
And softly closed your gaping mouth, seemingly speaking in silence
The silence of life eternal
Soar to the heavens our little hero
Back to your maker our little warrior
Your mission is complete
Your job is done
You've won the battle
You've sown the seeds of life, truth and love
You will always have a place in the heart
of all that cared for you and knew you
You will always speak to the core of their being
In their care of patients old and young
For you defied the odds and
You taught us all compassion, love , and care
Sleep in peace, little angel, our miracle
For you live forever.
I will hold you as you take your last breath
I commit your soul into God's arms
As the angels come for you and soar into heavenly bliss
Goodbye baby miracle, eternal life is yours.

March 29, 2012.

You're so good to me

God, you're too good to me
You spoil me beyond my imagination
You pamper me more than I deserve
When I think you could do no more,
You still keep giving and loving me

You always know what's best for me
You plan my life out to the last detail
There's nothing left to chance or luck
All is part of your divine order
You anticipate my needs
And give them to me before I even fathom them
And you give even more than I could ask for

You cater to my whims material and temporal
Like I can refuse nothing my daughter asks so sweetly or persistently
So you can neither refuse our most earnest requests,
no matter how trivial
Cause you love us more than our earthly parents could
You loved us so much you took flesh and bore suffering for us
So much you gave your only beloved son for our sake
How could you not give us our daily bread indeed.
We only need to ask and believe and it will be done
According to your will

Even when things appear to go wrong
I remind myself that you know and you allowed it
Because you love me and will not let any harm come to me
Because you are my own Father, who art in heaven
I believe in your love,
I trust in your divine mercy
And I submit to your Holy will
You truly always turn everything to good for my soul

Lord, you're so good to me, it brings tears to my eyes
Thinking of how much you love me, mere mortal and sinner
No matter how often I fail in my duties, you still love me

No matter when I forget to thank you, you still love me
Countless times I've broken my promises, and you love even more
No matter if I deny or betray you, you still love me
You are too good to me my Lord

You overwhelm me with your goodness
You keep filling me with your treasures and love
Pressed down. Shaken through, filled up till it runneth over
Your goodness to me knows no bounds
Even when I fall, you raise me up with your love
Even when I lose, you win me over with your love
Even when I cry, you bring me joy with your love
Even when I hurt, you soothe my pain with your love
O God you're so good to me

Like a beloved child, my chances never run out with you Father
Ever tender, ever patient, ever loving, ever merciful
Come into my heart and stay forever
Let not envy or avarice dwell within me
Let not anger or malice dwell within me
Let not fear or despair dwell within me
Let all kindness and joy spring from me
Let all mercy and love spring from me
Let all hope and faith spring from me

I will praise you with all my heart and from the highest mountain
I will spread your goodness to all I meet
I will let all know the secret of life - love and love again and again
Casting your cares to your Lord and He will lighten your burden
Uniting all acts, thoughts, desires, emotions, good or bad
To his holy sacrifice of the cross and the sacrifice of the mass
So He looks not on our sins but on the debts paid by his beloved son
To appease His justice and draw His love and mercy on us.

I will praise you O God for your goodness
In all my works, acts, joys, sufferings, triumphs and defeat
I will sing always of your goodness and countless blessings in my life.
For you are worthy to be praised and you love to be praised
And when we thank you for your goodness, You bless us even more

You honor all who honor you
So with all my heart, I thank you my lord and savior
For your goodness to me and tender love to me
I thank you for your divine mercy
I praise you for your glory and might

You fulfill even the innermost longings of my heart
You anticipate my needs, even when I do not voice or know them
I love you with all my heart, my Lord
Teach me to love you more and more every day
Daily I will sing and praise your love and mercy
Even with my last breath on earth,
I commit my last moment on earth to you O lord
Even if I cannot speak at that time,
I offer those moments in love and thanks to you my Lord

You speak to me in the depths of my soul, all my life
You have taught me from your Heavenly lips
Light infuses my soul from above
So that as I now read the words of your saints and martyrs
I see my own words and life within
I recognize truths known only to my soul
And realize they were indeed given to me from above
God is the original author of such work
and reveals to whom He pleases sinner and saint alike, as He pleases
O how you love me, to reveal to a sinful child such divine treasures
You stoop so low my King, all for love of me.

As unworthy as I am You still love me,
Not for anything I did or could do.
..Just because you are love and mercy
O Lord, you're so good to me,
So good, so good, O so good to me.

April 28, 2012
Chicago, Ilinois

Physicians: a spiritual ministry of healing, love and life

"Physician heal thy self" our Lord said unto himself
Yes, he was a physician – the divine physician
A healer of infirmities: both physical and spiritual
By a touch He made the lame walk, blind see, cured lepers and fevers
By a word, He cast out demons, renewed hope, and changed lives

Like so, all physicians are not just healers, but ministers of God
We are given the grace of participation of this divine ministry
Like most priests and ministers of God,
But we are even more blessed, because unlike priests and ministers
Physicians have the most contact with the sick, dying and unborn.
We are closest to humanity at the start, peak, and end of life
We should be true healers of infirmities
of not just the body, but the soul

We should be open to God's divine grace
That the living Christ may continue His ministry of healing through us.
We need to be His hands, feet, voice, and one in spirit with our savior
So by our hands we can heal infirmities, not just physical but spiritual.
With our voice, we can cast out fear, doubt and despair and instill
hope, faith, life and renewed vigor and spirit
With our knowledge, we can impart wisdom of science
but also of the divine significance of our work.
By our presence, we can share in their pain, joys, and sorrows
Showing compassion and mercy to them, like our divine mentor to us.

As physicians we should not miss an opportunity
to heal the spiritual along with the physical with a touch, a smile, a
kind word, a presence, unspoken compassion
That alone can stir the divine within everyone we meet
so the Holy spirit may ignite the souls and renew their lives

As physicians we are there as life is formed
We should preserve and protect it, not extinguish it
As we partake in this co-creation by safeguarding every life
Every life is paramount - "Ndubuisi", each soul a vital part of this earth
Regardless of age, physical ability or disability, or deformity,

color, or race or potential contribution to the society,
Every life is to be respected and honored
And when the creator calls it to Himself,
every life should be given the dignity of a holy death

 As physicians with the greatest contact with the dying on earth
We should bring peace, faith, hope and joy of God's love at the end
We should offer opportunity for sacraments of baptism to the young,
reconciliation to all, and healing and extremeunction to the dying.
We should help reunite loved ones and make peace,
though suffering is prolonged a bit longer, for suffering is redemptive.
We should bring them the peace of knowing they are loved by God
and His mercy is free and running unending like a fountain for them to
drink of even up to the last moment, they will be washed clean
We should help them see the face of God by our smile,
the truth in our eyes, our voice, our demeanor in this divine ministry
At the moment of death, God is present with Jesus,
and the Holy spirit and Mary and the angels and saints

The devil and his angels are present too trying to win souls over as
they hold on to anger and bitterness and despair
and regret and hate and their sins go unrepentant.
On whose side are we going to fight the last battle for souls
Will we let the devil win by ignoring our duty to reconcile souls ?
Or are we going to win souls for eternal life
by bringing them peace, baptism, and reconciliation by allowing
ministers to get to them or helping them ourselves
Or even saying a quiet prayer for them if they cannot pray for them
If you are neither warm or cold, I will spit you out, says our Lord
By not fighting, we allow the devil's triumph in the last battle for souls.
Let's treat the dying with compassion, dignity and reverence
for the holy presence around them; so others may emulate

Physician heal thyself, the people will say unto Jesus
Jesus needs us physicians to heal Himself- all are of His own image.
Will we not participate in this divine healing ?
Do we not see Christ in every patient we encounter?
He was once a helpless fetus in the womb of Holy Mary,
totally dependent on her accepting God's will and faith in unknowns

He was once a growing child and blossoming youth soaking in
knowledge at her feet, and from his teachers and elders
Humbly accepting the truth and living obediently
He that is all knowing and all powerful, yet humbled himself for love
When we meet the youth do we impart God's love and truths to guide
as we heal or watch over their physical infirmities
At his prime, despite His good deeds he was made an outcast,
despised by men, unjustly accused humiliated, crucified.
When we meet the outcasts and oppressed and poor in our world
Do we ignore or wipe their faces like veronica, or lend a hand like the
Cyrene, and speak in their defense like Nicodemus or Pilate?
Do we let them feel the comfort of God's mercy and His arms of love.
We may be their only contact with the divine.
Do we lose that opportunity to bring Christ to them?

God, Jesus, and the Holy spirit need us to be one with them
Physicians and all healthcare workers, nurses, therapists alike
In this divine ministry of healing of bodies an d souls
Of bringing God's lost sheep back to His fold like a good shepherd
Let us speak, and they will hear His voice and will come back to Him
For He knows His sheep and His sheep knows Him.
We can only do this if we open ourselves to God's love and mercy
We have to freely accept this union, for His love does not coerce
We should believe His Love, Trust His Mercy, and Submit to His Will

Thank you Divine Physician for this grace on your humble servants
Teach us to serve those you've entrusted in our care, like you did
Teach us to love them the way you would
Teach us to care for them, like you would, O divine physician
Teach me to be like you for I am your image
But Let all not see me, but only you
May I decrease that you may increase
But take my hands, my feet, my voice, my touch, my mind,
my memory, my spirit, my soul, my conscience,
my weakness and my strengths and make them yours
That it may be not I that lives, but you that lives in me so
"Physician, heal thyself" .

April 29, 2012, Chicago, IL

This Sensitivity and Scruples of mine

I tire of you this sensitivity and scruples of mine
My mind labors on trivial thoughts
I beat myself up for laboring on them
Then I torment myself for beating myself up for laboring on them
And I resolve to put my mind on God more often

My impulsiveness gets the better of me sometimes
And I say or do what I should rather not
My flesh is weak no matter how well-intentioned my mind is
Then I torment myself for giving in to my weakness and impulsivity
Then I cry for tormenting myself
And I resolve to be more meek and humble

I am negligent of my promises to God
My soul tortures me for breaking my promises and resolutions
I weep for my sins and misery
And I call and plead for God's mercy
Then I weep even more for being so weak in faith and not trusting in
God's mercy and strength during my time of weakness
And I resolve to be more steadfast in my love for God

I speak before I can hold my tongue
I am anguished at the pain or sorrow I have caused another
I cry bitterly for being the cause of such anguish to another
Then realize I am being too sensitive
And I cry even more for crying so much
And I resolve to show more love and compassion to others.

Each day I will work on them till I conquer these ills
Like an athlete trains his body to be in shape for a game
I will train my body and spirit for this spiritual battle
Cutting out my weaknesses, one day at a time
Persevering in my strengths, one day at a time
With the help of your divine grace
For I truly can do nothing without your strength O lord
I can do everything if you are with me O Lord
So stay by my side and do not let go, else I perish for I am a weak

Heavenly Hosts and patrons given divine mastery over such malady
St. Faustina and St. Therese you suffered
and overcame such sensitivities
I pray you intercede for me for divine intervention
to overcome my sensitivity and scruples
As oversensitivity is a sign of pride and mistrust in God
I will keeping trusting in God's mercy, when all appears lost
I will accept humiliation so I can learn humility
And will rise each time I fall into this malady
Till His grace lifts me high.

April 29, 2012,
Boston, Massachusetts

Come to my aid, O Holy Mother

Come to my aid O Holy Mother
I need you now mummy, more than ever
I need you now to visit me like you do in my time of need
Come with your humble presence into my heart
Infuse my soul with your purity of heart and mind
Intertwine my will with the will of your son
O you model of love, mercy and faith

Come to my aid O Holy Mother
I am at the pinnacle of my life
I am at the brink of destruction
I am at the center of my faith
I am at the core of my destiny
I either fly or fall
Bid me fly to your succor, holy mother
For therein lies peace, love and God.

Come to my aid, O Holy Mother
Mediatrix of all graces
Ark of the covenant
Seat of wisdom
You have never turned away your children in need
Patient, loving , doting mother
You anticipate my needs before I imagine them

Come to aid, my refuge and my intercessor
Lead me to your son, who you bore in your womb and nursed
Bid me to do whatever he says, for the wine is running out,
Bid him turn this water of life into the wine of his eternal blood
That He may flow within me to replenish, revive, invigorate, restore
Graces, wisdom, faith, love and above all humility
In accepting, following his divine path to the cross and salvation.

May 2, 2012,
Chicago, IL

The Waves of Life

Sitting under the palm tree along the shore
With the grainy feel of the sands under my feet
I see that as uncountable as the grains of sands were, so are my sins
And I marvel as the waves wash away the sands
To the bottom of the sea never to be seen again
So are my sins washed away by His precious blood
In the Ocean of His fathomless mercy
How great thou art, my Lord
Your mercy knows no bounds

Staring into the deep blue horizon
At the edge of the waters of the Atlantic
Caressed by the gentle winds
I watch the rhythmic splashing of the waves
Swishing, billowing, asynchronously in the deep blue sea
I watch the undulating ripples in the waves
Up and down, over and over on a constant baseline
So like the rhythm of our earthly sojourns
The ups are like the high peaks of the waves, still pulled by gravity
The downs seem abysmal but do not go beyond the baseline
So indeed are the waves of our lives
Driven by the winds of fate and providence

On my highs, keep me humble , O Lord
As I drink in your grace and consolation
May I praise you for your goodness
For you are worthy of all praise and glory
And gather strength for the anticipated nadir
I am gathering graces and assurance of your love and kindness
To prepare me for the inescapable drop from the hill of my life

In my lows, save me from despair, O Lord
May I remember your mercy and compassion
And know that this too shall pass
And imbibe strength and consolation
From your body and blood
For you are closest to me in times of misery and desolation

Even when I do not feel your presence
For in suffering, I resemble the crucified Christ
And share in your cross
You are with me always,
may I remember that in the valleys of my life

Hills and valleys, highs and lows
That is the journey of life on earth for all, none can escape it
But with faith one can glides peacefully through life's peaks and dips.
The closer you are to God, the deeper the valleys,
Because the more God entrusts you with his passion
And the more you resemble Him in His suffering
And the humbler you become, your peaks become higher
Cause He dwells in a humble heart
And bestows more graces on you
To share in the glory of His crown after the cross

The lows of life are when we receive graces
And nourishment for our earthly journey
To empower us to climb to the peak of the hills
So we should welcome these vital resting points in life
For here our Lord communes with us in our misery
The highs are where we receive graces
 to sustain us through the steep fall of the valleys
At our high, may we not forget to instill in ourselves these free God-
given graces, else we lose our balance during drop to the valleys

May my highs, not be too high that I forget your goodness
May my lows not be too low that I forget your mercy
And may I always remember that you alone are the constant in my life
Keeping me steady and firm along the rocky, billowing tides of life
With your blood like ocean waves drowning my sins
Into the depths of your mercy through the peaks and crests of the tide
Till I dock home in my odyssey, at last like the ships
Home in eternal rest, in your bosom.

May 5, 2012,
Fort Lauderdale, Florida

It's not You, It's me!

I could find many reasons why you are wrong
I could say all the ills you've done to me
I could try to prove how I did nothing wrong
I could show how much you need to change,
But it's not you, it's me

It's not you, it's really me
That was wrong on every count
I'm the one guilty of any ill
And I'm the one that needs to change
So it's not you, it's me

I should not seek love, I should give it
I should not count ills, I should forgive always
I should not look glum, I should be happy
That Christ loves me so much, He died for me

Dare I complain of ills done to me
When my sins He bares without a word,
He accuses Himself daily of my transgressions
He didn't defend Himself on my account
He loves unconditionally even as I ignore Him
Dare I ever think I'm blameless and count sins of others?

It's not you, it's me that need to change
Change the way I respond and react to you
Change the way I view or analyze things
Change the way I think or act on things
And do nothing but one thing only
Love like He has loved me

It's not them, it's me
I need to forgive as He has forgiven me
My stage is here; My mission starts now
I need not wait for the glorious time to prove my love
I need not wait for the peak of my life or career
I start now in my every day and minute, living and loving

Doing every little inconspicuous act out of pure love of Him
That shed His blood so dear for my sake

Yes, It's not You, It's me
I'm sorry for the ills and pain
I'm sorry for the misery and sadness
I'm sorry I didn't love you just as you are
For He loves me just I am
Despite my sinful nature, and daily failings
He still loves me even more.

Yes, It's not you, it's me
I need a change of heart, a heart more meek
I need a change of soul, a soul more loving
I need a change of mind, a mind more peaceful
I need a change of conscience, one more trusting
And accepting of God's call to love
A Christ-like love that bear all things
Patiently, lovingly, forgives all things,
And continues to love
through the highs, lows, imperfections and joys.
Yes, It's not you, it's really me.

May 6, 2012
Fort Lauderdale, FL

Teach me O Mother

Teach me your trust and your kindness
Teach me your meekness and humility
In accepting the will of God in your life
Teach me to receive Christ in me, like you did
Teach me O mother, teach me

Teach me to go forth and do God's will
Teach me to care for those in need
Teach me to serve and be merciful to all like you did for Elizabeth
Teach me to bring Christ within me to all
Teach me, O mother , teach me

Teach me to come to you with my problems
For you anticipate them before I do and bring my needs to your son
Teach me to trust and obey your son, and do as He says
So that the waters in my life will be turned into wine
Fruit of the vine and blood of salvation
That will renew my life forever more
Teach me, O mother teach me

Teach me to dedicate my life to God
Teach me to persevere and bear all trials with love
Teach me, to seek Christ in all I do
Teach me to bear all sorrows patiently
Teach me to find Him in the Eucharist
Teach me to nourish my body and soul and be born again of the spirit
And br guided by the life-giving grace of the holy spirit
Teach me the inner life through prayer and the sacraments
Teach me, O mother, teach me

Teach me love him, like you do
Teach me, to follow him through His passion, like you did
Teach me to love Him at the foot of the cross
Teach me to hold Him in my arms, like you did
Teach me to follow Him till the end
Teach me, O mother, teach me.

                    May 7, 2012,   Fort Lauderdale, FL

Teach me to Love, O Lord

Teach me to love, O Lord
To love the way you love me
Pouring out my heart without reserve
Trusting my heart, future and life
Opening up myself without fear
So the one I love can know and feel me as if we are one

Teach me to love O lord
To love the way you love me
Starting and ending my day with thoughts of my love
Filling pieces of my everyday with thoughts of my love
Thinking of ways to show my love
Thinking of ways to bring joy and laughter
To protect my love with my life
To give up self-pleasures for my love's happiness.

Teach me to love O Lord
To love the way you love me
To bear suffering and pain for the one I love
To seek to bring peace and progress to the one I love
To delight and rejoice when my love is happy
To weep and show compassion when my love is hurt
To tend, to care and nurture till my love is healed

Teach me to love O lord
To love the way you love me
To forgive easily, to apologize readily, to ignore flaws and negatives
and focus on strengths and positives
To erase past hurt by constantly renewing my love and commitment
To be humble and gentle at all times
For my love and I can only be one
when we make up what each other is lacking.

Teach me to love O lord
To love the way you love me
Kind and patient with my love's faults
Slow to anger, quick to make up

To confess all ills as truth only can heal
To avoid keeping silent when I hurt,
instead letting my love know my pain
so together we can conquer all obstacles,
 survive storms, recover from hardships and heal from wounds
And our love united will flow to all around us.

Teach us to love, O lord
To love ourselves the way you love us, just as we are.
To renew our love each waking day and promise
to love each other forever
and be faithful to our holy vows of marriage for better, for worse, in
sickness and health, to love each other till death do us part
And help each other love God more each day.
Mary mother of love, guide and protect us
Holy Spirit, source of love fill us to the brim, pressed down and
overflowing to all around us that they may be touched by God's love.
This plea we offer in union with Christ's sacrifice on the cross to
the God of love .

By Olachi Mezu-Ndubuisi
July 25, 2012

Put me back Together

Put me back together
Like pieces of a jigsaw puzzle
I have fallen away from you
I am lost in the haze
Unrecognizable
A shadow of myself

Put me back together
Like parts of a broken doll
My head dismembered from my adorned body
My heart misplaced in a heap of rubbish
Broken
A shame to myself

Put me back together
Like a soldier lost at war
I have strayed from my troops
I have abandoned my pledge
Exiled
A traitor to myself

Put me back together
Like the rays of the sun
I have lost my glow
I have lost my warmth
Cold
A shell of myself

Put me back together Lord
Lead me back to your fold, like the lost sheep
Embrace me with your mercy, like the prodigal son
That I start anew living and loving
The life, you have destined for me
My plea I will resound unceasingly
Till you put me back together again

December 13, 2012.

I Will Always Take Care Of You

"I don't want to grow up," 5 year old OlaRose said sadly,
"If I do, will you stop taking care of me?"
"No sweetie, I will never stop taking care of you? When you grow up to have kids of your own you won't need me always to take care of you"
"I don't want to grow up nor have kids. I just want you to take care of me all the time."
"I will always be your mummy, sweetie even if you grow up. I will always love you and take care of you."
"Would you take care of me always," OlaRose asked.
"Yes, baby, I will always take care of you."
"Even when I am six years old and can tie my shoes?"
"Yes, baby even when you are six."
"Even when I can take a bath by myself, can cook and drive a car, and I am tall and grown up like you?"
"Yes, baby even when you are grown up like me"
"Even when I become a doctor for babies just like you."
"Even then baby, I will always take care of you even when you are a doctor for babies just like me."
"Forever and ever and super-duper ever? " She asked anticipation
I hesitated for a second and then smiled,
"Yes, baby I will always love you and take care of you for as long I am with you. But I know for sure God will take care of me and you for ever and ever and super-duper ever..."
She smiled and hugged me.
"I love you mummy forever and ever and super-duper ever..."

January 11, 2013

By this I Shall Prevail

What is man that you mind him
What is the son of man that you care for him?
You have the authority to drive out unclean spirits.
They abound in our world today: the many faces of evil:
Lies, greed, envy, false witnesses, lust, money
Neither by my speech nor by words will I prevail against unclean spirits
But receiving and being the body of Christ
By my silent witness in my actions day to day
By my humble armor of truth through all storms
By my demeanor that embodies one word:
Serenity! Sweet, innocent serenity of mind, body and soul!

Jan 16, 2013
Chicago, Illinois

The Daughter of the Most High

I am destiny's pride
I am faith's muse
I am love's joy
I am hope's rays
I am the daughter of the Most High

I am beloved by the Father
Though walking on deep troubling waters, I will not tremble or fear
 For my eyes rest on the prize ahead
God's eyes rest on me loving, steadily
I will not falter
He is my shield and armor
Even in the thicket of flying arrows
None shall reach me
For I am under the protection of the King
If God is my anchor
Whom shall I fear, mere mortals?

He keeps his promises
His word is life and eternal
Even though all crumbles around me, through the fire, I am preserved
His arms embower and embrace me
Keeping all evil away
Even though they howl and bark, they cannot touch my soul
For I am the gift, the treasure, the pearl
The apple of His eye.

He answered me before in my hour of need
He will answer me again
He knows my troubles before they surface
He shields and protects all are according to His divine plan'
He allows the misery to manifest His power to the heathens
I will hold my head high and march forward with faith, trust, and love
I will smile amidst turmoil, for I am the daughter of the most high God.

January 30, 2013

God is With You

Dearest mummy, All shall be well ! You are under the care of St.
Joseph; protected by Mary and beloved by God.
Do not be afraid; We love you, mummy.

I love you mummy God is with you; Do not be afraid.
Mary our mother embrace mummy with your gentle arms,
Caress her soul and reign peace and joy in her heart.
We thank you Lord for choosing her to share in your passion;
for thus you sanctify her soul and prepare her for heaven.

Sweet Lord, look on our tears and allow our mother some more time
on earth with us: to nurture, love, and guide us her God-given charges.
Extend her earthly pilgrimage, so she bears the cross a little longer.
She brings more souls to love and know you on earth for your glory.

Give her strength to bear this suffering, and submit to your Holy Will.
By her suffering she has bought salvation for herself and loved ones.
Father, we need her and love her so much; but you love her more.
May your mercy overcome your justice, for her earthly work remains
May she continue to honor you through her counsel of young souls.

Arise dear mummy! Smile and be joyful for you are beloved by God
Chosen you were to share his passion; His grace is sufficient for you
He never left your side or took His gaze away from you.
You have triumphed over the evil one.
By your suffering you are sanctified

We are thankful for God's blessings and healing!
He is indeed a tender, loving, and merciful Father
His heart strings are stirred by the repentant heart and cries
Of his children like a doting parent.
Jesu Ufam Tobie! Jesus, we trust in you.
We believe in your divine mercy and submit to Your holy will for You
allow only what is good of our soul.

March 2013
Johns Hopkins Hospital Cardiac Critical Care Unit, Baltimore, MD

Book Four

The Way of Trust and Love

The Path You have chosen for me

Through which way will you lead me Lord?
I'm at crossroads now
Which path should I take, Lord
Each path looks as bright as the other
But only one path leads to my salvation,
Enabling me to do your will, to be your instrument
The path you have chosen for me

Fog abounds on this path, Lord,
Do let Your light shine on me
When I unite my will with yours, all I touch turns to gold
All doors open wide as I approach
Let me not take the path of damnation
I will crawl through the thorns
I will push through the fog
I will climb through the prickly thicket
I will run on hot coals
As long as it is the path you have chosen for me

Pain cripples me on this path, Lord
I trust in your mercy and compassion
Obstacles and detours placed my way by the evil one
Will not touch or harm me
And will only serve to accomplish your will in my life
As this detour leads indeed to your path
You have placed a thorn in my flesh,
That I may not become too elated
That my heart may not be proud
So carrying the cross you have chosen for me
And leaning on your graces, eternal love and unfathomable mercy
I accept this cross, fog, and pain O Lord
And offer all for your glory and honor
As I make my way through the path you have chosen for me

April 16, 2013

Come Sweet Suffering

Come sweet suffering stay with me
Come sweet pain, where's your sting
Come sweet humiliation, make me meek

Come, sweet suffering, fill me with the presence of the Most High
With His body, my soul is nourished
With His blood shed for me, coursing through my vessels
Drowning in his mercy, no ill shall befall me
Any snares I fall into are for the good of my soul
That God may be glorified in my misery

Come sweet pain, do not depart from me
Try me in a furnace like gold
Sieve me like diamond
Unearth me like precious pearls
I am a hidden gem, God's own jewel, His Ola
His plaything, his whip, his footstool
His possession to do as He pleases
To use to ease His suffering inflicted by lukewarm souls
To alleviate the sting of a thorn, the agony of the lance,
The unbearable pain of his ischemic organs,
Hemorrhaging for love of man.

Come sweet humiliation, I accept you willingly
I bear you patiently that my soul may not become proud
For I am nothing and exist only by His mercy.
I unite you with the passion of my savior
That you may become for me a saving grace
Come prune and tend my soul, sweet pain
That I may resemble my suffering Lord
So God can recognize his own image in me
When my soul rises to Him at the end of life's sojourn.
So come sweet suffering,
Guide me back to the path of salvation

April 17 2013
Chicago, Illinois

The Way Ahead: In Thanksgiving and Trust

I move ahead along life's path
In thanksgiving and trust
I thank you O my God
For the beautiful and rainy day
The bounty and the lacking
The praise and the scorn
The friends and the foes

You know my hearts desires
You fulfill my deepest longings
Even those I have not voiced or thought of
Even before I fathom them in my soul
Your goodness surpasses all treasures or earthly joy or love
Your fulfill my needs beyond my wildest imagination
Indeed, pressed down, filled to the brim and runneth over.

Any wish you do not grant
Is either not good for my soul or it is not the time
But you grant it at your own time and in an even better way
Truly you pamper me beyond compare
I am in awe of your goodness
And so undeserving of your kindness and mercy

Henceforth, I move along life in confidence
Trusting in your goodness and mercy
Thanking you for my every second – a gift of love
Entreating your help always, like to a beloved, doting father
I will be neither hesitant, fearful or ashamed in my succor to you
For even trifle, worldly, mundane things
For you want my happiness and joy on earth as I praise you
But this joy sometimes, will be found in the cross

When a door closes in my face
Or plans lay ruined or dreams crushed, I will not despair
For the road block is your plan
to redirect me to your chosen path for me
And the evil that men plan for me are allowed by You

And part of your plan for my salvation
To get to the rainbow, I have to go through the stormy clouds
To get to the zenith of the mountain,
I have to climb its rocky and steep terrain
I will pray for guidance and perseverance in my daily tasks,
I will go with reverence to the doors ahead
Till I find the one open one that'll lead me to your will in my life

So, I will wait patiently through hail and storm for your voice
Even when I feel alone, I know you are close to me
Even if the wolves howl and fire erupts around me
I know your wings of love surround me and shelter me
I will learn to quiet my soul, as it yearns to despair
And remember your goodness, your promise and your steadfastness
I'm thankful for my past,
I'll be steadfast in my present,
And I'll entrust my future to you, O Lord.

For at the peak of the mountain
At the end of the storm
And after the dark night
The light of your glory, mercy and love shines unsurpassed in splendor
The crown and prize is more than I deserved or imagined
For You give the best to all who let you make the choice in their lives
And nothing happens to me, unless you allow it
All things, whether good or bad in my life, is for the good of my soul
And part of your Holy Will for me.
So, I believe in your love,
I trust in your divine mercy,
and I submit to your Holy Will in my life, O Lord.

July 14, 2013

I am What I am

I am what I am
This is who I am
I am where I am supposed to be
At this very moment in the cosmos
This is what I am supposed to do
There are no mistakes, coincidences, chances, or accidents
All is known by God, ordained and allowed by Him
As part of His plan for my odyssey,
Each day is a page in my life story
Written from the beginning of time by Him who Is.

This is who I was destined to become
I am God's beloved
Made in His own image
To be fruitful and multiple in words, works, and love
To use his gifts for love of him and neighbor
To each His own special gifts and place in the world,
To each his own wondrous cross
To each His own –all for the glory and honor of God
To use and share with all that needs or seeks
And He will replenish even more than you have shared
He nourishes us with His body and blood to transformed us into Him
That He may live, walks , moves and talks through us
And touch His people – that share in His one body

I am what I am
This is who I am
An imperfect sinner
But still, He loves me like no other
So much that He gave His life for me
And daily gives that love like an endless fountain
Till He calls me to eternal life with Him

July 14, 2013

Fill me with Your Love

A desperate moan from the depths of my being
That of longing and unfulfilled desires,
Impatient I am of when my soul will be one with yours
Frustrated I am of my shortcomings and sins...
Tired I am of my imperfections
So aware I am of my weakness without you

Fill me with love for you, O my God
I give you my free will
Increase your love in my soul, O my Love
That's all I ask for
Not riches, not fame, not success, not gold or silver
I ask solely to love you like you love me
So I can love my neighbor like I should

Where is your love in me?
It is so close, yet so elusive
It's within me, yet so distant
I tire of my sins, over and over
Give me strength to overcome them
Chip away daily at my vices, like a craftsman
Train errant graces like a dedicated athlete in the gym
That I may grow in love for you
My actions oppose my desires for pure love of you

Come to me, O love
Come into my heart
Course through my body, veins, mind and spirit
Feed my heart , pumping life through my arteries and being
Direct my mind
Close my eyes to sin
Seal my lips to slander
Curb my desires
Guide my feet
All in your path of love

Fill me with Love
Love for neighbor, when unrequited
Love for foe, even when hounded by malice and falsehood
The love I feel appears conflicted
Like the sting of wounds though the battle won
Like the smell of spice in a cloud of sweet fragrance
Like the taste of lemon in a drink of nectar

The love you fill me with turns sour so quickly
So, my soul will not be elated or my heart proud
So, I can offer my pain and love, though sour to you
To rise even more fragrant and sweet
as moans while drowning in your ocean of mercy
Fill me with your love, sweet and sour
Fill me with you love, as I cannot live without.

July 23, 2013

Learning to Love

I said to my Lord in my dream - I love you Lord
Teach me how to love you daily more and more
Show me what to do for I know not

You know how to love me - You just don't want to do it
You have my grace within you
It is your will you hold on to
The choice is yours to unite your will with mine daily
To guide you in your thoughts, emotions and actions

If you want to show that you love me
The next time you work, you will come away tired
The next time you eat, you will come away hungry
The next time you give, you will come away empty
The next time you speak, you will finish lovingly
The next time you dress, you will finish gracefully
The next time you spend, you will finish modestly
The next time you serve, you will finish wholeheartedly
The next time you are angry, you will guard yourself silently
The next time you are humbled, you will bear it patiently
The next time you are wronged, you will forgive willingly
The next time you sin, you will flee to my mercy contritely
The next time you pray, you will do so like my child trustingly
And whatever you ask, you will receive unsparingly
What you desired and did not ask will be given to you abundantly

If you do just these in your everyday to your every encounter
That is the best way to show you love me
And grow daily in love with me more and more
And you and I will be one

I awoke in love and invigorated
I love you Lord, teach me daily to love you more and more
As I now do what I do out of pure love of you

August 8, 2013

Pray in Suffering

Pray even in suffering, let your soul not be troubled
When things don't go your way
Know that God is trying to get you to go in a different direction.
Keep pushing other buttons till you hit the right one.

When you pray in suffering, do not be afraid
Fear, despair or excessive worry means a lack of trust in God.
No matter what happens, trust in God.
He is real and loves you more than anyone on earth!
He allows suffering on His beloved, to bring them closer to Him
He only communes deeply with the suffering like Him.

Pray, for we do not battle flesh and blood, but principalities.
The devil never sleeps, prowls like a hungry lion, waiting to devour.
But with prayer and love we will defeat him.
So arm yourself with God's armor of trust and sword of prayer,
helmet of peace, and staff of love.

In suffering say, "Jesus I trust in you.
I offer my suffering up and unite them with yours on the cross.
Take control of my life, and thy will be done in my life.
Mary, my mother, I fly to your protection, take my offering to your
son, who never refuses what you ask.
Holy Spirit walk with me, guide my thoughts and actions
and move all hearts I encounter to do God's will."

God only allows what is good for our souls, even suffering
When we turn to Him, He showers unmeasurable graces on us
In suffering, pray, then act and God will direct the rest
If despite praying and honest efforts, things do not go your way,
Though difficult, know and accept that it happened as God willed.
If you feel peace or calm in your soul with a decision or event,
Even though spontaneous or out of your control,
That is the presence of the Holy Spirit and sign of God's will.
So pray and trust God in all things, even in suffering.

August 17, 2013

Fires of love

I see you my Lord
On fire on the cross
burning with love for me
With yearning, I run to you
I throw myself into your burning furnace of love

Set me ablaze with you my love
Light up the cold, dark cisterns in my soul
That I may yield only warmth from this fiery heat
Set my heart on fire forever
so my blood burns with truth perfusing my organs
Rekindle any flickering flames
That they send out only flickers of peace

May I shimmer with the light of your grace
Glow with the touch of humility
Purified by the heat of unwavering trust
Smothered with the ashes of compassion
Only to be set ablaze with fires even more fierce
So that united in suffering and love with your fires of life
I may die to self in your burning flames
And you now live forever in me

August 18, 2013
Chicago, Illinois

Give me your Heart

Take my heart O Lord
And make it more like yours
Transform my heart to be
A loving heart for all
A suffering heart for you
A burning heart with love
An enduring heart in trials
A silent heart in persecution
A humble heart in success
A trusting heart in uncertainty
A brave heart in fear
A forgiving heart when wronged
A giving heart in plenty
Take my heart O Lord,
And make it more like yours

August 25, 2013
Chicago, Illinois

The Way of Grace

God's grace is freely given
To whom he pleases, when and in any manner he pleases
It is not earned, deserved, or acquired by our own efforts
On my own, I am prone to sin, iniquity and vices
Despite my efforts, I am incapable of any good without God's grace
My efforts at best are clouded by pride, self-love,
I am unable to forgive ills of others, but instead bear grudges
And yet expect God's unwavering mercy

I run to you for succor O Lord
I hide under the cloak of your mother's love
I offer my sins, weak efforts, and vices to her
That she may present them with love to you
She, the perfect disciple and messenger of love
That you moved by your mother's request
You trade my sins for your graces and love
As I wait with patience and longing for her showering of graces

I will not be afraid of the future
I will not be afraid of failure, despite my weak and sinful nature
I will trust in your mercy and compassion
With bold steps , I will walk the way
The way of life with your mother
With my eyes fixed on the cross of salvation.
Rising after each fall, beneath the weight of my cross
Stopping to comfort others despite my pain and offering
In silence and humility, accepting all I encounter on this sacred path
Basking with the inner joy of communion with my Lord
Nourished by his body and blood
Sustained by maternal grace when given
And patiently accepting if no grace received
Knowing it lies therein within – regardless of corporal senses or not
Strengthened with the hope of the beatific vision
Which begins not after life, but here on earth?
Taking one step at a time along the way of grace.

Oct 10, 2013, *St. Stansilaus Koksta Church, Chicago, Illinois*

Dream so Elusive

Dream, O cherished dream so elusive
I had you within reach
But gone you are now into thin air
Like a puff of smoke

Joy, O joy so elusive
I was one with you
Basking in your radiance
Now gone you are dispersed into black clouds
Like a stormy night

Peace, O peace so elusive
I found you it seems
But only for a moment
Now gone you are into the abyss
Leaving a restlessness in the quiet of my soul

Love, O love so elusive
Reunited for a fleeting moment
But ghosts of the past again have resurfaced
And gone you are forever it seems
Leaving the ever familiar sorrow in my heart

Joy, Peace, Love, a dream it seems
Yours to gift and take as you please, O Lord
To you will I trust my soul, heart and destiny
Uniting with your passion through life's sojourn of darkness
Awaiting your gift of eternal joy, peace and love
A dream no more.

March 25, 2014,
Madison, Wisconsin

In Your Presence

In your presence, I feel love
In your presence, joy returns
In your presence, I know
It will be okay

In your presence, I feel peace
In your presence, faith returns
In your presence, I remember
It will be okay

In your presence, I feel whole
In your presence, hope returns
In your presence, I trust
It will be okay

In your presence, I feel you
In your presence, light returns
In your presence, I arise
It'll indeed be okay.

April 7, 2014
Madison, Wisconsin

Love You from Afar

A sacred bond denied,
Though the past forgiven, the pain remains
The ghosts of the past, keep us apart
So I will love you from afar

A love so deep, it is hollow
A love so strong, it is weakened
A bond seared by scars of past betrayal
So I will love you from afar

There's a love greater than this
All giving, it transcends all scars
Closer to it I'll draw from its nourishing richness
While I love you from afar

April 8, 2014
Madison, Wisconsin

To Where ... To Whom?

Torn between two worlds
Locked between two fates
Lost between two paths
To where do I turn ?

Left to my devices
Left to discern my path
Longing for guidance
To whom do I turn?

Trapped within my being
Looking within myself
Leaning deep for the truth
To where do I seek?

Lofty thoughts abound
Loathe humanities weakness
Longing to purge my flesh
To whom do I go?

I go within to listen
I go within to hear
Words of love, comfort and hope
Guiding me to the shore of peace

April 20, 2014
Madison, WI

As you arise, may I rise with you

As you arise today
May I rise in faith with you
As you arise today
May I rise in hope with you
As you arise today
May I rise in love with you
As you arise today
May I rise in compassion with you
As you arise today
May I rise in humility with you
As you arise today
May I rise in joy with you
As you arise today
May I rise in patience with you
As you arise today
May I rise in truth with you
As you arise today
May I rise in endurance with you
As you arise today
May I rise in suffering with you
As you arise today
May I rise in silence with you
As you arise today
May I rise in glory with you

April 20, 2014
Easter

Feed my Soul

Help me O Lord to feed my soul
the center of my being
From whence springs my free will
with which I make the choices
That control my heart, mind and body.
Guide   me O Lord to nourish my soul
With your presence daily in quiet prayer
With your body and blood weekly, in grateful reverence

For a soul starved of life-giving food is dead to God
Only this food can bring you closer in union with God
Without which, you are a slave of your passions
Without which, you are lost to self
Without which, your free will is carnal and all about self

Like an athlete trains his body with discipline
A physician trains his mind with dedication
A lover trains his heart with sacrifice
So must I train my soul with prayer
It takes discipline, dedication, sacrifice and practice to train one's soul
A step back and all the graces are lost

A nourished soul is enriched and free
Free to make the choice to
Nurture the body modestly, Nurture the mind humbly
And to love abundantly without reserve

A nourished soul is filled with knowledge -Knowledge of self
Knowledge of mastery of body, mind and self
Knowledge of the beauty of our humanity as divinity's image
Knowledge of discernment of God's will
That can be only discovered by faith, blind trust
and feeding your soul with prayer
So Lord, help me daily to feed my soul through this Odyssey till my
free will leads me home to you for aye

April 21, 2014

Lay it all on You

O what Love is this, my Lord
You gave your life for me
O what love you give my love
You emptied all on the cross for me
All the water and the blood
Every drop in your body
You laid down your life for me

O what Love is this my Lord
All you ask for is my trust
In your mercy and your love
For your love is all I need
For Your blood shed so dear for me

O what love you give my Lord
You bared your precious body for me
All you ask for is my sins
And all my fears,
And all my worries and all my needs
To lay it all on you on the cross

O what love you give my Lord
I accept your Love, my Lord
I will cast all my fear and doubts and needs
All my troubles and failures and worries
On you on the cross, I will give all my trust
You are the author of my life
You knew me in the womb
You named me your treasure, precious jewel
Nothing happens to me unless you allow it
Good or bad, it is all for the good of my soul
I may not see it now, but it always turns out for my good
Pain and suffering, loss, failure and shame
In time you use it all for the good of my soul

So I cast it all on you on the cross
And I lay it ... all of it

No holding back, I let it go
I give it … all of it, all my trust to you,
No matter what life throws my way
I will stand firmly in trust and love
through the pain, the hurt, the sadness , the joy, the failure
And lay it all on you on the cross
So you can unite it with your suffering on the cross
And wash me with your water and blood that I may be cleansed
As I feed my soul with your light and love, and you live in me
Through the days of my life
 So I lay it all on you on the cross

O what love this is beyond all love
That you died on the cross for me
You still love me despite my failures my weakness
You love so much
You died on the cross and shed every drop of blood for me.

O what love this is
All you ask for is my trust
That you may bear all my burdens
and you complete the love that is lacking in me
I embrace the cross as I lay it all on you on the cross.
I will trust in you, my love
I will start and end my day with you
Daily I fall in love again
Contemplating this love you have for me
Such that I will lay down my life for you
As you laid it down for me on the cross

April 27, 2014
Divine Mercy Sunday

Seven year old OlaRose

So graceful, So kind
So compassionate, So cheerful
How blessed I am
To be the mother of seven year old OlaRose

So gentle
So giving
So pure of heart
So loving
How cherished I am
To be the mother of seven year old OlaRose

Always happy
Always helping
Always thinking of Heaven
Always longing for God
What have I done to deserve
Seven year old OlaRose

"How old will I be in heaven?" she asks.
"In heaven, will all our family be there?
In heaven, will Obiola and I be together?
In heaven, can we be any age we wish to be?
Even though we grow old when we get there?
I wish me and Obiola will be seven years old
and you will be the same age as now ?
Will you still be our mummy in heaven?"
I smile in joy, "I will always be your mummy."

How I want to freeze the time, this moment,
this love with seven year old OlaRose.

May 31, 2014

There's no place like home

There's no place like home
Mezuville, the home of my birth – missed for so long
Tall, tree-lined avenue with sprawling beautiful flowers
Orchards with fresh, tropical fruits of the earth
Towering buildings of timeless decor
Sleeping to the symphonic chirping and hooting
of the night birds and creatures
Waking to the mellifluous crowing and chirping of the avian
at the first rise of dawn

There's no place like home
Regal statues relating stories of heritage, history and nature
Adam and Eve in their garden with Adam
holding the torch of life (a new redemption)
The patron –papa at the first gate watching over the hearth
Tiger, with gaping jaws, renamed "Violet" by OlaRose
Mom and Dad mounted at the home gate
In warm welcome to all to their dream hearth and nature's paradise

There's no place like home
Cherished memories of childhood abound
Laughter, and joyful patter of feet of ten siblings
through rooms and open doors
Fun games in the playground, exploring the estate
in pretend adventures
Our doting parents guiding, instructing,
molding us to care, share and love beyond compare
Birthdays, holiday celebrations,
constant flow of guests welcomed with open arms and door
Listening to the French tapes as we laid the table
for our meal and did our chores
Making garri from cassava, making pap from corn,
helping in the pig, goat, and poultry farm
Listening to folktales and learning prayers and psalms
when electricity is no more at night

There's no place like home
The hustle of bustle of Emekuku, a community with soul and heritage
The busy open market stalls,
haggling for the best price of choice food and goods.
People walking on foot for miles,
buckets in hand to fetch water, farm tools strapped on heads
Children strapped on their backs,
faces filled with joy and gratitude at each day of life
Three hour long church worship a meeting of souls full of praise,
dancing with hearts of joy and need
Giving joyfully from their widow's might
trusting deeply that the jar of oil and flour will never run out.
The bent, frail aged and the strong, bustling young ,
most sick and hungry,
All in their Sunday best: head ties, wrappers,
 gowns and coral beads in a communion of love

There's no place like home
Thankful for God's blessings, my family returns to the hearth
Laden with medicines and aid to care for the sick and needy
My heart is filled with joy and bliss
as I tend to their wounds and ailing bodies
Caring for the sick and needy ,
listening of heart breaking stories of need
Yet hearts filled with gratitude and blessings
for compassionate care received
So inspired are we by their hope and joy and strength
Receiving much more than we could give to them
All with hearts to love and hands to serve - caring for thousands
Reminiscent of the biblical crowds cared for and fed by Christ –
the divine healer in our medical mission

There's no place like home
Most memorable is sharing this experience
with my miracle baby OlaRose
A pure and innocent soul, skipping in joy,
laughing gleefully at all sounds: the hooting owl , the rustle of leaves
Enjoying native foods – 'oka and ube', gulping her soup "ofe" and garri
Relishing the nectar of succulent oranges, grapes and cherries

she plucked from the trees
Delightfully experiencing the customary loose tooth toss over the roof
and a visit from a tooth fairy too
Swinging in the playground,
exploring every corner of the estate and gardens
Running through the open doors and rooms in the house
Asking to look at my baby pictures to see our resemblance
Requesting to sleep in my childhood room
and share my childhood bed
Learning our native Igbo language studiously
with her cousin BiancaRose
Learning from her teacher, they call "*onye nkuzi*"
that "*Ntutuisi*" means hair, and
Exclaiming with joy that "*Ibolachi*" - goodmorning
has mummy's name
Picking colorful flowers from the orchards, naming the animal statues,
Chasing lizards and butterflies, counting birds,
petting the sacrificial ram
Playing with the hens – after grazing her feet
in the traditional welcome
So delighted to be part of the medical mission is she –
my seven year old bundle of joy
She indeed is a testament of God's love for me – His precious jewel
As I relive my childhood through her eyes,
I soak in the familiar smells and sights of Mezuville, Akwuosa.
From the "tropical dawn" to "songs of the hearth",
Indeed, there's no place like home.

July 27, 2014
Mezuville, Akwuosa

The Odyssey Begins

Here and now, the odyssey begins
Not waiting till the time is right
Not waiting till perfection arrives
Not waiting till the fullness of time

Here and now, the odyssey begins
This second is the right time
This imperfect you is the chosen one this time
The mission given this minute never returns

Here and now, the odyssey begins
Ready or not, here it goes
Soaking up the dawn, reminiscing at the dusk
Learning from each missed step, the next step a sprint

Here and now, the odyssey begins
With your shield and armor
Of prayer, trust and love
Through the thresholds of life, you'll cross to shore

Here and now, the odyssey begins
The Odyssey of the Soul to its maker
Through the waves and tides, through storms and winds
Not wavering in peaceful trust in Him that leads

August 10, 2014
Madison, Wisconsin

Uniting with God's Will

I offer you my free will
I seek to follow your will in my life
Wherever it may lead
Despite my weakness and selfish desires
I offer you my free will

My heart mourns an earthly loss
But my soul rejoices in finding you
I am here, Lord
You have called and I answered
My life is not my own
Loaned to me – renewed for a purpose
Lead me where you will
Do with me whatever you will

I am imperfect, marred, unworthy
Yet you have chosen me
And loved me like no other
You have pursued me like a jealous lover
Stripping me of all attachment and possession
You want me for yourself
I am totally yours
Fill me with your being

My spirit though willing, my flesh is weak
Ruled still by carnal desires
Purify me like unpure gold in a furnace
Mortify me till I am ablaze in humility
May my intentions be only out of pure love of you
I give you my bleeding heart
Wash it with your love
Ignite it with fires of your love
Make it a pleasing sacrifice
Keep those dear to me in your gaze , O Lord
Do not let one go astray
Till we reunite in your Kingdom

Your will be done, O Lord
You have cared for my every need,
more than I could ever wish for
Why would I worry that this skipped your gaze ?
This deep longing of mine.
All knowing, All powerful, All loving Father
It happened because you allowed it
Help me to offer this pain willingly, without remorse
And accept the treasure of your love and sacrifice
Accept the life you have destined for me
All paths and experiences and failures and joys and mistakes
Mistakes are only missed opportunities, now new directions
Nothing is by chance, but all is known to You
And all were to prepare me for this moment
Of total abandon to your Holy Will
I accept your will in all things
For nothing happens to me unless you allow it
For you give the best to him
That offers their will to you
And let's you lead them through your chosen path
For yours –though rocky and narrow is the path to salvation
And always for the good of our souls.
I offer you my free will
And unite it with your sacrifice on the cross

Yes, Lord I am here of my own free will
I love you above all things
I am sorry for having offended you
Never leave me, O Lord
Keep me always by your side and in your sight
And do with me whatever you will

August 12, 2014
Madison, WI

Measure Me , O Lord

Measure me O lord, level and flattened
That I may decrease while you increase
Measure my joy O Lord
That I may not become elated in my accomplishments
Knowing that of my own, I can do no good and I am nothing
All good comes from you, through you, in you and for you alone

Measure my pain, O lord,
That I may not wallow in self-pity
But rejoice in my tears knowing that I share a part of your passion
And that through suffering, I am drawn closer to you

Measure my love, O lord
That it may increase only for you
And decrease to self-interests and desires
For you alone loves me beyond compare
Pampering me beyond my wildest imaginations.
Who am I that you love me so, mere sinful mortal
You take me to the mountain peak to touch the skies
Measure my joy, so full else I burst
Out of pure love of you

Measure my fear O lord
That I may trust you and only you
You guard me from all evil
And only allow what's good for my soul
Even road blocks, become spring boards to greater heights
Derailed, the narrow path becomes the chosen one to salvation
Mistakes, become missed opportunities now new directions
In darkness, light shines forth from my soul
Alone you fill me with your presence
Slander becomes chants of accolades, all to your glory
I marvel at your divine plan, my majesty
Whom shall I fear, mere mortals?
So my love, measure me, Level, flattened
That I may decrease while you increase

August 30, 2014

I am Afraid

I am afraid, give me courage
I am sad, give me joy in suffering
I am tired, give me strength
I am alone, be with me
I am hungry, feed my soul
I am injured, heal my wounds
I am persecuted, help me show compassion
I am broken, fix me up
I am lost, show me the way
I am in darkness, shine your light
I am misunderstood, help me show understanding
I am ignorant, give me wisdom
to know that all comes from you and for your glory
I am sinful, show me mercy
I am humiliated, help me accept it
I am in despair, give me hope
I am embowered by malice, help me show love
I am losing my dream, help me trust in your will
You allow this suffering , Lord, to draw closer to me
I offer it up in union with your passion on the cross

Help me to love more; Help me to care more
Humiliate me, Lord that I may decrease and you increase
I offer all my pain, suffering, humiliation for your honor and glory.
Help me to see the pearls in these ashes of pain
Help me hold dear the treasures buried in this cloud of darkness
I asked for the gift of humility, love, and a share in your passion
Help me now to accept these graces, offered in the golden cup of gall
Help me love my detractors with burning tenderness only you can give
Help me care for others with love, my gaze fixed on you, crushed by
the weight of the cross, bleeding from pierced thorns
Help my soul sing with joy for every ill done to me, not caring for ego
I offer my pain, ignorance, humiliation to you for your honor and glory
and rejoice cause that's when you love me even more

September 6, 2014

Love in War

Love is won not by noble speeches or prolific writing
Or flowery talk or convincing demeanor
But by silent humility
Caring, loving in silent action
Letting God's work proceed in hearts

Over scrutiny of my every action
Is allowed by you
Because you expect higher standards from me - your love
I have failed you with my arrogance and self-interests
I submit to your oil of purification
Purge me in the furnace of humiliation
Till I blaze aglow with love for you and all around me

Evil is conquered not by
Powerful conferences or convincing witnesses
But my silent humility
Caring and sharing and loving
Giving up the fight
And giving in to love for all
So God may win the battle of hearts

There are no true victors or vanquished in love
There's no war in love
We're all pilgrims on earth
The militant fighting the unseen battle of souls
Put on your armor of truth
Cloak of justice, shield of trust
Helmet of love and sword of humility
With eyes raised to the cross of victory
Till the odyssey leads you home to paradise

September 6, 2014

My Offering in a pink bow

Here is my humble offering Lord
Laced in a pink bow
By your mothers gentle hands
Sprinkled with glitter and fragrance from the angels' wings
Look not onto my humble sacrifice of humility and ego
But at the love with which I offer it
The joy with which I give it
Unite it with your passion on the cross
All glory to the father

I was blind, now the scales are lifted from my eyes
I was deaf , now I can hear the murmuring around me
I was ignorant, now I know what love expects of me
I thank you for helping see, hear, know

Only God can heal and save, no other
He uses all around Him, king of hearts
He will care for them regardless
He can use anyone for this purpose

Thank you for helping me see, hear and know
What love demands of me
A sacrifice of humility
To trust and believe in those around me
To trust that God will use them as well
To accomplish His will in these little ones
For He is the King of all hearts.

Here is my humble offering Lord
Laced in a pink bow
By your mother's gentle hands
Sprinkled with glitter and fragrance from the angels' wings
My offering of humble sacrifice of love and trust in you
In union with your sacrifice on the cross
To the glory of the father

September 7, 2014

Longing For Heaven

I can't wait to go to heaven, says OlaRose
I can't wait to see Jesus and Obiola
I can't wait to see my room in heaven
Filled with all the treasures

Yes, you can, OlaRose, I say
You can wait to go to heaven
For God has more work for you on earth
More sacrifices to make to help him

For each sacrifice you get a precious rose in heaven
Soon your room will be filled with roses , sweet and lovely
For each sacrifice you help Jesus on the cross
So he does not suffer so much by himself

Then, I want to help Jesus on the cross
And get a rose for each sacrifice I make
We will start a rose club in heaven
Me, BiancaRose, UreAnjali Rose, Nanny and Aunty KC –
all the Roses in our family
You can come to our Rose club mummy and all our family too

Yes, sweetie, your "Rose Club" sounds fun
I would love to come to it sometimes
For now our work on earth remains
For God made us to know, love and serve him here on earth

"And when we are done with our work here," says OlaRose
The angels will bring our wings so we can fly to heaven
O, I can't wait to go to heaven mummy
I will make lots of sacrifices each day till it's time to go to heaven

Mummy and OlaRose

September 9, 2014
Madison, WI

I offer it All to You

My burden is heavy,
You're asking to carry it
So, I offer it you
That you may replace it with your feather light love

My fear of failure holds me back
You're asking for it
So, I offer it to you
That you may replace it with trust in you

My anxiety imprisons my mind
You're asking for it
So, I offer it to you
That you may replace it with your peace

My desire to control my destiny cripples me
You're asking for it
So, I offer it to you
That you may replace it with total abandon to your will

My longing for instant results tires me
You're asking for it
So, I offer it to you
That you may replace it with patience in your daily word

When I offer all to you – my worries, fears, free will
You transform them to amazing gifts, beyond my imagination
You complete what is lacking in my unworthy human efforts
All I need to do is trust, offer, and seek to love like you have loved me

September 25, 2014

Love is Sacrifice

Love without sacrifice is empty
Love with no sacrifice is incomplete
Love without sacrifice is not true
To love is to sacrifice

Sometimes love is not enough to hold a dream
A sacrifice is needed to make it come true
Without which, the dream remains a dream
In the shadows of what could have been

Love without sacrifice is hollow
Love with no sacrifice is shallow
Love without sacrifice is not real
To love is to sacrifice

Sometimes, the sacrifice is too much to bear
A sacrifice that love demands
Without which, love is let go
In the depths of what will never be

Love and sacrifice are one and cannot be apart
For our savior loved so much He sacrificed His life for me
True love should not separate one from this eternal truth
So indeed, this love I'll let go than sacrifice the love of my Lord

September 25, 2014

I know why you are so happy

"I am so happy", I said as we drove home from the chapel after school
"I know why you are so happy, mummy," says OlaRose
"Why do you think, my love?" I asked.

"You're happy because you have Jesus in your heart
and He fills you up."
Yes indeed, she was right.
Spending time in adoration of the blessed sacrament
Fills me up with such love, joy and peace unknown to this earth

I say to OlaRose,
"Yes my love, I am happy because I have Jesus in my heart
Do you know how you can have Jesus in your heart?"

"Yes, mummy, by talking to Him, eating communion bread,
reading the bible, and being kind to everyone we see."

"Yes, my love, We should learn about God by reading his word
Spend time with Him by going to see Him in the blessed sacrament
Even better, let Him come into our hearts
by eating his body and blood
And when we help others and are kind to them,
even though they hurt us
We are helping Jesus on the cross."

Also, there is another reason I am so happy, OlaRose."
"I know mummy. You are happy that I am your daughter."
"Yes my love, you are the best gift from God I could ever wish for.
And I am so happy you are my daughter."

September 25, 2014

Have you seen Jesus on the way today?

Have you seen Jesus on the way today?
Stripped, beaten, hungry, bleeding,
But so in love with you
If you have not seen Jesus today, you are holding on to your pain
For He stands right before you offering His love, joy and peace

Have you seen Jesus on the way today?
Do not despair for our sins are ropes with which He draws us near
When we turn our backs to heaven by our sins,
we come face to face with Jesus on the way to Calvary.
Only then can we feel His love and mercy so real
Our sins are opportunities to accept God's grace in our lives

Have you seen Jesus on the way today?
Asking that we give him our struggle with sin and accept His love
Life is a daily struggle against our sinful human nature,
Some walk to him, deaf and blind to the howls of the flesh,
Eyes fixed on the crown of glory on the crucified Christ
their souls soaked in humility and penance
Others behold the cross, but are distracted by worldly pleasures,
And turn their backs to heaven, only to meet Jesus face to face
In torn clothes, tortured, shamed by our sins, but so in love with us.
He beckons to us, "Give me your cross, my love, that I may carry
Your iniquities and suffering I have borne
Give me your sorrow, anger, pain, betrayal,
And I will make all things new!"

Have you seen Jesus on the way today?
He reaches out to us offering his love and mercy, freely given
It cannot be forced on us because of our divine gift of free will
God loves us because of our sins and despite our sins
We then lean on him and let Him bear our cross and burdens
And turn to behold His cross ahead, shinning the path to salvation.

Have you seen Jesus on the way today?
Do we ignoring His offer of love and mercy
To bear our cross along the path from Calvary to Heaven?

Do we take our cross from him, choosing to carry our guilt and burden
despairing over our sins, the sure path to Hades?
As long as you live, Jesus will always meet you along the path
When you accept His divine mercy and turn towards heaven,
You do not see Jesus 'cos he walks alongside you in same direction,
but guided by faith and love, learn to trust that He is always with you
When you falter through sin, you come face to face with Him.
Take a second from your pain and self-pity, and look at His face of love

Have you seen Jesus on the way today?
You encounter Him when you turn away from Heaven
Do not reject His love and mercy of Christ.
Sins, mistakes, shame, loss, grief, misfortunes are blessings in disguise
Christ's rope of salvation, calling us to Him against our human nature
These stumbling blocks are our detours that can bring us back to God
Through self-knowledge of our human weakness and nothingness
And understanding of the all-knowing, loving and powerful God
Who loves us so much that He took on human flesh
to feel our pain and guide us back to Paradise.

Have you seen Jesus on the way today?
Stripped, beaten , hungry, bleeding
But so in love with you
He will do amazing, beautiful things in your life,
If you will only allow Him.
Please, look for Jesus on your way today, through life's odyssey

September 26, 2014

Come to me Spirit

Come to me O Spirit of Life
Fall on me like the dew fall at dawn
Renew, invigorate, and revive
That I may live for you

Come to me O Spirit of Truth
Shine on me like the rays at dawn
Ignite, illuminate my soul
That I may know that you live in me

Come to me O Spirit of wisdom
Descend like the fall leaves in abundance
Enrich, overcome my soul
That your work may flow through me

Come to me O Spirit of Peace
Blow like the breath of dawn
Abide within me and make thy home
That my will may be united with thine

Come O All Knowing and Powerful Triune Spirit
Infuse me with your grace
Transform my meagre efforts and quest for truth
That all may be for your honor and glory

October 26, 2014
Madison, Wisconsin

For Your Eyes Only

They will look but will not see
My heart, my life, my love
Encased, enclosed, hidden
They will read but will not know
My words, my mind, my will
Embowered, entwined, unknown
They will listen, but will not hear
My voice, my breath, my spirit
Engulfed, transformed, whispered
For all are for your eyes only my Love
Only you see my soul,
Only you know my love
And only you hear the murmuring
In the depths of my being
Hidden to all, despite what they see, know and hear
All are for your eyes only, my love
Giver of life, love and truth, Amen!

October 26, 2014

I will love Again

Was that love? Why then gone without a trace?
My bruised heart fearful
Now closed to love's door
Yet a glimmer sheds doubts
Was love my destiny? Or is there another ?

I will love again
Broken and deserted
I'll heal and mend
Hopes dashed, wishes lost
I'll dream again
Tears dried, sorrow lifted
I'll smile again
Memories painful and ruined,
I'll build new ones
Faith lost, doubts abound, I'll believe again

I still believe in ever after
I still long for true love's promise
Through my pain and hurt
I'll immerse myself in God's love
And let divine love heal, soothe and renew
And be open to the fruits and yearning

I have so much love in me; and so much love to give
Love is a truly a choice
So despite the hurt, pain, loss, fear, doubts, and uncertainties
I can, will and choose to love again
Drawing from God's fountain of love
Thankful for my gift from God – my joy
Precious and pure – my OlaRose
Given to see me through life's storms
A source of delight and pure joy at all times
A reminder of God's eternal love for me.
With a joyful resolve, I will indeed love again

November 18, 2014

My Heart Stirs

The dark clouds descend
My hearts stirs
I see through the darkness
To the glimmer of light beyond
I claim my joy
Given to me by the eternal light

Dreams shatter, hopes dashed
My heart stirs
I dream beyond the limitations
To the eternal destination
I claim my hope-filled dreams
Fulfilled beyond my imagination
By the maker of dreams above

The door shuts, obstacles block my path
My heart stirs
Redirected past the closed doors
I climb and soar above the obstacles
To reach heights beyond my wildest imagination
My true destination ordained by
The way of life above

Empty, forlorn, forsaken
My heart stirs
I will drink from the fountain of love
My cup of blessings full, pressed down and running over
Overwhelmed and overflowing with goodness
Satisfied beyond my desires
By the bread of life and blood of salvation.

The murmurings and slander abound
My heart stirs
I listen beyond the noise to the sounds of the trumpet of victory
I am the daughter of the Most High
His wondrous works in my life
Will be murmured about even louder till the ends of time.

Anxiety returns, uncertainty and fears
My heart stirs
I remember the fears of yesteryears,
Gone in a puff of smoke
So shall today's illusions
Evaporate in a cloud of faith
I believe without knowing tomorrow
For I trust in He who knows tomorrow
Be it done to me according to His word.

My heart stirs knowing that the author of my life
Is yet to write the best chapter of my life
The most amazing things, He will yet do in me, have not been written
His will for me is accomplished despite obstacles,
mistakes, seeming misfortunes
Like a jigsaw puzzle, every misplaced or mismatched piece
is vital to the final outcome
The molding of my soul like clay
The masterpiece- that I am yet to become
Only if I abandon myself completely to the divine carpenter
To chip away at imperfections
To test the gold in blazing furnace of flames
And ignite love beyond compare within
So I am beautifully and wondrously made
Known to Him before my soul's existence
A mirror image of my savior - in suffering and in glory.
So craft me, divine craftsman
When my heart stirs.

December 4, 2014
Madison, WI

Maria, full of grace

Maria, full of grace pray for me
Maria, immaculate conception, help me be pure
Maria, meek and humble, teach me humility
Maria, handmaid of God, show me how to serve
Maria, help of the sick, teach me compassion
Maria, intercessor with Christ, anticipate my needs
Maria, mother of all, be my mother dear
Maria, spouse of the spirit, give me peace
Maria, joy of the angels, teach me joy
Maria, vessel of honor, help me seek truth
Maria, queen of heaven, pray for me
Maria, bosom of love, enrich my love
Maria, your son refuses nothing from you,
Maria, please secure my soul with God

December 8, 2014
Feast of Immaculate Conception

Choosing Joy, Love, Peace

Joy is a choice
Love is a choice
Peace is a choice
Joy, love and Peace
Today I choose you

I have no control over what people's thoughts, words or actions
I can only control my thoughts, words and reactions to them
So I choose peace where there's strife
I choose to understand when misunderstood
I choose to be joyful when others would expect me to be mad.
I choose to love even when I've been treated with malice.
I choose to speak well of others though they've spoken ill of me

For when joyful in every word or action
Love radiates from within
With love comes peace of heart and thoughts
So I choose joy, a name I bear
I am joy and will live in joy – through pain or gain.

You can take away accolades and praise
You can take away your praise
But no-one can take my joy, love, and peace
Divine gifts freely bestowed to me from above
Unless I let them

Joy, Love, and peace
Virtues hard to acquire
Virtues easy to lose
You will become mine
if I make the choice
to hold on to you in my everyday

Dec 13, 2014

Only You know my Heart

I will not show my pain
For no words can convey
The hurt I feel in my heart
Only You know how I feel even more than words can say

I will not show my sorrow
For no words can convey
The grief I feel in my heart
Only You know how I feel even more than words can say

I will not show my fear
For no words can convey
The panic I feel in my heart
Only You know how I feel even more than words can say

I will not bare my heart, for no words can convey my emotions
Only You can comfort, bring peace and joy, justice and truth
I will draw close to you in suffering
Drawing strength from your mere presence
Knowing and Believing that you make all things new.

December 14, 2014

Waiting in Joyful Hope

I wait in joyful expectancy
My heart ready to be filled
By Joy beyond compare
From a boundless cosmos of joy

I wait in peaceful expectancy
My soul ready to be embowered
By peace beyond compare
From a limitless tornado of calm

I wait in loving expectancy
My being ready to be consumed
By love beyond compare
From a fiery ocean of love

I wait to receive Joy, peace, and love
Gifts from a babe in swaddling clothes
God made man, on earth he stooped
My sins he bore to gift me life and hope

I wait in joyful, peaceful, and loving hope
A slave no more, the daughter of the King
Abundant blessings bestowed on me according to my faith
O what greater love than this.

December 21, 2014

Suffering I Embrace You

Suffering,
You are my saving grace
My cup of salvation
I drink you with joyful thirst

Suffering,
Your sting is gone
I embrace your thorns
With warmth and love

Suffering,
I used to be fearful and anxious of you
I did not understand why if God loved me
Why he would let me suffer so?
Soon, I grew to accept that you existed

Suffering,
I soon knew that I suffer because God loves me
Through my suffering I was sanctified
He bears my suffering with me
I only need to trust in Him and accept His love
His grace is sufficient to overcome all

Suffering,
Still, I tried to pray you away
Relieved when you were gone
Living in fear of your lurking
Defeated when you returned

Suffering,
Now I understand you're my ladder to heaven, I fear you not,
I expect you, welcome you; and I am battle ready
I am embowered with divine weapons of love, peace and joy
Willing to be molded like clay, refined with fire like Gold
Ready to bear your scars of victory,
With which my maker will know me

Suffering,
Please come and stay
Your bring my sins and imperfections to light
My opportunities to receive God's grace and mercy
And become a victim of His love
Through you my soul is cleansed and healed
My character is refined and my love tested

Suffering,
You are my road to Calvary
Death to self, like Christ on the cross
If borne with patience and love
You exalt me to higher heights
Drawing me closer to my suffering Christ

Suffering,
Victorious I am over you
I can offer you up with every sting
Numb to pain, gall tastes like nectar for real
Because of the unshakable trust in He who knows tomorrow
Believing the suffering is leading me to
my abundance, my victory, my destiny
Not just for aye but for here and now

December 21, 2014

Ten Mantras

Silence is golden
Words have power
Happiness lies within
Sin is a choice
Sacrifice is rewarding
Error is human
Forgiveness is divine
Life is a trial
Free will is sacred
Humility is power
Peace is renewing
Love conquers all

January 1, 2015

Today

Today is the first day of the best year of my life
Today, I accept my humanity, but claim my divine heritage
Today, I unlock my doors of opportunities
Today, I reap my harvest of success
Today, I release yesterday's sorrow
Today, I embrace tomorrow's happiness
Today, I am thankful for the daylight
Today, I am grateful for the approaching dusk
Today, I give my all in faith
Today, I receive God's all in love
Today, I know will be a great day
Today, I expect graces in abundance
Today, my cup of gall will be tomorrow's drink of nectar
Today, I will bear my sufferings meekly,
Today, an even better tomorrow is only a heartbeat away.
Today will be great, but my best days are yet ahead

January 4, 2015

Wounded Soul

A wounded soul you are
Tormented by pains of ages past
Bleeding from self-inflictions
Howling like a hungry wolf
Changing colors like a chameleon
Rambling like a demented neurotic
Circling like a hairless chicken
Haunted by deceit and lies
Unable to help yourself
Driven by carnal needs
Bloated with egoistic views
Yearning for understanding
Self destruction abound
Your own worst enemy
Strength misused now weak
Lacking in moral conscience
From whence sprung beauty so pure
Bounty, now hollow emptiness
So blessed, yet seemingly cursed
One can only feel pity for you, O wounded soul

January 21, 2015

Free at last

I'm free at last
My heart is light
The burden lifted
My conscience is clear
The guilt dissipated
My day is bright
The shadows gone
My horizon is clear
The fog disappeared
My future is amazing
The past renewed
My path is unknown
The thought exciting
My will is united
With Him in whom I trust
I'm free at last
To live and to love

January 21, 2015

I'm content

Some dreams may not come true
Some hopes could remain unfulfilled
Some tasks may be unfinished
Some pain may still linger
Some treasures may remain unearthed
Some goodbyes may be forever
Yet, somehow, I'm okay with that

Trust in divine mercy and Faith in God's love
Hope in divine providence and Knowledge of God's goodness
Brings peace in the storm and unwavering faith in the midst of doubt
All things, though caused by our sinful human nature
Are known to Him and allowed by Him, but not caused by Him
He uses them ultimately for our own good

So, I will trust like a little child
Pining for more candy, but its mother says no
Trying to touch the fiery flame, but her hand is knocked away
Petulant, crying, but deep down knowing it is for her own good
I may not see it now with my finite, human vision
But the all-seeing, all knowing, all loving father does
So He shields me, detours me, stops me, slows me down
Or closes hearts and influences actions, even of others

So, trusting with the heart of a child climbing on its mothers knees
With no fear of rejection, even though just chastised fiercely
I trust, I believe, and I submit to your Holy will
This too shall pass and in time it will be revealed
What marvel you've in store for me, beyond my wildest imaginations
Surprise me, O Lord, as I wait, in joyful expectancy
Despite the pain, suffering and loss, Your love dissipates all fears
Though a fallen creature, your graces instills confidence
And peace in the heat of the storm rests within my soul
So at this moment, with unanswered prayers and unfulfilled desires,
I'm content.

January 22, 2015

Your Grace is all I need

My days are joyful, because your grace is all I need
My nights are restful, because my heart rests on yours
Your murmurings in my soul alluring, Your breath of life invigorating
Your seeds of greatness bearing roots within me, awakened by faith

Despite storms, my boat sways peacefully
I can walk on water, as long as my gaze rests on you
In Your image, I'm beautifully made, overwhelmed by your goodness
Stumbling blocks are only stepping stones to greater heights
Ordained by you, before I was formed in the womb
With confidence I strive through life with my armor of faith,
Sword of truth, Power of my words, speaking faith, love, and hope
Believing in your mercy, holding on to your peace
I can tell your loving peaceful nudging of my spirit
Distinct from the nagging restless thumping of the evil one
I will not worry or lose my peace, 'cos all is known by you,
allowed by you, and will be used by You for the good of my soul

Words cannot convey how much I love you
You need my arms to hold, my heart to love,
My voice to speak, my legs to journey
I am yours and yours alone, be it done to me according to your will
Despite the chaos my earthly eyes sees, or doubts of my feeble mind
No weapon or flying arrows shall touch me
Even if they kill me, I will not die but will live forever
I will claim my victory for I am blessed and loved beyond compare
By the creator of the universe – my Abba, Father

Your grace is enough for me for I trust in your goodness and mercy
You complete what is lacking in my efforts
My blessings overflow as you raise me high, all to your glory
Not by my effort or good deed or hard work, but by You
Who makes the impossible possible, and ordinary extraordinary
Guide me and always lead that I may follow with unwavering faith
Through forest and storms, thorns and blizzards
O how I love you so, Your grace is all I need.

February 3, 2015, *Madison, Wisconsin*

Weekend Spiritual Retreat at Valley of Our Lady Monastery

Friday, February 6, 2015 - Vespers:

"Lord, what is man that you care for Him? Mortal man that you keep him in mind. Man who is merely a breath, whose life is like a passing shadow. Lower your heavens and come down... reach down from heaven and save me, draw me forth from the mighty waters,..."
Psalm 143a

Dear Family,
We are in a lovely sanctuary, quiet, serene, peaceful and welcoming, nestled in the woods in rural Wisconsin. We were welcomed by young Sister (Sr.) Christina Marie, a picture of serene joy. She showed us the simple but comfortable guesthouse with a kitchen and living room. It happens that we are all to ourselves as the other lady guest postponed till Sunday. They are a cloistered convent, and do not come out in public except those with specific duties like doorkeeper or cook or postulants. They are a congregation of 21 sisters from 24 yrs to 81 yrs according to Sr. Christina Marie.

We arrived at 4:20 p.m. and after putting away luggage, we went to the chapel for vespers (5 p.m. prayers). They sang the psalms in Latin from their cloister above the chapel looking down - hidden from us below. In the pews with us were just two elder sisters. After Vespers, Sr. Christina Marie kindly served us dinner: neatly laid out fish with batter, vegetables, potatoes, and applesauce with hot tea. It was delicious. We ate alone after an older sister chatted with us.

We will return to the chapel for compline (6:30 p.m. prayers) and then benediction. They sing all the prayers with their soft, angelic voices.

After benediction, we'll shower and go to bed. It's a simple and peaceful life. Makes you forget life's troubles and bustle. All seems frivolous and you remember what matters - your eternal soul.

OlaRose is enjoying the experience and the sisters love seeing her. I'm emailing to let you know we arrived safely and are fine. Have a good weekend. Love you all.

Always,
Olachi

****

Saturday, February 7, 2015 1:15 AM
Subject: Valley of Our Lady Monastery -- Peace

Psalm 37:
...Trust in the Lord, and do good...Commit your way to the Lord, Trust also in Him, And He shall bring it to pass. He shall bring forth your righteousness as the light. And your justice as the noonday. Rest in the Lord, and wait patiently for Him; Do not fret because of him who prospers in his way... cease from anger and forsake wrath; Do not fret - it only causes harm.
... For evil doers shall be cut off; but those who wait on the Lord, they shall inherit the earth.
... The steps of a good man are ordered by the Lord, And He delights in his way. Though he fall, he shall not be utterly cast down, For the Lord upholds him with his hand.
...For the future of the blameless man is peace.
... The salvation of the righteous is from the Lord; He is their strength in the time of trouble. And the Lord shall help them and deliver them... Because they trust in Him."

Dear Family,
The loud yet carefully quiet bang of a rustic bell woke me up at midnight - I guess for their prayers. They have another one at 3:50 a.m. OlaRose is sleeping peacefully and soundly. We are in the same building with the sisters, separated by walls from their cloister. You do not hear a sound from their rooms or quarters. In the chapel

yesterday, I would hear an occasional cough amidst their silent meditation - a reminder of their humanity and the choice they have made to seek God in the silence of their hearts, to hear him and commune with him in a way so profound, it's alluring.

OlaRose was wondering yesterday at bedtime why they go to church so many times and I explained that they have different prayers for each part of the day. She loves their food, though. There is an old TV in the living room of the guest house, but we did not use it. We are enjoying the serene quiet. OlaRose brought her journal and plans to write in it every day while we are here. She wrote that "It is very peaceful and calm here." I do agree.

Their life is a simple thanksgiving to God - singing psalms at every third hour or so (Liturgy of the Hours). We glimpsed 1 or 2 of the young sisters kneeling with head bent in adoration in the chapel. They walk away back to their cloister for prayers with eyes lowered (seemingly closed) in serene meditation.

I marvel at the peace they exude and that is infused in this hidden life and sanctuary. Is it possible to acquire this peace in our busy life? What about that firm conversation you need to have, wrong impression you need to correct, rebuke you need to give, assertion you have to make. There is so much we feel the urge to do in our every day. Is it really needed to have that last word, win that argument, correct that wrong impression, and put that person in their well-deserved place? Can we forgo those urges and see that they don't change our lives and the day still is bright and didn't stop, or get prolonged by that last justification we needed.

It seems more rewarding to maintain control of your emotions, not giving in to disturbing your inner peace and sanctuary, withholding that retort or word, smiling in silence instead of an angry glare. Guarding jealously our thoughts and words, for they do indeed have power in them, releasing into existence only that which we wish on ourselves: peace, love, joy, and understanding, no matter the provocation! There is already someone whose vow it is to fight our battles, seek vengeance on our behalf and take stock of ills done to us and reward us double fold - our Father, the Creator of the universe!

"Fear not," He said. "My peace I give to you, my peace I leave with you." We do have that peace always within us - the peace no human love, praise or possession can give. We always have a choice of peace or fear or unrest in our everyday. We need to make the choice to live with joy and love and peace.

My free will is God's most powerful gift to me. I get to choose peace or fear every minute by my thoughts, words and actions. Someone can say mean or hurtful words or do something bad to me; that's their choice and I cannot control that. What I can control is how I react to them. If they decided to ruin my day, my joy, my peace, why would I agree with them and give in to anger, bitterness, hatred, revenge and poison my thoughts, mind, actions, day and future? Those negative emotions only lead to one negative decision or choice after the other. It is a cycle or spiral I have within me to end or halt at any point by the decision to act differently - just like that. God, in addition to His free will, has given me the grace to overcome temptation. His grace is sufficient for me and I will never be tempted beyond what I can bear.

I will endeavor to use my choice wisely and decide to control my emotions, hold my tongue, keep my peace, and hence my joy. That choice to ignore that remark or spiteful action brings me peace and determines how my day proceeds and ends. The evil one will always tempt us using coworkers, strangers and even loved ones, but remembering that this is a daily battle for my soul will help me keep the peace and choose what words I release into my life.

I'm going back to sleep... We'll sleep in (skip 5 a.m. prayers at Matins) and join the sisters for mass in the chapel at 8 a.m. Goodnight!

Love you all,
Olachi.

Subject: Valley of Our Lady Monastery - My Desert Place

Dear Family,
Read if you can, save it if you can't ... So long a read but I feel I should share my wrritings with you, my loved ones. I am rested, renewed, joyful and ready for the rest of my journey. Ngozi, your patience and spirit must have been nurtured from your experience living in a convent school - it is beautiful here.

Saturday February 7, 2015,
Prayer at Terce: 7:45 a.m.

Psalm 120:
I lift up my eyes to the mountains, from whence shall come my help?
My help shall come from the Lord Who made heaven and earth...
...The Lord will guard you from evil. He will guard your soul...
Hymn: Now Holy Spirit, one with father and with son. Come quickly penetrate and fill the souls that thirst for you...

After a hot morning shower, we had breakfast in the guest house kitchen. It was well stocked. We helped ourselves to orange juice, hot chocolate and buttered wheat bread. We joined prayers at Terce at 7:45 a.m. followed by a lovely mass at 8am.

Our young, angelic guest mistress, Sr. Christina Marie is so sweet. She left a note on the Liturgy book for OlaRose beginning with "Dear chore lover".. inviting OlaRose to join the sacristan at 10 a.m. to clean the chapel." (See attached). OlaRose was so ecstatic. She had told the sister yesterday when we arrived that she loves chores, and I had told her the sisters do chores like baking, cooking, sewing, cleaning, setting tables, laundry, etc. It is so nice that they are allowing us participate in their life, though they are cloistered.

At mass, Fr. Joseph talked about how Christ retreated to the desert with his disciples for prayer and solitude in the midst of the crowds following him, seeking miracles and his words of hope. The sisters laughed at his jokes from their cloister above the chapel. It was nice to know they had a sense of humor. During communion, we were surprised to see that all the sisters came down the cloister stairway in a single file for communion. They were a beautiful, serene vision in their white habit - all 24 or so, eyes lowered, faces serene. OlaRose was happy to see them all. A couple sisters joined us in the pew for mass and you could see they were pleased to see us too. She has been so well-behaved, as usual, observing the silence easily with joy. It seemed as if today, the veil of the cloister was opened for us and we began to see the sisters as they are: women with the same needs, struggles, fears, desires, who have freely made a choice to live for God - a choice they have to renew everyday with God's grace.

There is such peace here, I cannot describe it. It feels like my desert away from the world ... I need to seek some solitude in my busy life. Not just being home alone, but a time to retreat into prayerful solitude (no TV, noise, or rambling in my brain) and listen to God. I am so grateful for this opportunity.

At 10 a.m., we met Sr. Marie Gabriel, the middle aged sacristan, so full of cheer and wit. We dusted and vacuumed the chapel with her. She was delighted to have us helping her with chores. She had not seen anyone quite as happy to do chores like OlaRose was. We spent 2 hrs merrily cleaning and talking with sister. Sr. Marie Gabriel was so kind and gave me some spiritual counseling. She encouraged me to take each day at a time to discern God's will in my life; but to live in the present and enjoy God's blessings in my life. She advises to receive daily communion and frequent confessions. "It sustains us," she said. "It's God's gift to you." She said she could not imagine living without daily communion or weekly confession. I was amazed she spoke to me for as long as we did. They do have normal views and feelings, and their silence now I understood was true admirable self-discipline indeed. Sr Marie Gabriel gave OlaRose and I warm hugs and told us how beautiful we were. She said OlaRose's sparkly red shoes reminded her of Dorothy in Wizard of Us. Soon, the bell rang for prayers at Sext (noon). The sisters filed in with soft patter of feet above the chapel from their enclosure and they sang hymns in Latin form their cloistered pews above, and then a yummy lunch with potatoes and cranberry sauce with green peas. Fr Joseph joined us for lunch with a family that was helping repair the flooring in the fathers' guest house.

We had prayers at None (2:15 p.m)
Ps125: "What marvels the Lord worked for us! Indeed, we were glad..."

After none, OlaRose and I took a brief stroll down the street next to the monastery, and she skipped gleefully around. It was so serene. When we returned, we got a couple items: rosary and medals from their craft store - all hand made. At 3:15pm we had scheduled to meet with Sr Mary Benedicta (who had replied my first email) and she spoke to us about their life. OlaRose told her she wanted to be a nun and a doctor. They all think it is sweet, and told her she will know as she grows up if that's what God is calling her to do, but she will have to finish college first before making a decision. The Cistercians are a reformed order of Benedictines and sustain their cloister through work inside the convent (craft work, baking altar bread), so unlike Carmelites that accept from age 18 yrs, you have to learn a skill or understand how to be independent or be used to responsibilities before coming to their cloister (their minimum age is 21 yrs). Sr Benedicta was so delighted with OlaRose, and said she hoped she will always be close to God as she grows up. Sr. Mary Benedicta is African American (a protestant convert whose parents divorced) witty, full of jokes and laughter. She had finished University and taught for a while before entering the convent. Sr Benedicta invited us to return to visit whenever we want, even at short or no notice. "We do not go into the world," she said, "and our only contact is when you come to us." You could tell that our presence had infused such delight and life in them too - it was mutual.

After joining the sisters for vespers (5 p.m. prayers) we had dinner with Fr Joseph alone. Dinner was beef lasagna - sister cook had outdone herself. Everyone was happy with the sister who had just begun her new assignment as cook this week. They rotate chores (cooking, cleaning, guest mistress, etc.). Sister Margaret Mary, the oblate director gave me some information about their third order oblates; and gave OlaRose a Benedictines medal as a gift, and chatted with OlaRose across the cloister separation. They just enjoyed her presence. OlaRose drew a picture and wrote a thank you card for the sisters - Sr. Christina was delighted and said she'd hang it on their board for all to see. We skipped compline prayers at 6:45 p.m. so Father Joseph and I could speak for a while.

I feel so well nourished spiritually from this retreat, and so pampered by God. I trust Him implicitly and believe all will turn out for my own good. In this sanctuary - this desert place, I have found what I need for the journey ahead and I am thankful: silence, communion with God, and obedience. I need to seek silence and a desert place to commune with God in my every day. I need frequent communion and confession. That'll restore in me that faith in God's love and mercy that no howling wind can blow away, like a reed I may bend but never break. Having the real presence of God in communion and adoration instills a trust in Him that unites your will to His, knowing that all will be for your good - even that meant for your harm He will use for your good. When hearts are hardened towards you, remember He is ruler of all hearts. Like He hardened Pharaoh's heart so that His power may be manifest in a greater way, so maybe He is allowing opposition around you, things not to go your way, hard work not to be fruitful in the immediate, so He can work a wondrous work for you later.

I need to be obedient to authority around me - except in matters that go against my moral conscience or faith. Even Christ was obedient to Pilate, even unto death and didn't even defend himself against false accusations. Through that surrender of self will, He conquered the world - opened the gates of heaven and won salvation for all mankind. If the devil knew that his masterplot to kill the son to God would do all this - 2,000 years and counting, he would not have done so. So, I have to submit to authority in my workplace, family, as they are God's instruments to guide me, even if to teach me humility. He can influence their hearts too. If I am filled with His grace from communion and prayer, His grace will flow from me to them. God has no feet, hands, or voice on earth - we are His body. He needs us to reach people that do not know Him or are so lost in pain and despair, they can't feel Him. Only by our example of humility, obedience and joy that people are drawn to HIM who rests within us, such that they understand that our works are blessed despite what they or others do to stop it, and they begin to long for what we have - our blessings, our joy, our faith. With time, they will realize that what we have is the grace of Christ. That's how we win souls for Him. Not by our fine speeches or wondrous works but our silent witness, humble demeanor, and loving example.

I know that God has done amazing things in my life. Look in your life and marvel at His goodness too. He's taken me places I have never dreamed of going. He has fulfilled my every desire, some even before I voiced or thought about them. He's done things that put me in awe above and beyond my dreams for myself. Why would I think He does not know or see my needs now? I remember that in the past, what I thought was the silence of God was actually heaven's behind the scenes massive preparation of unprecedented blessings in my life - that manifested at a later time. So, now I will bear patiently, wait faithfully, live joyously, and trust lovingly, that He will fulfill His divine will in my heart.

God is so good and loves me so. Anticipating life's struggles and my times of doubts, He gifted me with a daily reminder of His love for me, a reminder of His loving mercy, a reminder of His divine power, and a source of constant "Joy " - my OlaRose. She is pure joy to all she meets and I've realize that she is my "Joy" too. He has protected this " Joy" fiercely and passionately over the years, even separating her from anything that could mar her soul. Thus, she is the joy and pure heart she is today. What is God's gift in your life? Look around you and see these gifts: your health, your success at work, your kids, your spouse, your life. He has a mission for you on earth that only you can fulfil. Your nature, passion, temper, indecision, even things people don't like about you - God put in you for a reason. He says you are fearfully and wonderfully made - such that after making you, on the sixth day he looked at this masterpiece — "you" and said, "This is good." He wants to do amazing things in your life, if you'll let Him. Thank Him daily for His goodness even in your pain, sorrow and lack; and He will turn all that was meant for your harm to unparalleled blessings. If we mere mortals can give our kids the best toys, good food, beautiful clothes, and want to make them happy, why do we think God our almighty Father in heaven cares any less for us. He cares about our every need: food, job, success, peace, companionship, etc. Didn't he bless Solomon with riches and gold even though Solomon asked only for wisdom? Didn't he feed thousands when they were hungry, or turn water into wine at a wedding? No need is frivolous or trivial for Him.

He wants us to be happy on earth and use whatever He gives us to serve him. We are a reflection of him, as our kids are a reflection of us. Who wants their kids looking sad and miserable and dirty? Why would we think God wants us to look sad, alone, unhappy and hungry all the time. Who would want to worship such a God or Father. He wants us to radiate such Joy that people are drawn to us, and want to have what we have, which is HIM.

Even my mistakes, seemingly wrong decisions, God has turned around for my own good. I have often wondered, could there have been a less tumultuous path to the same destiny if I had been patient and trusted God in the midst of my troubles? I am realizing closed doors are detours God plants in our way, stumbling blocks are stepping stones to greater heights. When filled with indecision, it's also okay to wait and do nothing if you can't discern God's will. God still will accomplish His will, with or without you (like Mordecia told Esther in the bible). He will use someone else to direct you. But I believe there is a better way to journey through life - living in the desert - nourished by his body, he lives physically within you such that you can hear Him clearly and you are guided more surely, so that when those obstacles do come from your human failings or choices other people make - which you have no control over, your faith is still steadfast, and you are able to wait with joyful expectancy, humble resilience, loving abandon to His will. That way the hills and valleys of life feel like a level, equanimous path to the shining goal ahead.

Tomorrow, we go back to our reality: school, work, doubts, fears, insecurities, uncertainties, everyday bustle. But I feel confident that I have the tools I need to face them. I may not have all the answers, I may make mistakes or falter; but I know how to get up after each fall and continue my journey, refuel with divine nourishment, respray myself with nonstick oil of renewed trust such that those doubts, fears and the dust of life do not linger or stick to my being. I will restart each day and minute anew, not live in my past but, *rather forgive my past and learn from it, embrace my present and enjoy it, and hope in my future and dream of it.* Those dreams my Dream maker above will fulfil above and beyond. I may not practice all I have written and resolved to do - Don't hold me to it. It will be difficult, but I surely will try. Even when I do not feel God's presence in me, I know He is there. The closer

I get to Him, the less He shows me external joy and emotions, because He trusts my love for Him does not need constant reassurance. I have to remain steadfast in those spiritually dry times. Sr. Marie Gabriel says she does not get frequent consolations - so their task is difficult going through everyday not feeling God. So, she says it is the Eucharist that sustains them - it's God's gift to you. I will accept this free gift and nourish myself with it.

OlaRose has lots of stories to tell her class and teacher who were fascinated when she told them she was spending a weekend at the convent. The kids were more shocked when the teacher told them that OlaRose would have no TV or toys the whole weekend.

Sunday February 8, 2015:
Prayers at Terce (7:45 a.m.) followed by morning mass at 8am.

As we packed our luggage this morning and got ready for mass, OlaRose said, "Mommy do you know that there is a statue of our Lady, Mary, in the chapel?" I asked if she meant the big statue outside the monastery, and she replied "No, there is a statue of Mary in the church." Not knowing where she was going with this I replied, "Okay, and..."
OlaRose added, "and, right beside the statue is a rose. A single rose flower." I smiled in confusion saying again, "and..."
She continued, "and there's Rose in my name. I saw it yesterday and thought it's there because my name is OlaRose."
My heart stopped. I didn't remember seeing a statue with a rose. I smiled slowly saying, "Maybe Mary is speaking to you, OlaRose. Sometimes God lets us notice or see things that others don't"
"But, it's there mummy, the sister saw it too," she said.
I smiled, "I'm sure it's there. But someone may just see a rose. But you saw a rose and thought it was there because it's in your name. God put that thought in your heart. That's how he speaks to you."
She looked confused, "but I didn't hear him or anyone speaking to me. I just saw the rose right there."
I continued, "Yes sweetie, you don't need to hear a voice when God speaks to you. He puts thoughts in your heart and mind, and you just know it and it feels peaceful. You should listen to that voice."
She smiled, " So what should I do?"

I said, " Just say thank you God and Mary."
She repeated with a smile, "Thank you God and Mary." Such simplicity.

So at church, during consecration, I suddenly felt the urge to turn around. Then, did I see the rose: a carved red rose with a golden stem right at the foot of the statue of our lady. I smiled and then a thought came to my mind: OlaRose was the "Rose" from a Rose (my mother) - God's precious gift to me, given to me to nurture, love and nourish with love of God. I cannot give her what I don't have. I have to take care of myself, my body, my health and my soul, and from my fountain, she will be full. It made sense and I felt humbled and blessed. If this was my mission on earth, I have to do it well and trust that God will provide all I need to accomplish it - despite my failings, experiences, sufferings like the carpenter, Joseph, was charged with the child Jesus and had to flee to Egypt to escape Herod's massacre. God did not send Angels to sweep them in a chariot to Egypt, but He sent an angel to warn Joseph. Joseph listened, obeyed and trusted that God would protect them and walked on foot pulling the donkey with Mary and Jesus to Egypt. God speaks to us all with thoughts, ideas, musings, through others - but we need to find a quiet place to listen to him. Find the Roses and treasures in your life today and nurture them.

Sr. Christina Marie, our lovely guest mistress kindly agreed to take a picture with OlaRose near her "Rose" statue after mass.

We'll leave after 12 noon prayers and lunch around 1 p.m. As Sr Christina hoped in her note, we did indeed have a grace filled visit.

Love you all,
Olachi

Silence and Obedience

Silence and Obedience ,
Fruit of all virtues
That which I need to grow in virtue
That which I seek to grow in love

Through which a soul grows in grace
Through which God draws a soul to Him
With which self-will is overcome
With which a soul is united to God

Silence within and without
With which one guards ones soul
Through which God speaks to a soul
Through which a soul hears God

Obedience to authority and superiors
Through which God guides a soul
Through which God humbles a soul
With which God accomplishes His will

Silence and Obedience
That which I've been missing
That which I now must practice
In my every day with your grace

February 7, 2015
Valley of Our Lady Monastery,
Prairie du Sac, WI

Take me To My Desert Place

Take me to that desert place
Where there's not a soul in sight
Where heaven touches the earth so
That all I have and need is You

Take me to that desert place
Where there's not a drop of water
Where I'm parched and dry with thirst
That only Your saving blood can quench

Take me to that desert place
Where there's no morsel of food to eat
Where I'm starved and frail with hunger
That only Your life giving body can fill

Take me to that desert place
Where though the world abuzz around
Where I retreat within to find
That only You and I exist deep in my heart.

February 8, 2015
Valley of Our Lady Monastery
Prairie du Sac, Wisconsin

Step by Step

Step by step, I'll learn to love
Step by step, I'll learn to give
Step by step, I'll learn to bear
Step by step, I'll learn to trust
Step by step, I'll learn to hope
Step by step, I'll learn to know
That you O Lord love me beyond compare.

Where next, O Lord
You work wonders in my life beyond compare
You take me to journeys in far places I have never dreamed of
I am ready for the task ahead
For you will provide exceedingly beyond my needs

What next, O Lord
You fulfil my wildest imaginations
My innermost desires you bring to life
More than I could ever even wish for myself
I wait in joyful anticipation for Your will in my life

Step by step, I've learned to love
Step by step, I've learned to give
Step by step, I've learned to bear
Step by step, I've learned to trust
Step by step, I've learned to hope
Step by step, I've learned to know
That you O Lord love me beyond compare.

February 9, 2015
Valley of Our Lady Monastery
 Prairie du Sac, WI

Today and Tomorrow

Today and Tomorrow, I thank you for your blessings
I thank you for my OlaRose - innocent, pure, happy soul
Thank You for showing me life with her eyes: beauty, trust, peace, joy
I thank you for the unknown tomorrow
I'm thankful that only You know tomorrow
I thank you that I don't know tomorrow
For today's bustle is indeed sufficient
Embowered by storms and howls, I place my trust in You
And remain in the palm of Your hand

Each moment I get to choose joy or sadness, peace or strife
I choose to keep my joy and peace, God's free gift to me within
Faced with fears of the unknown, failures, and weaknesses
I place my trust and faith in You my kind, loving Father
Knowing that You know my needs and care for every detail of my life.
And what's meant for my harm, You will use for my good.

I must be close to my God-ordained destiny
I must be about to enjoy His massive blessings
For the enemy's angry breath and treacherous unrest sound so close
I will not let this cowardly villian win by giving in to despair
I will not let him steal my peace, my joy – my gifts from God

God strengthens my soul, for I am the daughter of the Almighty.
I will not be derailed from my path, my mission.
I will trust each thought, word and deed to Him
Knowing that He allowed this storm to wash me to a treasure island
I'll not fear the storm and turbulent waves, for He sleeps in the boat

God will line up the waves to lead me safely through this storm.
I pray for the grace to see His hand, the wisdom to discern and act
The humility to know when things are beyond my control
And the faith to allow Him to do the rest
Indeed my Joy I'll keep
So for today that is, and for tomorrow that will be, I thank You.

March 7, 2015

Let Go, Let God

Sometimes we lack courage to make the right decisions in our lives
But God loves us so much,
He makes those decisions beyond our control

A God who loves us beyond compare
Who wants only our good
The Almighty creator who we call Father!

There is peace in letting go
Of things beyond your control
Knowing that they were, are and will always be in God's control

So when the unexpected happens, I'll be still
In the storm, I'll be calm
When injured, I'll still heal
In sadness, I'll keep my joy

Crushed, I'll still rise
Broken-hearted, I'll still love
Betrayed, I'll still trust

In doing so, my soul remains at peace
In trusting God, He becomes my defender
In losing to the world, I win for Christ
So I'll let go, and let God!

March 20, 2015

Expectant Blessings

I'm looking forward to tomorrow
I linger expectantly about the future
Something beautiful is about to happen
Something amazing beyond my wildest imagination

I wonder what's around the corner about to happen
I inhale expectantly this breath of anticipation
Something big is about to be revealed in my life
Something magnificent beyond my vision

You take me places I have never even dreamed off
You amaze me with blessings, beyond what I deserve
You shower me with graces, above my needs
You take me to heights, I could never reach on my own

You sustain me daily,
Revealing your goodness one glimpse at a time
Else my human heart would not contain such blessings
Such joy and bliss, beyond that which I wish for myself

I am so humbled by your unconditional love
I am in awe that You exalt me to lofty heights
I am so underserving of the gifts you give me
Even my misfortune, you turn to great fortune

Your plan indeed is a mystery
I am learning to trust you in good or bad
Knowing you have the world in your hands
And All shall work for the good of my soul

So as the storm brews around me and dark obstacles appear
I brave the storm, knowing clear skies are ahead
I step on the obstacles, knowing they propel me to greater heights
My heart is still, my soul is calm awaiting in peaceful expectancy
Knowing that the blessings I am about to receive are beyond compare
                                                    March 28, 2015

No more Tears

No more tears, I'm numb to pain
I'm indifferent to the storm
I've no more tears

No more tears, my soul is at peace
My heart is at rest
My cup of joy is full
I've no more tears

No more tears, I trust in God
I believe what's meant for my harm He'll turn to my good
I offer all to you who knows tomorrow
I forgive my past, I'm thankful for my present,
I'm hopeful for my future of joyful peace, tears or no tears.

No more tears, for there's a peace that comes from knowing
That when things are beyond your control
They were, are and will always be in God's control
There's Joy in these tears - the joy of knowing that God loves me so
So much, He shed every last drop of blood for me
Why do I think He let this little detail slip his divine plan
I trust all as God's will
I accept, I surrender, I offer it all
So no more tears

Just one last tear, for all I've survived
Tear drops are transformed to diamond
Pearls for these ashes rise to sunlit skies
Rainbows appear in the stormy horizon
Golden rays of His smile dries the one last tear
Tried with fire, I emerge as gold
Happy, content and at peace,
for I've earned a crown for these thorns,
So no more tears.

April 27, 2015,
Madison, WI

Truth

"What is truth?"
This age-old question, asked Pilate to Jesus
Are there different kinds of truth?
Like shades of black, white, then gray?
Half full, half empty, and somewhere in between?

It's unbelievable that the inflictor
Can also feel like the victim
Your mind sees what it wants to see
Rainbows, color blind, or just blind

What is truth indeed?
Does it change because someone refuses to proclaim it?
Does it morph based on our perception and will?
Does it get silenced by a louder voice?

There's only one truth
It's not gray, it's white with black edges
It's a glass with 50% water
It's indestructible, its' undeniable

Truth is eternal
Truth liberates from bondage
Truth empowers you to freedom
Truth is invigorating when incapacitated

Seek it to find it
Keep it to treasure it
Know it to live it
When hidden, it shines from within

Truth is louder than WORDS
Voiceless, yet it can't be silenced
Keep it from all, but it remains known to your soul and its maker
The eternal WORD – Who is "TRUTH"!

April 29, 2015, *Madison, WI*

No Compare

Who can I compare to you?
Who on earth ? Who on earth?
Can compare to you my Lord
My God and my All, there's no compare
Savior of my soul, there's no compare
Creator of the world, there's no compare
You speak and there's life, there's no compare
Alpha and Omega, there's no compare

Who can I compare to you?
Who on earth ? Who on earth?
Can compare to you my Lord
If I lose it all, I'll still have you
If I die, I'll live in you
Heartbroken alone, your love heals me
Lacking all, you're enough for me
Misunderstood, you understand
Abandoned, lost, you give me hope
There's no love on earth, that compares to you
Your love is my all, it's enough for me
No one on earth, compares to You

May 8, 2015
On top of the clouds, on the flight to Baltimore

No Why's in Love

Why? Why not?
I accept, no questions asked
I trust, no questions asked
That is the way of love

I want to love completely
So I need to trust completely
And cast my worries on Him completely
And give of myself to Him without reserve

I asked for a love that gives without reserve
A love unconditional for all seasons
A love the burns with fires unquenched
I found that love in You
Who have been in me since the beginning of time

Why? My mind wants to ask
I don't care to know, my heart offers
It is because He deigned it so
He who loves me so, He died for love of me
So I trust Him completely with my life
This love of my soul, and author of my destiny
I'll accept His will in my life
And go where He leads

I love You with all my heart
I dedicate my heart to you
A promise made at deaths door, almost forgotten
A promise claimed since that moment life renewed
A sacrifice offered for a promise, I will keep
So my love, do with me whatever you will

Show me the way my love
Teach me to love you as You deserve
Teach me to love you as You love me
I've searched all my life but never found
For such a love no human can give

Show me what you want of me
That I may do your will; I offer you my free will
And accept whatever you want for my life
For I know and trust that it is good for my soul

Closed doors are only detours back to your path of life
I thank you for my closed doors
Stumbling blocks are stepping stones to greater heights
I thank you for my stumbling blocks
Moments of pain are opportunities to seek your love
I thank you for my pain

Your love completes me
Your love excites me
You anticipate my needs
You feel my pain
You never tire to listen to my soul
Your love is more than I deserve
Your love is enough for me

Lead and I will follow blindly in trust
The path of life may be rocky and thorny
But your love numbs the pain
I humbly let go of my past
I peacefully embrace my present
I joyfully anticipate my future
Awaiting the abundant graces and blessings you've prepared for me
I trust completely and offer all to you my love
The ups and downs, the good and bad
The successes and failures, and thank you in advance
That you allowed them because You love me so
They are my guiding light to eternal life with You
So, there are no more whys in my life;
I trust you - no questions asked,
Because I'm in love with You.

May 10, 2015
Mother's Day

I found True Love in You

You know my needs and my heart, before I think or speak
You feel my pain and my hurt, before I realize I'm wounded
You give me peace and joy, before I long for them
All my life, I was looking for love
In all the wrong places, people and things
Each time I thought I had found it, it felt wrong, lacking, and wanting
I could not settle or be satisfied, for I was seeking a perfect love – YOU

You stood by silently, patiently, waiting for me to know and love you
You were there to soothe my pain through the hurt
You were there and never left my side
How could I treat you so, MY LOVE?
Now, I know it's You I need and want
You are enough for me, the love I've always longed for
That stands by illness and health, good and bad times
A love that gives without counting the cost, even till the breath of life
You alone can love me the way I long for

Thank you my love for letting me share in your passion
I have felt the pain of injustice and betrayal that you felt
I have felt the loss your mother felt too, with You lifeless in her arms
I now know how you love despite it all, for I'll love just the same
My heart is light and joyful, despite the pain
My soul is peaceful and loving, despite the loss
I have always been yours, but true love does not coerce
You let me seek the whole world wide
Till I found you again and again

I have found true love in YOU, indeed
And marvel how you love me beyond compare
You pamper me beyond what I deserve
You fulfil my innermost desires, even before they form in thought
Thank you for letting me see the love of the world; it pales to compare
Thank you for showing me the world's glory, fleeting and worthless
All I have and need is you, my love!
Teach me to love you more daily more and more

May 12, 2015

Jesus I trust in You

Jesus I trust in you
I trust you with my life
I give you my pain, my broken heart, and my tears
You alone know my anguish
You alone can comfort me

Jesus I trust in You
I long to hear your voice
Please show me the way
Bid I come to you, and I will follow in blind trust
Wounded, maimed, I will crawl
through hot coals and thorns to get to you

Jesus I trust in You
You allowed this to happen, so it must be for the good of my soul
This pain must be needed to purify me
This suffering must be needed to prepare me
To receive the never heard of before blessings you have for me
Your silence is indeed your busy orchestration and preparation
of momentous graces in my life

Jesus I trust in You
Hear my voice and my prayers, O Lord
I give you my heart and my love
I give you my free will
Help me love even though I've been hurt
Give me strength now that I am weak

Jesus I trust in you
Help me discern your will in my life, no questions asked!
Where does the path lead now?
You kept your promises of old, I remember and I am comforted
I believe You are always with me, a constant witness to my suffering
My pain is nothing compared to your suffering on the cross for my sins

Jesus I trust in you
I forgive all that have hurt me
I love all that have caused me pain, and seek no justice
Through my suffering, I'm drawn closer to you
So sweet suffering, where is your sting?
This obstacle only serves to elevate me to greater heights
Such that I see a glimpse of God's glory
You have not cause this ill - a result of man's abuse of his free will
but You have allowed it for the good of my soul

Jesus I trust in you
Give me peace in my soul in this storm
Give me hope in your love in this despair
Give me joy in my heart in this sorrow
My heart is aglow with the fires of your love
I am filled with sweet awareness of your love, amidst this gall
Shield me in your wounds where the evil one cannot reach
Only You are the Way, Truth and Life

Jesus, I trust in you
You who raised Lazarus from the dead
You who turned water into wine
You who fed thousands with a couple loaves
Bring forth the same power of life from within me
To resurrect these dormant dreams in my soul
To turn these bitter waters to sweet wine
To multiply the work of my hands

Jesus, I trust in You
I arise renewed, invigorated
I am armed and battle ready for the odyssey ahead
Lead the way, warrior Prince,your warrior princess follows
We will conquer the world with love
So, Jesus, I trust in You

May 12, 2015

Birthday Gift

My birthday offering to you, O Lord, is my free will
Take it and do as you please
A song of praise, my lips will ever sing
Of your goodness, love and mercy

You called to me my Lord, Here I am
You wooed me so passionately, I succumb lovingly
You are the answer to my every wish
You alone know the deepest desires of my soul

I ponder your goodness and mercy
I am rested and indeed have found peace in your love
Staring at the waters and the heavens above
your greatness is a beauty

Why would I ever worry, when you bear my burdens
Whom shall I fear, when you are my Father, the Almighty
When things don't go as I wish
I lay them in Your hands, for they are indeed as You wish
You who know the past, present and future
You who alone cares and loves more than any other
You who wants only what is good for my soul
You who alone allows what is good for me
You who are in control of all things

Nothing can happen unless allowed by you
Even if it brings pain, hurt, loss, sadness, misery
You will always turn it into good - all a part of my destiny
So I trust in you dream maker, my Divine majesty
It took me this long to find this peace in your love
The peace of knowing that all things work out for my good
If I entrust them in your care
No matter what it looks like or how impossible it seems
You are the God of possibilities; You give me more than I deserve
You always forgive and not count my ills
You will always redirect my path when I stray
You always use my stumbling blocks as footstools to greater heights

So I thank you for my open and closed doors
I praise you for my smooth and thorny paths
I exult you through my joys and sufferings
I will still love through my heartache and betrayals
You who makes a way through a thicket and fog
You who can move mountains and hold the sun still with your face
You who can give life to buried dreams with a breath
You are my everything my love; Keep me always with you
I know you are always by my side, even closer to me when I suffer
I offer to you - my free will; my all

Do with me as you wish
When undecided or astray, please use others to redirect me
and leave me no choice but to return to you
I am but a child and do not know what is good for me
I accept whatever life may bring with tranquility
Knowing you are the author of my life,
and the odyssey of my soul does end in victory over sin and death
So your majesty, paint this portrait of my life as you please.

My best life is still ahead
Your most wondrous works yet to revealed in my life
Your amazing gifts to me yet to unfold
You've blessed me beyond my wildest imagination
You've taken me to places I could only dream of
You've loved me with a love I've always longed for
I'm happy and content in your love, O Lord
It took this long but I'm ready for the odyssey ahead
Step by step, I follow where you lead.
I will not be afraid in the storm
For you sleep in the boat with me
Even when I can't see or feel you, I know you are with me
So let it be done to me according to your word
So on my 39th birthday, my gift to You is my free will.
My Lord, My King, My love, My All

June 16, 2015

How Could You Still Love?

I'm asked, "How could you still love
When you've been hurt so much?"
How could I not still love? I answer
For He who is LOVE lives within me
And has loved me no matter what

I'm asked, "How could you forgive
When you've been wronged so much?"
How could I not forgive, I answer
When I've been forgiven all my sins
By He who bore them all

I'm asked, "How could you move on
When all seems to be lost?"
How could I not, I answer
When He that I trust leads the way
And I follow not missing a step

I'm asked, "How could you still dream
When your dreams are shattered?"
How could I not, I answer
When He that makes my dreams has created
New dreams of life, love and hope beyond my imagination

I'm asked, "How could you find peace
When such unrest abounds?"
How could I not, I answer
For I trust in He that knows tomorrow
Who allows only that which is good for my soul

I'm asked, "How could you still be happy
When such misery will be understood?"
How could I not be full of Joy, I answer
I am loved beyond compare
With a love that brings eternal JOY

July 2, 2015

I've Found that Place

I've found that place of peace
I've entered into that desert place
I've come to that sanctuary of rest within
Where nothing matters but Your love

I've found that place of hope
I've entered into that abyss of trust
I've come to that ocean of faith
Where nothing matters but Your love

I've found that place of joy
I've entered into that canyon of bliss
I've come to that peak of contentment
Where nothing matters but Your love

I've found that place of strength
I've entered into that valley of faith
I've come to that rock of courage
Where nothing matters but Your love

I've found that place not far ayonder
But right here within me
In the core of my being
Where everything fades into oblivion, except You and I

July 2, 2015

Thank You

I want to thank You for my closed doors today
I want to thank You for the things that didn't go my way
I want to thank You for my disappointments and failures
I want to thank You for my humiliations and mistakes

I want to thank You for the stumble that slowed me down
I want to thank You for the harsh word that left me speechless
I want to thank You for the news that halted my impulse
I want to thank You for confusion that left me undecided

I want to thank You for redirecting me
I want to thank You for making a way
I want to thank You for leading me along
I want to thank You for lighting the path

I want to thank You for there are no coincidences
I want to thank You for every piece of the puzzle
I want to thank You for your Holy Will in my life
I want to thank You for my memorable Odyssey

July 2, 2015

Thy Will Be Done

Thy will be done
Despite my indecision
Despite my fears and limitations
Despite the obstacles I see
Despite the disapproving noises I hear
Despite my mistakes and wrong choices
Despite my misfortunes and mishaps
Despite my trials and tribulations
Despite my pain and suffering
Despite my wrongful speech
Despite my weakness and lack of courage
Despite the wrong path I took
Despite my impetuous nature
Despite my humiliations
Despite my desires
I accept your will in my life, good or bad
Thy will be done, O Lord, to me as you please
For I trust You with all my heart
And know that Your will leads my soul back to you

July 12, 2015

Who am I?

Who am I? I am God's beloved
I am nothing without Him
Where am I? I am where He leads me
I am lost without Him
How can I? I can do all things with Him
I can't do anything without Him
What have I? I have all I need in Him
I have nothing without Him

Adversity is God's way of leading me to His chosen path
Adversity is the pain before the prize
I will persevere knowing that nothing can derail my destiny
I will be at peace knowing there's no mistake or coincidence in my life
Unanswered prayers mean something bigger and better awaits
Come pain or gain, I will always give honor to God
As in trust I wait, praising His goodness and thankful for His love

God's plan for me is bigger than my mistake
My wrong choices cannot keep me from my destiny
God will always offer a way back to His plan for me
So long as there's breath in me, I will call on Him for succor
He'll answer, for He bears no grudges and forgives shortcomings
He allows humiliations, so I see my nothingness and need Him more
He allows misfortune to propel me to greater heights closer to Him
His love has no end, even when I stray in thoughts, words, or deeds

I lost love in the world, but found love in God
I lost my name in the world, but found myself in Him
I was lacking in the world, but found abundance in Him
I was sorrowful in the world, but found joy in Him
I was anxious in the world, but found peace with Him

Who am I? I am His beloved
Where am I? I am where He wants me to be
How can I? I can by His mercy, power, and love
What have I? I have everything because I have Him

September, 9, 2015

None of that Matters

I may not fit in
I forget my words sometimes
I'm not part of a crowd
But none of that matters
Because He loves me just as I am
And I love me too

I may have nowhere to go
I may have no one to talk to
I'm not alone or down
But none of that matters
Because He's always with me
And will never leave me

I may make mistakes or poor choices often
I may be weak and inconsistent with my resolutions
I may disappoint others because I'm not perfect
But none of that matters
Because His plan for me stays true
And nothing can derail me from my destiny

September 3, 2015

Fix My Eyes On You

I'll fix my eyes on you, O Lord, less I falter and fall
When my gaze falls away from you O Lord, I become weak and fearful
You fill me up, when I am empty
You give me strength, when I am weak
You lift me up, when I have fallen
You show me light, when I am lost

If I don't have it, then I don't need it
What I want or need, please choose for me
Let it be done to me like you will
For you only allow what's good for me
If it happened, then that was your will
I'll still trust you and give you praise, through joy or suffering,
For all roads lead to the destiny, You choose for me

My life story is already written,
You know the beginning and the end
Unruffled by each passing scene, I'll follow your steps in light or dark
When suffering comes, I delight in it, keeping my peace and joy
For it has come to lift me up to heights beyond my imagination

When trouble comes, I'll praise you in it
Those closed doors, are only detours to where you want me to go
So, I will go without a word, trusting you with all my heart
You love me beyond compare like no other, O my Lord and my God
So when this pain comes and stays, I'll cling to your love
And remember you taught me to trust and love through your cross
So, pain you will not take away my joy
You're my victory over the world, over pride – by which I am free

I'll still dream beyond my boundaries
I'll still love despite the pain
For one has shown what love is, by His death for love of me
No pain can stop my destiny, one of unsurpassing splendor
All I need is to fix my gaze on you.

September 16, 2015

The God, I serve

I want to tell you about the God, I serve
He is a fixer-up and a world connector
He is a record-breaking, life-changing, Ever living God!

Before I think it, He does it
While I dream it, He fulfils it
When I can't find it, He shows it
When I make little efforts, He magnifies it
When I can't finish it, He completes it
When I make a mistake, He covers it

When I don't know it, He teaches me
When I don't feel it, He touches me
When I can't love, He loves me
When I don't succeed, He promotes me
When I'm lonely, He hugs me
When I'm empty, He fills me
When I'm sorrowful, He gives meJjoy

Whatever I ask, he gives it to me
Not just my heart's desire, but more than I could ever wish for
For He knows what is good for me
And He who owns the whole world and ayonder
Loves me beyond compare
So, I trust Him with my heart and life
Whatever may come my way, I will not fear , worry or be sad
Because He will always turn it into a greater good

This cross is not my downfall, but will indeed make me great
It will bring forth my impurities
So He can polish them like gold
That I may shine bright like His star, His joy that I am
That is the God I serve
Who I can call Abba, Father

September 17, 2015

Father Knows Best

Father, you know best
Lord, you are awesome
You are a master architect
Indeed a supreme author
You plan my life superbly

Nothing is left to chance
Every moment, hour, day
Is in its exact time as ordained by you
Every person, I meet , word spoken, or experience had
Is just as you planned it

If only I could see the future
And know that which worries me so
Will indeed be resolved with time
I would not worry so much today or now
I would spend my "NOW" praising you

But just as I begin to worry or despair
I realize that I really should not worry
But trust that you will resolve it
Like you've done of old for me

Suddenly, the issues disappear
Then, I regret the moments I panicked
The wrong choices made in fear
Just as suddenly, you gave me another opportunity
In the present moment
To correct the wrong, and I did

I'm sorry for not trusting
I'm sorry for not believing in your love
I'm sorry for thinking I need to act to change my fate
I can do nothing without You
Nothing can happen to me, unless for my own good
So, thank you Jesus
I love you so much

Even though, I do not still know tomorrow
I will not fear, worry or be anxious
I will trust you completely, no questions asked
Like a child trusts its mother
I will embrace your love so lovingly
Like a child in his mother's arms
I will love you completely,
Like 8 year old OlaRose loves me

Knowing that I love her with all my heart
and that all I do for her is for her own good
Even when not desirable, she sees it soon enough
And she says *"Thank you, mummy!"*
And in that moment, I try to teach her to trust completely
I ask her , "Will I ever hurt you, baby?"
And she always says with a smile, *"No, you are my mummy."*
Do you trust me, baby?
She says with confidence, *"Yes, you are my mummy"*
"Even when I tell you No, do you believe that I love you?"
She always says, *"Mummy, I know you love me*
even when you say No to me,"
"Everything I do is for your own good,
even if you don't get what you want," I said
"I know, mummy," she says, *"I love you even when you say No,*
because you know what's good for me."
I smile and say " Yes, sweetie, mummy knows best"

In the same way, "Our Father in heaven knows best."
He knows best what we need
He knows best when to give it to us
If He doesn't give it, then either we don't need it or
Something bigger and better is planned in the future or
This difficulty that we loathe is needed to get us to our destiny
Father, You know Best
Help me trust, believe, and submit to your Holy Will in my life!

October 8, 2015
On plane flying from Chicago O'Hare to New Orleans

442

I live for Him

I faced my greatest fear, and I'm still here
I faced my biggest disappointment, and I'm still hopeful
I faced my deepest sorrow, and I'm still joyful

I lived my most treacherous pain, and I still breathe
I lived my most painful heartache, and I still love
I lived my most agonizing tragedies, and I still trust

I've suffered my harshest judgement, and I still have mercy
I've suffered my darkest nights, and I still have light
I've suffered my longest loneliness, and I still have you

No matter what I've faced, lived, or suffered
I'm still so full of Hope, Joy and Love
Because they were all known by You, allowed by You,
and will be used by You for my own good
You who loves and courts me like no other
Who has pursued and possessed me like an obsessed lover
Stripping me of all human love and attachment
Wanting to fill my being with all of You
 till I overflow with Your love and joy

No matter what tomorrow brings
Fear, disappointment, sorrow, pain, heartache,
tragedy, judgement, night, loneliness
I fear not, for You are with me
I worry not, for You hold me in Your embrace
My heart is light with peace
My soul is steeped in joy
My spirit is nestled at rest
For all shall be well in the end
I need not know tomorrow to trust
I need not see the end to believe
I am content with the knowledge that I am loved by You

I am steadfast in the truth that
Your mercy surpasses all my faults and failures,

Mistakes and mishaps, suffered or self-inflicted
I am strong in the conviction that Your love overcomes all my
weakness and inadequacies, poor judgement and spontaneity,
misguided or well-intentioned actions
I am Your beloved, Your daughter, Your bride, Your joy,
Your precious jewel, Your priced possession, Your plaything, Your Ola

Nothing can happen to me without Your permission,
so whom or what can I fear?
You can bounce me like a ball
Rest on me like Your footstool
Raise me to the mountain
And Allow me to fall into the depths of the valley
But no harm can come to me, because You hold me in Your face
As long as I keep my gaze at the cross
I willingly embrace and carry it, and go where You lead
With joy I walk,
In peace I stride,
With love, I act
In faith, I move
For I would rather suffer the greatest pain according to Your will
Than experience the greatest joy according to the world
Because Your pain bringing sweet joy that lasts forever
And the world's joy brings everlasting sorrow.

So I praise you Lord for my now
I thank you for my yesterday
I praise you for my future unknown
In all I offer you glory
May all be to your praise
May your will be done at all time
I believe, trust, and submit to Your holy will.

October 10, 2015

That You May Live Through Me

Lord Jesus, show your face
Let your presence be felt
Let your voice be heard
That you may see with my eyes

Lord Jesus, walk with me
Live through me
Love with my heart
That You may heal with my hands

Lord Jesus, your will be done
Give me your patience to persevere
Your strength to endure
Your humility to trust
That your will will bring forth good in my soul

Lord Jesus, Prince of peace
May your peace be with me
Give me silence in persecution
Give me joy in suffering
That my soul may rest in you

Lord Jesus, fountain of mercy
Forgive through me
First me, for ills done to you
And others for ills done to me
That I may love as you did

November 1, 2015

Praise to God, our Light

He is the light
That illuminates the path to victory
His light infuses strength for the journey
Even in dark paths, His light, though seemingly dim, is ever present

There's no humanly way possible,
I could do all I need to do in my own strength and stay sane
His blessings amaze me daily
He completes anything that is lacking,
And gives me beyond what I deserve,
In a moment, arranges things that I thought impossible,
And turns my mistakes into blessings!

Sometimes, God allows us to experience
misunderstandings, humiliations, or judgement,
deserved or undeserved
These are necessary for our own good
Through trials, we remember
that we are nothing without His grace

So, when things don't go my way,
it turns out God was only leading me
through a necessary dark tunnel into amazing light and goodness!
That darkness is the only way to the blessing
So, why turn back or be afraid, if He is with me
and it will always end up for my own good?

Keeping my gaze steadily on Him, who leads me
I'm learning to be patient and walk expectantly in dark nights
for they fade into nothingness with the light!
All glory to God, our light! He loves to be praised.
He blessings chase me down, overtake me and WOW me!
When I praise Him, He does even more!

November 1, 2015
Madison, Wisconsin

I am Free

I am free
I was free
My maker made me free
I have the power within to stay free

I am not a slave to my desires
I am no slave to my body
I am no slave to my fears
I am not what friends or foes say I am
I am not what anyone may think I am
I am who God my maker says I am
I am the best me he made me to be
I am a child of the Almighty God
I am made for heaven not earth

I am His perfect creation, there's none like me
Despite my imperfections, I am his masterpiece
He made me with all that I need
That which I don't have, I don't need
My life story has already been written
It ends in victory over sin, illness and death
No bad luck, loss, pain or betrayal can stop it

He completes what I am lacking
He is enough for me
He gave me this powerful gift of free will
To make choices, mistakes, missteps, that always will detour to Him
He also gave me the free will to call on him when I err
And He will make all things new and well again
With His no grudge holding, everlasting, ever living LOVE
Through this love -so pure, so good, I am free
Despite the chaos, turmoil, lack, hurt, and wants, I am joyful
His love is all I need – It sets me free to live and love
I claim my freedom now, today and all the days of my life

November 11, 2015

I am madly in Love with You

I am madly in love with you
You overwhelm me with your love
You surround me with your presence
I feel you with every breath of mine
I feel my heart palpitating, as your heart touches mine
My blood boils in ecstasy, as your blood courses through my veins
My soul soars, watching you move above the firmament

Ardent lover, your passion is unmatched
Your read my mind and soul like no other
Before I wish it, you grant it
My desires, you command the heavens to fulfil
My crosses, you make feather light with your love
My pain you take away, leaving me with joy
The Joy you give is beyond my imagination
My tears overflow daily like a baby in awe of your love
A love like no other, that I've dreamed and longed for all my life
Only to find it within me, neglected and alone
It took a spark of love to reignite for eternity
Now it burns fiercely, my heart can almost not contain it

Heavenly Potter, You mold me like clay
Artist of beauty, You make me a masterpiece
Ancient of days, You wrote my past
Light of the world, you illuminate my future
Quiet brook of living waters, You fill me with your peace
Fountain of life, You quench my thirst;
Saving bread, You nourish my soul

Thank you for loving me, choosing me, and blessing me
My tears of joy at your goodness, You turn to jewels in my life
The plots of the evil one, You turn to my victory.
I am so madly in love with you, my love

November 24, 2015

I Remain

I wait patiently; I linger hopefully
I accept serenely; I move on trustingly

The day of the Lord will come
The will of the Lord will be done
The God of Justice and Peace
Always triumphs in the end

Truth cannot be clouded
Light cannot be hidden
Words can be twisted
But in the heart, the truth remains

I stay joyfully; I abide peacefully
I trust lovingly; I live abundantly

I forgive wholeheartedly; I understand compassionately
I stand firmly in truth and faith, for His mercy has no end
I loved passionately; I love passion-filled
I will love faithfully, for His love knowns no bounds

Life passes on
Trials come and go
Tides rise and fall
I remain steadfast in your love, the Alpha and Omega

I remain unmoved and unruffled, Come rain or shine
Your love and word never fails
In time, your glory will be manifest,
O Almighty, my Love and my God

No betrayal or lies can turn my love sour
My soul soars instead to imaginable heights
For my crown increases with each cross
So in trust, I remain….

December 1, 2015   *Pikesville, Maryland*

Direct my Steps

Direct my steps O Lord, so I do not falter
Guard my thoughts O Lord, so my heart is ever turned to You
You feed my desires O Lord, even the faintest longings of my soul
I trust You my God with my heart, my soul, my all
May I live for you alone – giving up human love, praise, or earthly gain
You complete what I lack with Your love
You are everything , all that I need
From my waking moment to the close of day

Direct my steps back to you, O Lord
I pray for guidance to live with love, joy and peace
To put You first in all things, and all others You will add onto me.
To resist the evil one's lure to old fights and worries, even if justified.
But to keep my eye on the prize to the road to salvation
Neither seeking praise, gain, relief, apologies,
Nor giving in to anger or bitterness, no matter if justified
To be the best me, God made me to be
To love unconditionally when the opportunity arises,
Because You love me, just as I am !

Direct my steps, O Lord
As I carry my cross through the dark nights
While you purify me, like gold in a fiery furnace
Till I shine and glitter purified, free of sin and impurities
Through the agony and loneliness of the dark night
I will trust in You and not despair
Help me accept whatever You allow in my life
deserved or undeserved; self-inflicted or inflicted by others
For it is for my own good
And through my suffering, I am one with you
You give me such peace and joy that the world cannot give
As I sojourn on earth to reach the beatific union in heaven,
Wearing the crown my suffering has earned
Do with me as you please, my love, as you direct my steps

Dec 14, 2015
Madison, Wisconsin

Today I Conquered

Today, I battled not flesh and blood, but principalities
Today, I fought the evil one face to face in his guises
An unjust judge; An angel of death
An innocent soul has joined the choirs of angels
On the birthday of namesake Papa Francisco – Christ's vicar on earth
On the day OlaRose was "Mary" in the school play
Heaven won this battle, the evil one will not prevail

There is a God who lives in me, breathes in me, and whispers to me
Show me your face, O Lord; but, only in my heart
In the darkness, shine your light
Humiliated, you rid me of pride
Heartbroken, you fill me with love
Spent, your invigorate me

There is a God, who's alive in me, loves in me, and abides in me
I offer up this loss and pain
What matters on earth is our eternal soul
Keep mine for heaven, O Lord
Rid me of material gain, human praise, and accolades
For as swift as they come, so they are gone in a second

If it pleases you, Lord to allow this, your will be done
For in the turmoil, you give me peace
I will cling to you as I'm ridiculed, and will endure all for love of you
I will love you even though I lose my heart's desire
Though tested like gold in a furnace, my faith will not falter,
I trust you with my heart and unite my feeble suffering to yours

For out of this sorrow, comes Joy
I remember your goodness and defeated the urge for bitterness
No matter what befalls me, You will never leave my side
My trust is in You, O Lord, for You alone can bring good out of evil,
So, I wait patiently, expectantly, joyfully
Thankful that I conquered the devil, today, and saw your face my love

December 17, 2015, 11:55 p.m *(close to midnight)*

In Joy I live

In Joy, I live my every day
Despite life's ups and downs, my Joy remains full
Joy is not external, but dwells within
Joy exists beyond happiness, which can come and go
My Joy is my eternal gift from the Giver of Joy above
A Joy, no human can give or take
For my Joy is mine to keep or lose
So, each day I choose to keep my Joy

In Joy I live and breathe and move
My zeal, passion, and energy coming from my Joy within
Words and pain may hurt, but cannot steal my Joy
Disapproval, poor judgement may sadden, but can't quench my joy
You do not know where I came from or what I've been through
You do not know how I got here or where I am going
And you cannot stop the person I am to be
For there's love in me that ignites my soul like a flame,
A constant fuel to my joy

In Joy I live my day to day
Though my future is now shaped by my memory, intellect, and will
For my past, my joy neither makes excuses nor has regrets
If I had to do life over, I may still relive the love, pain, and trials
I may still make the same choices and so-called mistakes
For I wouldn't give up my journey, my cross or my life for another's
They're perfect for me and helped me become the "me" of today
Though drawn to such flawed love like a moth to a flame
Out of the flaws came such beauty and grace – gifts on high
There's no coincidence; All were known by Him before I was formed
Leading me to find my Joy and true perfection of love in God

In Joy, I live and love
My Joy cannot be silenced , it's speaks without words
My Joy cannot be hidden, it shines even in the darkest nights
So, In Joy I live, for my name is " Joy"

February 19, 2016

Through this Odyssey....Above the Clouds, I soar

Above the clouds, I will soar through life's Odyssey
Above the clouds, laden with stormy rain and turmoil, I ascend
Above the clouds, where there's stillness in the blazing sunlight
Above the clouds, tempestuous and turbulent
Above the clouds, where joy and peace abound, there I'll reside

You alone know my heart and the deepest longings of my soul
You allow only what is good for my soul
Life events are consequences of our choices and choices of others
All things in my life, you use for my good, even if beyond myr control
So I worry not for earthly troubles and above the clouds, I will remain

You designed my life like a masterpiece, a story like no other
Every pain, tear, joy, encounter, person, mistake, impulse
None, a coincidence, no experience, wasted or unnecessary
For all are parts of my life's story, my odyssey
Despite the evil one's bumps, twists, turns, ups and down
All paths redirect to you, and in time, fall in place
For the end of this odyssey, you've written in victory
So above the clouds, I will rest

No-one knows the mind of God or the will of God
All one can do is believe and trust that all shall be well
So, I offer up that which I cannot control
To Him who is the Almighty who allows only good in my life
And so why worry about the known, unknown, or known unknowns
So above the clouds, I'll stay

The joy you give is not of this world
The peace you bestow is indescribable
Joy and Peace abide within me no matter what comes from without
Your body and blood sustain my faith in your love and mercy
So, I soar above the clouds to you my love,
in this Odyssey of my soul

March 6, 2016

Visible, Tangible, Audible Faith

Can you see my faith, Lord?
I don't see a way
But I'll take a step forward
Trusting that You'll open a path ahead

Can you touch my faith, Lord?
I don't feel strong
But I'll work like I am
Trusting that you'll give me strength

Can you hear my faith, Lord?
I don't know what to say
But I'll speak words of life
Trusting that you'll give me wisdom

What I want may not be what I need
My wishes for me, may not be God's for me
So in faith and trust I walk, knowing that
He who loves me so will only allow the best in my life

Faith is alive
I want to live a visible, tangible, audible faith
Trusting that You'll complete what I lack, O Lord
Believing that I don't have it, because I don't need it
For You are all I want and need.

March 8, 2016

Playing Your Part

Life's a story and you're the star!
Playing a part written just for you
Life's a cruise and you're a passenger
Riding through the undulating waves

In life's thickest plot or deepest waters
Fear not the roaring storm or dark sinister plot
Remain at peace and draw strength from within
Looking ahead to the guiding light
For your story and journey does end in victory

Be thankful for your past, and learn from it
Be joyful in your present, and love in it
Be hopeful for your future and dream of it
For closed doors are detours to your Divine destiny
Obstacles are stepping stones propelling you to greater heights
Mistakes are not missed opportunities, but new ones
So live each moment with joyful expectancy through life's Odyssey

Yesterday's thorns are indeed tomorrow's crowns
So, live today with joy
Love today with passion
Dream today with a vision
And wake up tomorrow to play your best **"you"** all over again!

March 30, 2016

Mature in Love – Thorns, Roses and My Will

When our love was new
I needed to hear that you loved me
Not once, but over and over
I needed to look into your eyes
Not once, but over and over
To be reassured of your love

When our love was young and tender
I needed to touch and feel you
Not once, but over and over
I needed to see your smile to light up my heart
Not once, but over and over
To be reassured of our love

Now our love is grown and mature
I need not hear you to know you love me
I need not see you to feel your presence
I need not touch you to relive our passion
I only need to taste you to unite with You
Body, Soul, and Divinity

Our love has grown over the years
Then, you gave me sensual delights as I desired
You revealed your love so unsparingly
You were unmatched in the passion with which you sought me
You've now won me over my love , You need not worry
I'm yours heart, body and soul

You gave me three gifts, divine and true: my memory, intellect and will
Before you formed me, You called me to be yours,
The true love of your heart
My path in life, thorns and roses, all planted before me
Their sole aim to lead me back to you
At the end of my sojourn

With my memory, I recall my sins
And how much I have hurt you, but you still love me
I recall most your goodness and mercy that endures forever
I detest my sins, as I am overwhelmed by your love
You have taught me from your lips
You lift me to the skies, and open my soul to commune with me
Above the clouds, heading to San Francisco, you reveal yourself
And I contemplate your majesty and my nothingness

You've overwhelmingly blessed me with your sights and insights
Even when I am unaware that I feasted on the table of Your Majesty
With grown eyes, I now recall and know
And I am humbled at your goodness
For greater and more loving have achieved with painful passion
Such graces that you so lavish on my tepid soul
I am so underserving of your love, mercy and goodness

With my intellect,
I seek to know Your will in my life with love and perseverance
My will is a divine weapon
That gives me the choice to turn to you or against you, my love
I trust not my carnal desires or inclination to sin
For on my own, I do that which I 'will' not
May I always seek to do your will because it is for the good of my soul
Now I'm mature in our love, I trust you with my free will
Do accept it as a humble offering of my eternal love

I want to become a slave to Your will
Your divine power gifted to me, to resist the devil and his guile
I give you my free will, so I can live free indeed
Unflattered by the evil one's colorful guise to the flesh
Unwavering in my trust and quest to do your will
For in doing your will, I rise quickly to greater heights of love with you
In seeking your will, I see you face to face, my love
In desiring your will, I am uniting myself to you
I'm all grown up now my love, your will is my sweet command

You make all things new
Through your will, I am transformed into love

In your will, I find compassion and mercy
From your will, I emerge renewed , invigorated
So I can love my neighbor, even when they don't love me
I can feel their pain, even when they persecute me
I can see their fears, even when they are blind to mine
I can hear their anguish, even when they are deaf to mine
I can know their loneliness, even when they slander me
And I can have compassion, even when rejected and ridiculed
For in seeing them , I see you ; and in loving them, I love you
With that unrequited, unbridled, unwavering love you have loved me
Through the darkness they cause me, I'm transformed into light
Whose rays cannot be hidden and reflect vigorously, Your presence

I am now grown and mature in love, my love
And know you are always with me, even in my pain and loneliness
To feel you, see you, and touch you in my dark nights
I need to seek to find, serve, and love my neighbor
So you send me more thorns than roses in our grown, old love
For through their sharp impale, I rise higher quicker to you
Faced with thorns, I do not fear
Its sharp prick fills me with joy
Faced with roses, I accept its fragrance in humility
A reminder of how sinful and helpless I am without your graces
Pleased with my humble offering,
You lifted me higher as the roses wither around me
I'm ready and willing my love, to live with thorns and roses
A sign of your love for me
A shorter and surer bridge to your ocean of love and mercy
Wherein I can drown myself in ecstasy
For thorns and roses become my crown of victory

April 11, 2016

With Love, there's no Fear

I told OlaRose how I am no longer afraid about suffering
because God allows suffering for my good;
and when I trust Him, I don't feel the pain of suffering
OlaRose then said:"I know what you mean, mommy.
* It happened to me one day."*
And she told me of how during her cousin, BiancRose's birthday
last month, while playing with friends and little ones,
their golf ball fell in a bush with thorns.
All feared to go in and get it
Some tried to use a long stick to reach it, afraid of the thorns
The little ones became sad, longing for the ball
"I didn't want them to be sad," she said, "so I went to get the ball.
I knew the thorns may prick me, but I wasn't afraid
A thorn did prick me for just second
And then, I didn't feel the pain anymore;
* and we were all happy I got the ball," she said*
I marveled how a nine year old knew so well what took me years
to understand that fear of suffering cripples our journey of faith
But suffering in Christ not only numbs the pain, but turns it to nectar

You fear because you trust not
Without trust, love can't grow deep
Love without roots, bears no fruit
Life without fruit, has no witness
For witness to truth, gives hope
Without hope, you are enslaved

Uniting your will with His, sets you free
When you are free, you seek truth
When you know truth, you love wholly
When you love wholly, you give more freely
When you are empty, you gain joy
When you have joy, you have peace
When you have peace, you have HIM
When you have HIM, you fear not
When you fear not, you LOVE even more

April 11, 2016

Today and Always

Give me courage to do your will
Give me humility to accept all from you
Give me strength to rise when I fall

Help me to persevere even when I'm weak
Help me to give even when I'm empty
Help me to be joyful even when I hurt

For with joy comes peace
For with peace comes love
For with love comes life everlasting

April 11, 2016

Face Life from Within

When life throws you a curveball
Don't just dodge it
Kick it back with the JOY of a winner
Knowing the POWER of He that lives within...

When life gives you lemons
Don't just make lemonade
Add a spoonful of honey and sprinkle some love
Trusting the GOODNESS of He who loves within

When life takes you for a spin
Don't just hold on
Lift you head up high and soar to the skies
Seeing the VISION of He who reigns within

April 22, 2016

Alphabetical Index of Titles

Y

www.ingramcontent.com/pod-product-compliance
Lightning Source LLC
Chambersburg PA
CBHW030907090426

42737CB00007B/125